Sarah McQuade

Nicola Davis

Paul Butler

Published by Network Training Publishing Ltd
Suite 1, Grimstone Grange Offices, Tadcaster, North Yorkshire LS24 9BX
tel 01937 833619 fax 01937 833512
enquiries@network-publishing.co.uk
http://www.network-publishing.co.uk

© copyright 2002
First published 2002

ISBN 0-9542623-0-1

Sarah McQuade, Nicola Davis and Paul Butler assert the moral right to be identified as the authors of this work.

All rights reserved. No part of this publication may be reproduced, stored in a retrieval system, or transmitted in any form or by any means, electronic, mechanical, photocopying, recording or otherwise, without either the prior permission of the Publisher or a licence permitting restricted copying in the United Kingdom issued by the Copyright Licensing Agency Ltd, 90 Tottenham Court Road, London W1P 9HE. The book is sold subject to the condition that it shall not by way of trade or otherwise be lent, hired out or otherwise circulated without the publisher's prior consent.

British Library Cataloguing in Publication Data
A catalogue record for this book is available from the British Library.
Commissioned by Tony Outhart
Project managed by Sue Chapple
Design and cover design by Wendi Watson
Edited by Jane Bryant
Picture research by Thelma Gilbert
Index compiled by Julie Rimington
Printed and bound by Printing Express, Hong Kong

Acknowledgements
The Authors and Publishers would like to thank the following people for their help in the development of this book:
Chris Buckley, Oakbank School
Tracey Barton, Southfields Community College, London SW18
Chamberlayne Leisure Centre, Woolston, Hampshire
David Lloyd Tennis Centre, Lordshill, Hampshire
Hamble School, Hamble, Hampshire
Bitterne Leisure Centre, Bitterne, Hampshire
Wildern Sports Centre, Hedge End, Hampshire
Rachel Messias

Photographs
All photos supplied by Empics Sports Photo Agency, except:
Action Plus (pages 138 (left), 170). Alan L. Edwards (pages 15 (bottom right), 83, 85 (top), 89, 113 (top, middle), 127 (bottom), 150 (bottom left), 152, 157, 185, 194, 200, 212, 256). Allsport (pages 202 (bottom), 260). Paul Butler (page 265 (top) Colorsport (pages 86, 119, 131, 134, 219 (top), 223 (left), 231). Richard Harris (page 196) Hulton Archive (page 223) Popperphoto (page 210). Science Photo Library (pages 38, 42, 59 (right). Roger Scruton (pages 73, 245). Mike Watson (pages 23, 24, 37, 90, 102, 103, 107, 114, 115, 129 (top), 143 (left), 153, 171 (left), 199 (bottom), 202 (top), 226, 248 (bottom), 250).
Cover photographs courtesy of Empics Sports Photo Agency

Illustrations
Jerry Fowler (pages 4, 6, 8, 9, 10, 11, 12, 13, 17, 18, 19, 21, 22, 23, 24, 25, 26, 27, 28, 29, 30, 32, 33, 34, 35, 36, 41, 43, 46, 48, 51, 52, 54, 55, 56, 57, 58, 134, 268, 270, 271). Cedric Knight (pages 49, 50, 104, 112, 172, 222, 231, 266). John Plumb (pages 68, 74, 77, 78, 79, 80, 81, 93, 94, 109, 137, 200). Mike Watson (page 84). Wendi Watson (pages 51, 60, 61, 63, 88, 162, 188, 240, 255, 262, 265).

Every effort has been made to contact the holders of copyright material, but if any have been inadvertently overlooked, the Publishers will be pleased to make the necessary arrangements at the first opportunity.

Contents

The body in action
Chapter 1　Anatomy and physiology　　3
Chapter 2　Fitness, testing and training　　59
Chapter 3　Factors affecting performance　　101

Human performance in sport
Chapter 4　Acquisition of skill in sport　　143
Chapter 5　Psychology and sports performance　　167
Chapter 6　Observing, analysing and improving performance　　185

Sport in society
Chapter 7　Current issues in sport　　195
Chapter 8　Finance and funding in sport　　217
Chapter 9　Organisation of sport　　245

Answers to revision questions　　268
Useful website addresses　　280
Index　　282

CHAPTER 1: Anatomy and physiology

The human body is a complex machine. It can produce a very wide range of movements and take part in many different activities, exercises and sports. In this chapter you will investigate the structure, function and location of each of these body systems. You will also identify the role or job that each system does in order that the body can move and take part in sport and activity.

The body is capable of producing a wide variety of complex sporting actions and movements

CONTENTS

The human jigsaw	4
The skeletal system	6
The muscular system	16
The respiratory system	27
The circulatory system	31
The nervous system	37
The hormonal system	46
The digestive and excretory systems	47
The energy systems	49
Revising anatomy and physiology	53

The human jigsaw

All the body systems operate together to make your body work. For example, when you run a 5 kilometre race you breathe faster than usual and your lungs expel (get rid of) more carbon dioxide and take in more oxygen. This oxygen is transferred to your blood and your heart works harder to pump your blood faster around your body. The blood carries oxygen to the muscles to give them the energy they need to continue working throughout the race.

Understanding how your body works is like piecing together a jigsaw. Each body system is a different piece of the jigsaw.

This chapter looks in detail at each of the body systems, so that you can understand how the human jigsaw is pieced together.

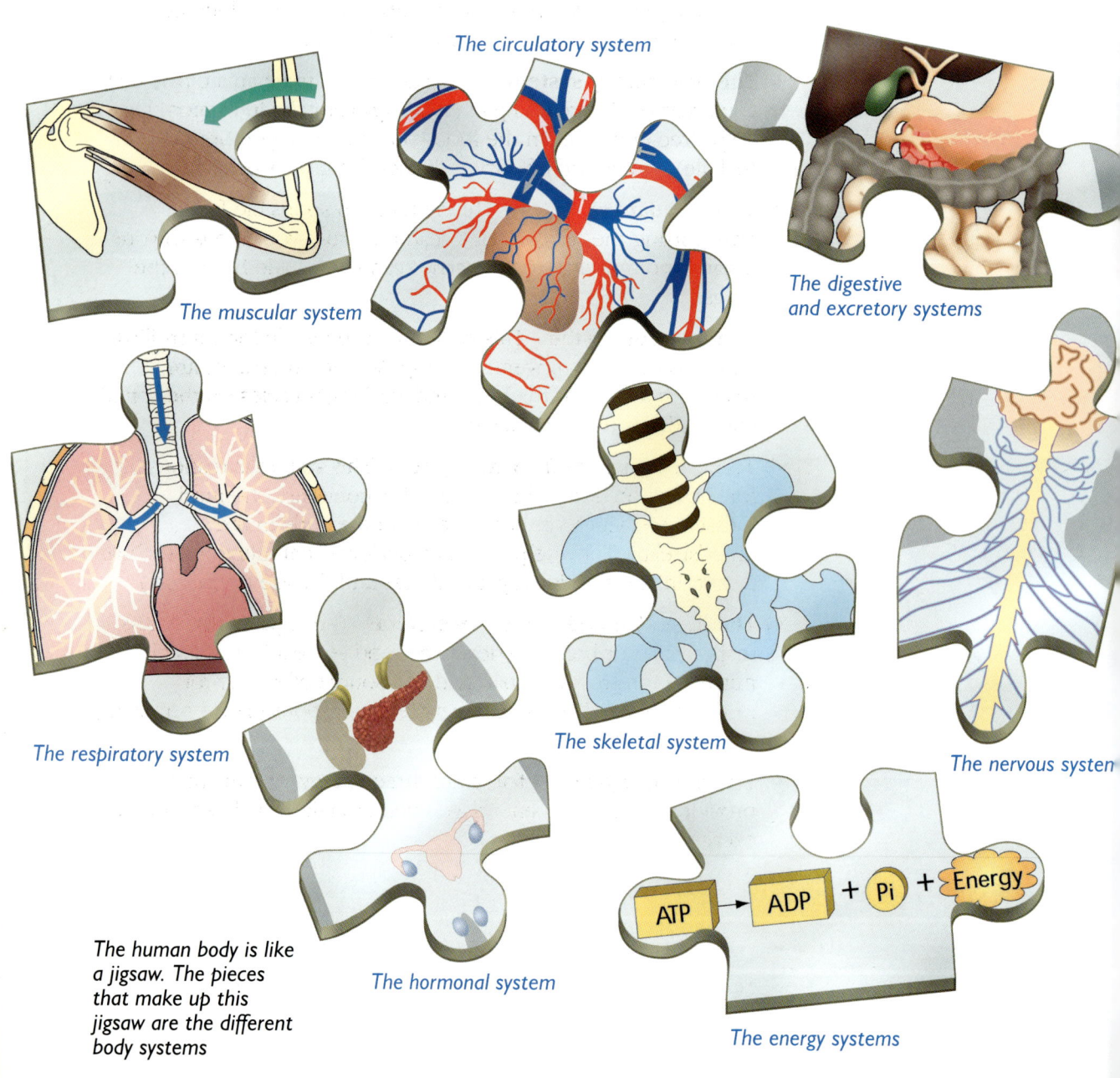

The muscular system

The circulatory system

The digestive and excretory systems

The respiratory system

The skeletal system

The nervous system

The hormonal system

The energy systems

The human body is like a jigsaw. The pieces that make up this jigsaw are the different body systems

4 Anatomy and physiology

The body systems

The human body is made up of a number of different systems. Each system has a specific job to do so that the body can function properly. These systems are:

◆ **The skeleton or skeletal system** This is the framework of the body. It is made up of a variety of bones which are jointed in such a way that movement can occur.

◆ **The muscular system** The muscles responsible for movement are attached to the skeleton by tendons. These are called **skeletal** or **voluntary** muscles. When the skeletal muscles contract (shorten), they exert a pull through the tendon which acts across each joint to make the joint move. Other muscles that have essential jobs to do are the **involuntary** muscles, which perform vital functions such as breathing and digestion.

◆ **The respiratory system** Respiration is the mechanism by which you breathe. By breathing in (inhaling) you take in oxygen that helps free energy from the food you eat. When you breathe out (exhale) you get rid of carbon dioxide from your body.

◆ **The circulatory system** This system is responsible for transporting the oxygen you breathe in from your lungs to your organs and muscles. It also carries carbon dioxide back to the lungs.

◆ **The nervous system** This system is responsible for controlling and co-ordinating movements. Impulses and messages are relayed to and from the brain and working muscles via the spinal cord and a network of nerves.

◆ **The hormonal (endocrine) system** This system is responsible for the production of hormones. Hormones are chemical messengers which are carried around the body in the bloodstream. They help the body perform vital functions such as digestion and the fight against illness and disease (immunity).

◆ **The digestive and excretory systems** The digestive system is responsible for breaking down the food you eat into valuable nutrients for growth, repair and as a source of energy for muscular work. The excretory system is responsible for removing waste products.

◆ **The energy systems** There are three energy systems that provide you with the energy you need to take part in sport and exercise.

The skeletal system

The body's frame is made up of more than 200 bones. When you are born, your skeleton has around 350 bones but by the time you become an adult, you will have only around 206 bones. This is because, as you grow, some of the bones join together.

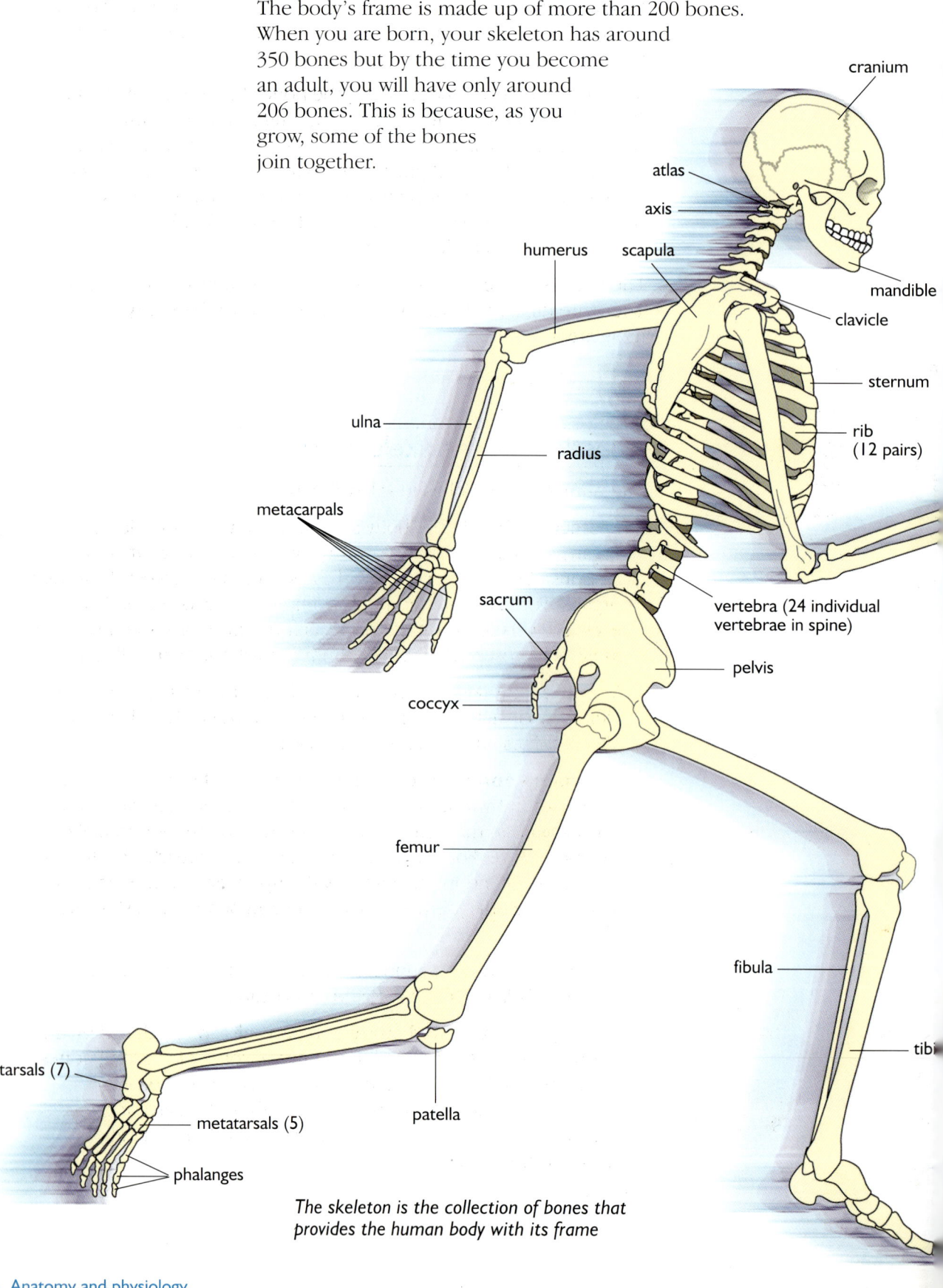

The skeleton is the collection of bones that provides the human body with its frame

Your bones vary in size, shape and function according to their location in the framework. For example, the bones in the skull (cranium) are flat bones designed to protect the brain from accident and injury, whereas the long bones of the legs and arms are used in movement.

As you can see from the diagram, the bones fit together at **joints**. The end of each bone is covered by a tough, smooth shiny substance called cartilage. The cartilage-coated bone ends are kept apart by a thin film of slippery fluid that works like the oil in a car. All of this is so that your bones won't grind and bump against each other when you move. The bones are held together by strong stretchy bands called ligaments.

The body is jointed in such a way as to allow movement to occur. There are different types of joints, which allow different types of movement.

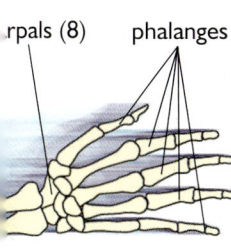

 joints, p.11

Functions of the skeletal system

The human skeleton has four key functions:

- **Protection** Within the body's frame are a number of delicate organs such as the brain, eyes, spinal cord and heart. It is the responsibility of certain parts of the skeleton to protect these vital organs. For example, the skull (cranium) protects the brain and eyes, the vertebral column protects the spinal cord, the heart and lungs are protected by the sternum (breast bone) and rib cage.

- **Support** The skeleton gives the body its distinct shape. It holds vital organs such as the brain and heart in place. The skeleton also provides attachments for muscles.

- **Movement and posture** Muscles are attached to the bones of the skeleton by tendons. When muscles contract (shorten), they exert a pull on that tendon which acts across the joint to make the joint move. For example, when the biceps muscle shortens it pulls on the tendon that attaches the upper arm to the lower arm across the elbow joint. As a result the arm bends (flexes) at the elbow.

   Muscles also work to support and hold the body in an upright position. This is referred to as your posture.

- **Blood production and storage** Blood cells are produced by the marrow, which is located in the centre of some of the long bones. An average of 2.6 million red blood cells are produced each second by the bone marrow to replace those that are worn out and are destroyed in the liver. Calcium and other minerals are stored in the bones.

The structure of the skeletal system

The bones vary in composition, size, shape and function according to their position.

Bone composition

Bones are made up of tissue that can take one of two forms:

◆ **Compact bone** is dense and hard, and forms the protective outside portion of all bones.

◆ **Spongy bone** is very porous (full of tiny holes). It is embedded in a web containing salts (mostly calcium and phosphorus salts) to give the bone strength, collagen fibres and ground substance to give the bone flexibility.

You can see the structure and location of both types of composition in the diagram of the long bone. Most bones contain both types.

A typical long bone

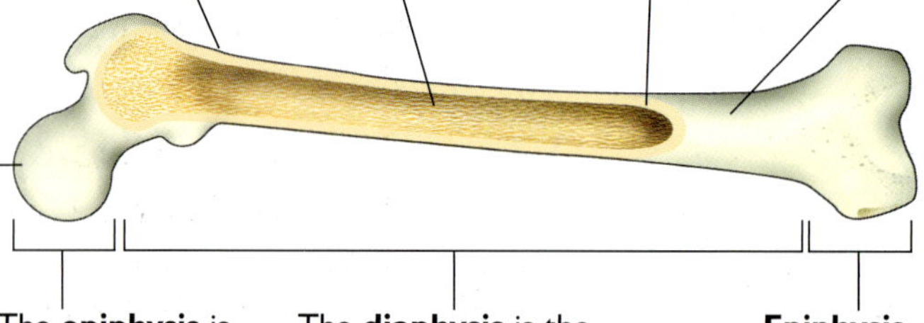

Compact bone is hard and strong, and is made of fibres cemented with calcium salts.

The **marrow cavity** is filled with a soft yellow pulp called marrow. White blood cells are produced here.

Periosteum is a tough fibrous cover for the bone.

Spongy bone is hard, light and very strong. In some bones red blood cells are made here.

Cartilage is a smooth and slippery layer that protects the ends of the bone where it meets other bones.

The **epiphysis** is the end (head) of the bone.

The **diaphysis** is the long shaft of the bone.

Epiphysis

Types of bone

The bones of the skeleton are divided into four types:

Long bones
Long bones are longer than they are wide and work as **levers**, which is how movement occurs.
Long bones are found in the arms and legs, and include the **humerus**, **tibia**, **femur**, **ulna** and the **radius**. They are not solid but contain marrow in the centre, so these bones are strong but not heavy.

Long bones almost always have a crucial role to play in producing any movement.

Flat bones
Flat bones have broad, slightly rounded or curved surfaces designed for the protection of organs and the attachment of muscles.
Examples include the **cranium**, **scapula** and **pelvis**. They consist of spongy bone between two layers of compact bone, and have a large surface area.

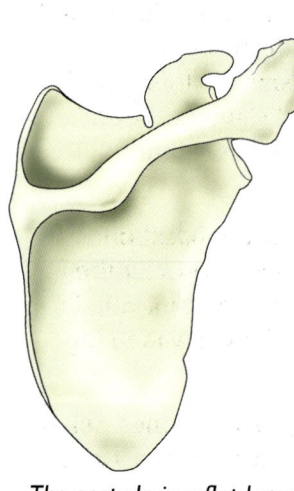

The scapula is a flat bone

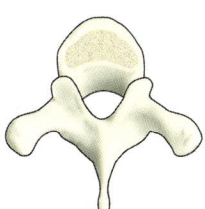

A vertebra is an irregular bone

Irregular bones

Irregular bones are all those that do not fall into the other categories. They have spongy bone inside and compact bone outside. They have varied shapes, sizes and surface features and include the **vertebrae**, bones of the face, some bones in the skull, and the **patella** (the knee cap).

Short bones

Short bones are short and cube-shaped. Examples include the **carpals** and **metacarpals** in the wrist and the **tarsals** in the feet. They are spongy, with an outer layer of compact bone, and as a result are light and strong and capable of fine movements.

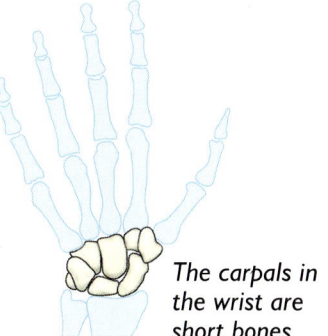

The carpals in the wrist are short bones

The skeletal frames

There are two distinct frames within the body's skeleton. These are called the **axial** and **appendicular** skeletons.

The axial skeleton

The axial skeleton consists of bones that form the axis (the central part) of the body. It is made up of the **cranium**, the **spine** or **vertebrae**, the 12 pairs of **ribs** and the **sternum**. The axial skeleton supports and protect the organs of the head, neck and trunk.

The skull or cranium

There are 28 bones in the cranium, 14 in the face and six in the ear. Most of them fuse (join together) during early childhood.

The cranium protects the brain, eyes and ears. The brain is responsible for the control and co-ordination of movement, and the balance mechanisms are found in the ear. The brain and the sense organs of sight and sound play key roles in the performance of sports skills.

The vertebral column

This is often referred to as the **spine** or the backbone of the human skeleton. Its main function is to protect the spinal cord from injury. It also plays an important role in almost all sporting actions because it allows a wide range of movement to occur.

The vertebral column is made up of 33 small bones called **vertebrae**, and is divided into five distinct regions. Each section has its own type of vertebrae and functions.

The skeleton is made up of two frames – the axial skeleton and the appendicular skeleton

Between each vertebra is a disc of **cartilage** called a vertebral disc. The combined length of all of these discs is about a third of the total length of the spine. The cartilage is a thick circle of tough tissue which acts as a shock absorber.

The vertebrae and discs move together in a wave-like action so that the spine is quite flexible. To understand this action in terms of sport and movement, think about sporting actions that require twisting and turning, for example in gymnastics, high-board diving, judo or athletics.

Seven cervical vertebrae These form the head and neck, and provide attachment for the neck muscles. The top vertebra, the atlas, fits into the skull and allows you to nod your head. The second vertebra, the axis, allows you to rotate your head.

Twelve thoracic vertebrae These are connected to the ribs and work to support the rib cage. They allow some movement, such as bending forward, backward, to each side, and some rotation.

Five lumbar vertebrae These large vertebrae form the lower back and provide attachments for the powerful back muscles at each side. A large range of movement is allowed here – particularly more bending forward, backward, to each side and rotation than in the thoracic region. However, as a result of this flexibility this area of the spine is more susceptible to injury.

The sacrum (five fused vertebrae) These vertebrae are fused together to form one bone, which is joined to the pelvic girdle. The sacrum is a very strong structure which supports much of the weight of the body. It also transmits force from the legs and hips to the trunk and upper body.

The coccyx (four fused vertebrae) This is the base of the spine. In our ancestors the coccyx used to form part of the tail.

The vertebral column protects the spinal cord and has five distinct regions

The rib cage and sternum (breast bone)

The rib cage consists of 12 pairs of **ribs**, which are joined to the vertebral column at the back. At the front the first seven pairs are attached to the **sternum**. The next three pairs are attached to the seventh rib and are called 'false ribs'. The last two pairs are unattached and are called **floating ribs**.

Look at the diagram of the skeleton on page 6 to see how the ribs form a dome-shaped cage around the heart and lungs. They protect the heart and lungs, and are also used in breathing.

The appendicular skeleton

The bones of the appendicular skeleton are attached to the axial skeleton. They include the **arms** and **shoulder girdle** and the **legs** and **hip girdle**.

The arms and shoulder girdle

The arm consists of a series of bones from the shoulders to the hands. The **humerus** ends at the elbow, from which the **radius** and **ulna** start. There are eight **carpal bones** in the wrist, five **metacarpals** in the hand and 14 **phalanges** in the hand.

The arms are attached to the shoulder girdle, which is attached to the vertebral column. The shoulder girdle is made up of the **scapulae** (shoulder blades) and the **clavicles** (collar bones).

The legs and pelvic girdle

The pelvic girdle is much heavier than the shoulder girdle because it has to support the body's weight through the legs.

The legs are attached to the pelvic girdle at the hip. The long single bone from the hip to the knee is the **femur** and it is the strongest bone in the human body. From the knee joint the **tibia** and **fibula** run down to the ankle, where they meet. The **patella**, or knee cap, is not attached to any other bone – its function is to protect the knee joint. The ankle is made up of seven **tarsals** and five **metatarsals**, and there are 14 **phalanges** in the toes.

The pelvic girdle is actually made of two halves (left and right), which are fused to the bottom of the spine at the sacrum.

ACTIVITY

The appendicular skeleton and movement in sport
- List at least three sporting actions that rely on movement of the arms and hands around the shoulder joint.
- Can you list three or more sporting actions where the movement of the legs about the hip plays a vital role?

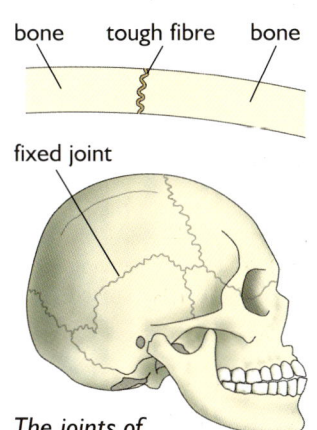

The joints of the skull are fused together

Joints

The human body can produce a wide variety of movements. Some of them are relatively simple, such as walking, while others are more complex, such as a swivel hips in trampolining and the lay-up in basketball. Movement is possible because of the joints between the bones.

There are three main types of joint:

- **fixed** or **immovable joints** (**fibrous joints**)
- **slightly movable joints** (**cartilaginous joints**)
- **freely movable joints** (**synovial joints**).

The skeletal system

Fixed or immovable joints (fibrous joints)
In this type of joint, the bones are in very close contact and are separated only by a thin layer of fibrous tissue. The joint is fixed and no movement is possible. Examples include the joints between the flat bones of the cranium, and the fused joints in the sacrum.

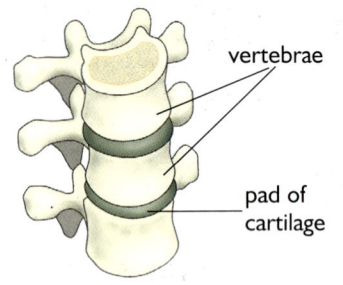

Slightly movable joints (cartilaginous joints)
The bones at these joints are connected by cartilage and only slight movement can occur. The cartilage acts as a cushion between each bone to prevent the bones from grinding against each other. In movement, the cartilage also acts as a shock absorber so that the bones will not jar when you run or jump. Examples include the joints of the vertebral column, and between the ribs and sternum.

Slightly movable joints allow only a limited range of movement

Freely movable joints (synovial joints)
Most of the joints in the human body are synovial joints.

Synovial joints vary in their external structure and function according to their location in the human body. However, they have the same composition (make up), designed to prevent friction between the moving bones.

A freely movable joint has a number of parts, each of which has a specific job to do.

The knee is an example of a freely movable or synovial joint

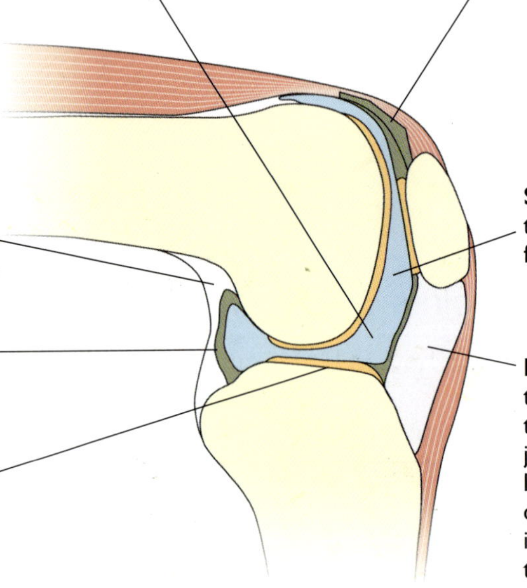

The **joint cavity** is the small gap between the bones that is filled with synovial fluid.

Tendons attach muscle to bone.

The outer sleeve is called the **joint capsule**. This holds the bone together and protects the whole joint.

The **synovial membrane** lines the inside of the capsule and produces the synovial fluid.

Synovial fluid lubricates the joint to allow friction-free movement.

Ligaments are bands of tough, fibrous tissue that attach the bones together across the joint. They support the joint, keeping it stable, particularly during exercise. Ligaments vary in size and shape according to the joint they are supporting.

A tough layer of **hyaline cartilage** covers the ends of the bone inside the joint. It protects the bones and reduces friction in the joint.

Synovial joints allow a wide range of movement. The main types of synovial joints are the ball and socket and the hinge joint, although there are six in total.

Pivot Rounded surfaces of one bone fit into a ridge or peg on another. Only possible movement is rotation. Example: between the axis and atlas in the neck.

Condyloid A mixture of the ball-and-socket and hinge joints. A rounded bump on one bone sits in a hollow formed by another bone or bones. The joint allows movement back and forward and side to side. The ligaments supporting the joint prevent rotation. Example: the wrist.

Saddle The ends of the bone are shaped like saddles and fit snugly together. Allows movement in two planes at right angles to each other. The only saddle joint is at the base of the thumb.

Ball-and-socket Ball-shaped end of one bone fits into a cup-shaped socket on the other. The most movable type of joint in the human body. Examples: shoulder and hip.

Gliding Flat or slightly flat surfaces move against each other, allowing sliding or twisting without any circular movement. Movement limited by strong connecting ligaments. Examples: wrist and ankle.

Hinge The head of one bone fits into the cavity of another. The joint only allows movement forward and backward. Examples: knee and elbow.

ACTIVITY

Understanding the structure of the skeletal system

On pages 8–11 some of the bones of the skeleton are named in bold. You should understand the structure, function and location of these bones.

Copy and complete this table:

NAME OF BONE	TYPE OF BONE	LOCATION	FUNCTION
	Flat		
Tibia			
Patella			
			Protection

The skeletal system

ACTIVITY

Understanding movement at the joints

1 Copy the table below and give an example of a joint in each category.
2 Identify a type of sporting action or skill in which that joint is involved.

	EXAMPLE OF JOINT	SPORTING ACTION/SKILL
Ball and socket		
Hinge		
Pivot		
Gliding		
Saddle		
Condyloid		

Types of body movement

The range of movement at any joint can be described using a range of technical terms.

Extension and flexion

Extension is the straightening of a body part to its normal position and **flexion** is the opposite (bending).

When you run you are continually repeating the same movements. Just before the lead leg strikes the ground it is extended, while the trailing leg is flexed.

Hyperextension

In hyperextension, joints are extended excessively. It can happen in gymnastic and diving routines, and in athletics as you clear a hurdle.

Flexion and extension occur during running. Hyperextension occurs when the joints are over-extended

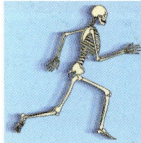

Hyperextension in sport
Which other sports or activities involve hyperextension? You may want to refer to photographs or video footage of sporting actions to help you.

Abduction and adduction

To understand this type of movement, imagine that a line has been drawn vertically (up and down) through the centre of your body from the top and middle of your head, down to the floor. This is known as the body's centre line.

Rotation and circumduction

These are circular movements.

Abduction is the sideways movement of a limb away from the body's centre line.

Adduction is a sideways movement, towards and even across the body's centre line.

Rotation is a turning movement, such as turning the head.

In **circumduction**, the end of the bone moves in a circle, for example swinging your arm 360° about your shoulder joint.

ACTIVITY

Understanding movement at freely movable joints

Copy and complete the table. Add your own example at the end.

TYPE OF JOINT	SKELETAL EXAMPLE	LOCATION	MOVEMENT CREATED	SPORTING ACTION
Pivot	Joint between atlas and axis	Neck	Rotation	Side to side breathing (lateral) in front crawl
			Extension	
	Knee			
			Circumduction	

The skeletal system

The muscular system

The skeleton provides your body with its frame, but the muscles give your body its unique **shape**.

There are hundreds of muscles in your body, from the very largest in your legs to the tiny ones in your eyes.

Some of these muscles work automatically. For example, your heart muscle (**cardiac muscle**) keeps on beating by itself and your body digests the food that you eat. The muscles responsible are called **involuntary muscles** because you do not have to decide when and how to use them.

The muscles you use to take part in exercise and sport are called **voluntary muscles** because you are in control of them. You use them to create movements, whether of the whole body (gross motor skills) or of a part of it (fine motor skills).

 skill acquisition, p.143

Denise Lewis has a very distinct shape. Her muscles have been defined by athletic training

Involuntary or smooth muscle

Involuntary muscles work without you consciously controlling them. Examples are found in the lining of the stomach, in the bowels, in the walls of the blood vessels and inside your eyes.

Cardiac muscle

The heart is a specialised type of involuntary muscle which contracts, or beats, rhythmically. As the heart beats, it pumps blood out of the heart to the lungs and around the body.

 the circulatory system, p.31

Voluntary muscle

Voluntary, or skeletal, muscle is the type of muscle used to perform sporting movements and actions.

These muscles give your body its shape. There are more than 600 of them in the human body. They are attached to your bones by **tendons**. Voluntary muscles account for over 40% of your body's weight.

Structure of skeletal muscle

Skeletal muscle is composed of thousands of long narrow **muscle fibres** or cells that are able to contract. The combined effect of all of the muscle fibres contracting is to change the length of the muscle.

The muscle can shorten or lengthen, but it can also produce tension without changing in length. An example of this is in a handstand, where the muscles of the arms and upper body are working to support the body's weight and hold the handstand steady when the body is upside down. This an example of **isometric** contraction.

Skeletal muscle needs to be observed under magnification to understand its complex structure

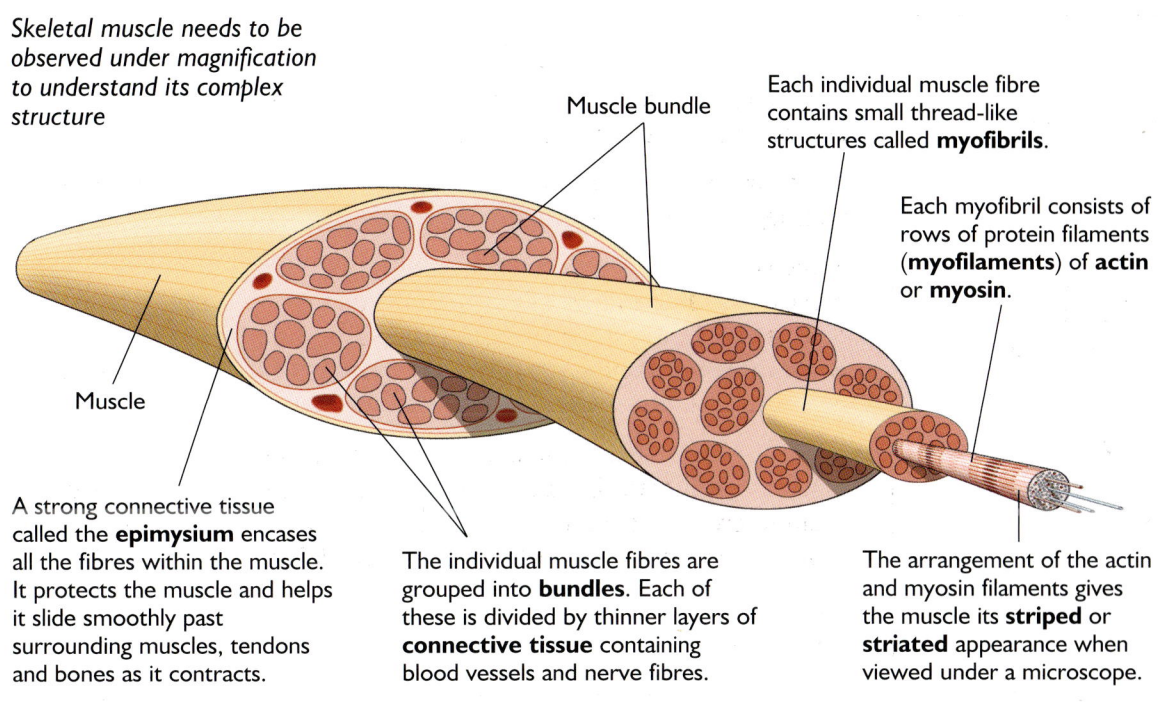

A strong connective tissue called the **epimysium** encases all the fibres within the muscle. It protects the muscle and helps it slide smoothly past surrounding muscles, tendons and bones as it contracts.

The individual muscle fibres are grouped into **bundles**. Each of these is divided by thinner layers of **connective tissue** containing blood vessels and nerve fibres.

Each individual muscle fibre contains small thread-like structures called **myofibrils**.

Each myofibril consists of rows of protein filaments (**myofilaments**) of **actin** or **myosin**.

The arrangement of the actin and myosin filaments gives the muscle its **striped** or **striated** appearance when viewed under a microscope.

The small, thinner actin filaments surround the thicker myosin filaments. When the muscle contracts (shortens), it is as a result of the actin filaments sliding over the myosin filaments. This movement is referred to as the sliding filament theory.

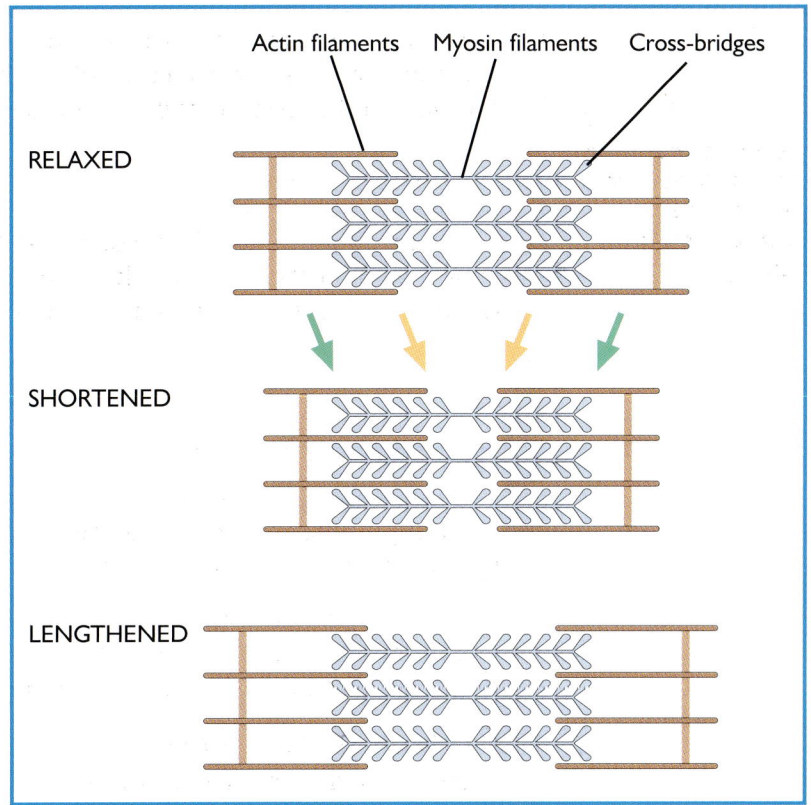

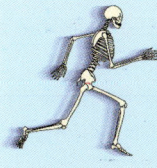

Voluntary muscle structure

Flex and then extend (bend then straighten) your arm. Can you see your biceps forming a distinct shape or mass as you flex your arm?

Think about the hundreds of tiny protein filaments in your biceps muscle which are working to make the biceps firm. What is happening to the muscle length as you flex your arm?

The muscular system

Skeletal muscle – location and function
All skeletal or voluntary muscles have the same internal structure, but they vary in their size, shape and function.

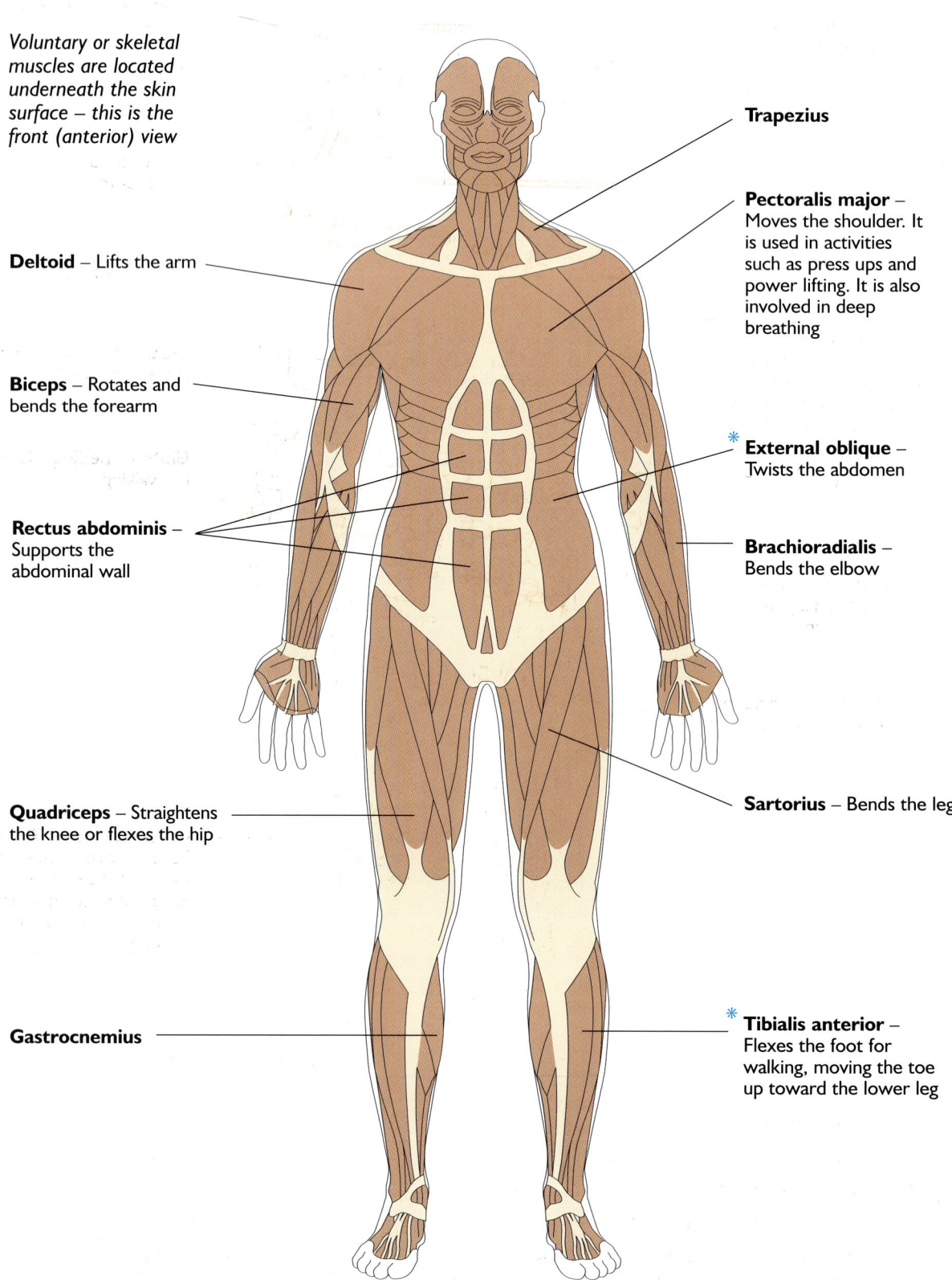

Voluntary or skeletal muscles are located underneath the skin surface – this is the front (anterior) view

Deltoid – Lifts the arm

Biceps – Rotates and bends the forearm

Rectus abdominis – Supports the abdominal wall

Quadriceps – Straightens the knee or flexes the hip

Gastrocnemius

Trapezius

Pectoralis major – Moves the shoulder. It is used in activities such as press ups and power lifting. It is also involved in deep breathing

***External oblique** – Twists the abdomen

Brachioradialis – Bends the elbow

Sartorius – Bends the leg

***Tibialis anterior** – Flexes the foot for walking, moving the toe up toward the lower leg

Back (posterior) view

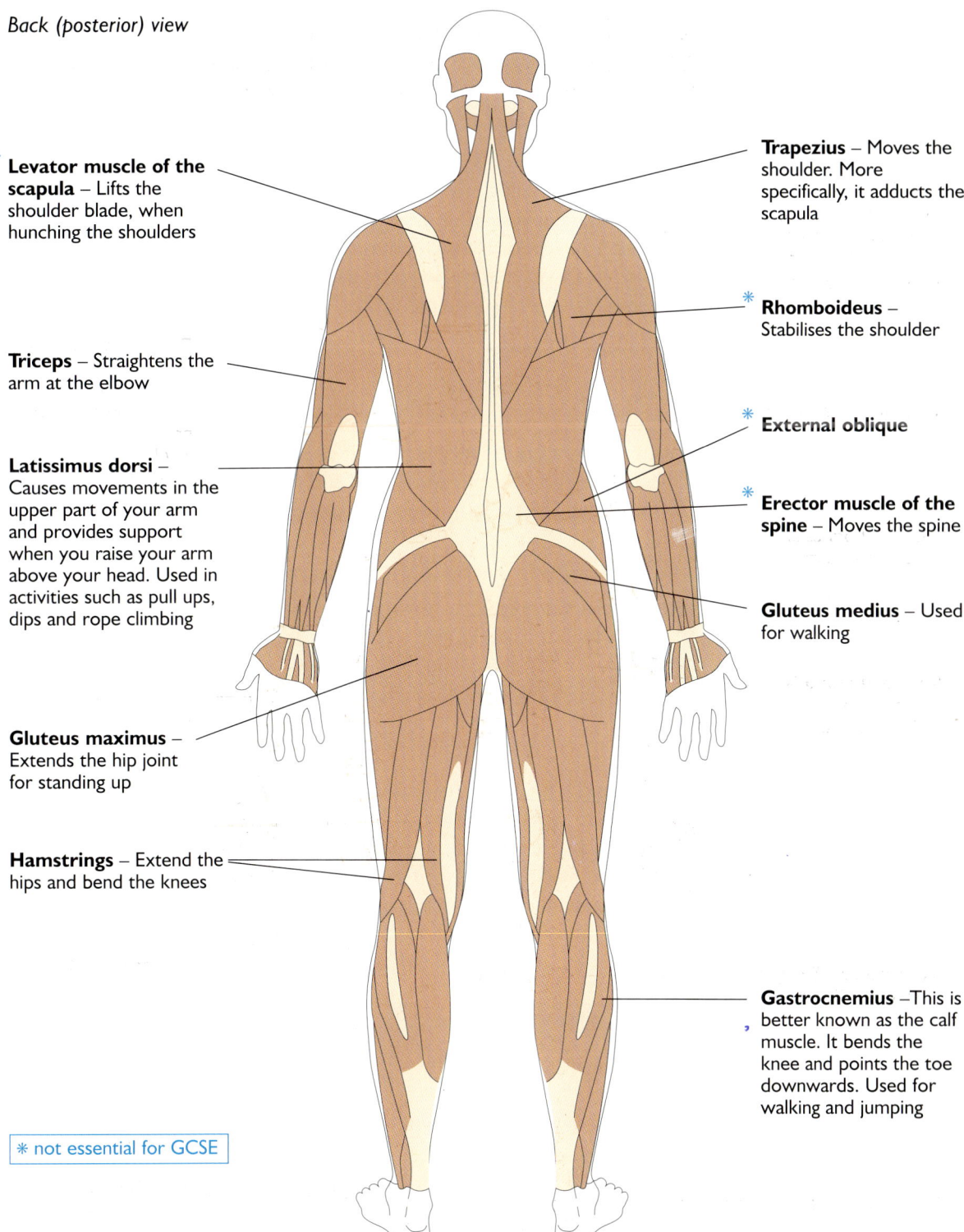

* **Levator muscle of the scapula** – Lifts the shoulder blade, when hunching the shoulders

Triceps – Straightens the arm at the elbow

Latissimus dorsi – Causes movements in the upper part of your arm and provides support when you raise your arm above your head. Used in activities such as pull ups, dips and rope climbing

Gluteus maximus – Extends the hip joint for standing up

Hamstrings – Extend the hips and bend the knees

Trapezius – Moves the shoulder. More specifically, it adducts the scapula

* **Rhomboideus** – Stabilises the shoulder

* **External oblique**

* **Erector muscle of the spine** – Moves the spine

Gluteus medius – Used for walking

Gastrocnemius – This is better known as the calf muscle. It bends the knee and points the toe downwards. Used for walking and jumping

* not essential for GCSE

ACTIVITY

Voluntary muscles and human movement

Make a list of six muscles from the diagrams.

Find that muscle on your body – contract it, then relax it. What sort of movement occurs when you make it work? At which joint is the movement created?

The muscular system

A 100 metre sprinter will have a higher proportion of fast twitch fibres to allow her to produce maximal effort

Muscle fibre types

There are two types of muscle fibre, **fast twitch** and **slow twitch**.

Fast twitch fibres

These are bigger and stronger than the slow twitch fibres. They contract very quickly and so are used in explosive or powerful movements like sprinting, jumping and throwing. An athlete cannot maintain this intensity or work rate for any length of time. This is because fast twitch fibres work without oxygen (anaerobically) but as a result they tire very quickly.

Slow twitch fibres

Slow twitch fibres contract slowly and with little force, but have a good oxygen supply and can work for long periods without tiring.

Endurance or repetitive-type activities, where the same movement is repeated over and over – in sports such as swimming, cycling and running – rely heavily on the work done by slow twitch fibres.

Most muscles have a balance of fast and slow twitch fibres. Many sporting activities rely on the different fibres at different times. For example, in a 2-kilometre rowing race, the coxless fours will use their fast twitch fibres at the beginning of the race to move the boat from a stationary start. They will depend on their slow twitch fibres when the stroke rate has reached a constant level but if the race requires a sprint finish the rowers will use the fast twitch fibres to increase their power output.

Fast and slow twitch fibres are distributed fairly evenly in the body. You are born with a particular ratio of fast to slow twitch fibres, which cannot be altered, although by training you can develop either type to contract more powerfully or more often. Swimmers tend to have a higher percentage of fast twitch fibres in their shoulder muscles (68%), long-distance runners tend to have a higher percentage of slow twitch fibres (74%) in their calf muscles.

Endurance athletes such as cross country skiers rely heavily on the work done by slow twitch fibres

Muscle action

Body movement is carried out by the interaction (combined work) of the muscular and skeletal systems. For this reason, they are often grouped together and referred to as the **musculoskeletal system**.

Muscles are connected to bones by tendons. Bones are connected to each other by ligaments. Where this connection occurs is typically called a joint. All movement occurs at the joint.

 joints, p.11

Muscles cause movement by contracting and relaxing – the muscle either shortens or lengthens. Muscles can only move bones by shortening in length and pulling on the tendon attachment.

For example, flexion at the elbow is produced by the contraction (shortening) of the biceps muscle and relaxation (lengthening) of the triceps. The contraction of the triceps and relaxation of the biceps straightens the arm.

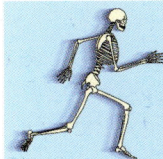

Muscle contraction and muscle length
Try bending and straightening your arm to understand the concept of movement by pulling. As you flex your arm, place the fingers of your other hand at either end of your biceps muscle. Can you feel the change in length as you alternately flex and extend your arm?

Tendon attachments

Muscles are usually attached to two (sometimes more) different bones by **tendons**. The points at which the tendons connect the muscle to bone are known as the **point of origin** and the **point of insertion**. The point of origin stays fixed, while the point of insertion moves.

The movement about to occur in the diagram is flexion at the elbow. In this movement the biceps muscle is contracting and exerting a pull on the radius so that the arm bends at the elbow. In this action the insertion moves towards the origin.

Muscles are attached to bones at the points of origin and insertion. The origin is where the muscle joins the stationary bone. The insertion is where it joins the moving bone

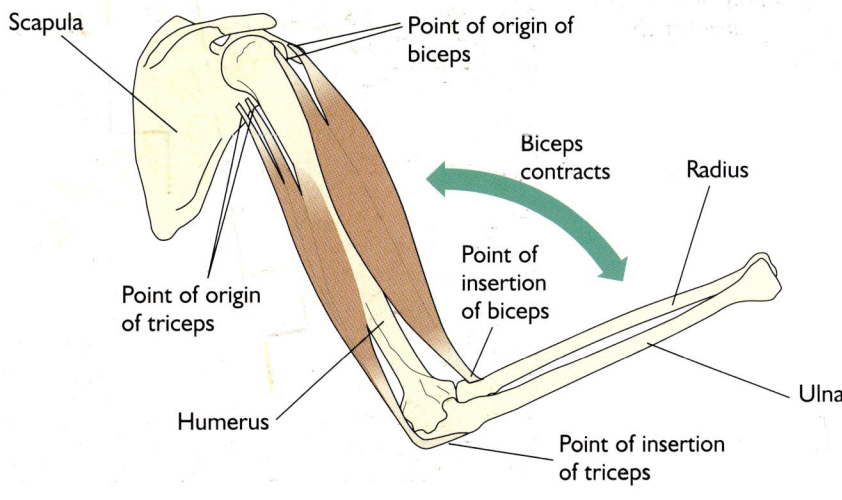

Working muscles

Muscles can only pull by **contraction** – they cannot push. If one muscle contracts across a joint to bring two bones together, then another muscle is needed to pull them apart. Muscles therefore work in pairs. These pairs are referred to as **antagonistic pairs.**

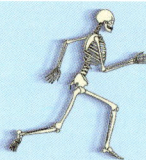

> **Antagonistic muscle pairs**
> Stand up, then flex and extend your leg at the knee. Now try walking and running. Can you identify which muscle is responsible for flexion of the leg and which for extension? Look back at the diagram of muscles of the human body (pages 18–19) to help you.

Skeletal muscles responsible for movement of the limbs can be classified according to their function or the job that they do:

◆ Muscles that bring the bones closer together are the **prime movers** or **agonists**.

◆ Their opposite, the **antagonistic** muscles, cause the joint to stretch out. For example, in the last stages of kicking a football (striking the ball and extending the leg forward in the follow through) the quadriceps is the **prime mover** or **agonist** and the hamstring is the **antagonist**.

◆ **Synergists** reduce unnecessary movement when the agonist contracts. They also fine tune the movement.

◆ **Fixators** steady parts of the body to give the working muscles a firm base.

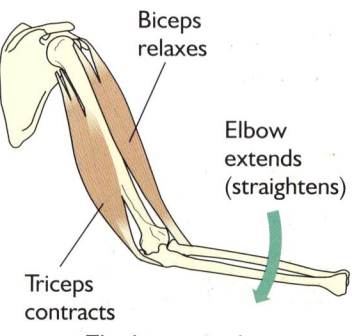

The biceps and triceps work as an antagonistic pair to flex and extend the elbow

The flexor muscle contracts to bend the joint

Synergists fine tune the movement and fixators give the working muscles a firm base

The extensor muscle contracts to straighten the joint

The antagonist works against the prime mover to control the movement

The prime movers are the main muscles that produce the movement

Sporting action and human movement occur as a result of the contraction of voluntary or skeletal muscle

Types of muscle contraction

All muscles contract, that is the muscle shortens to produce tension. There are three different types of muscle contraction:

- **isotonic**
- **isometric**
- **isokinetic**.

Isotonic contraction

Isotonic contraction can be divided into two types:

- **Concentric** This occurs when a muscle shortens. It is usually seen in the work done by the prime mover or agonist.
- **Eccentric** This involves the development of tension whilst the muscle is being lengthened. It is seen in the work done by the antagonistic muscle.

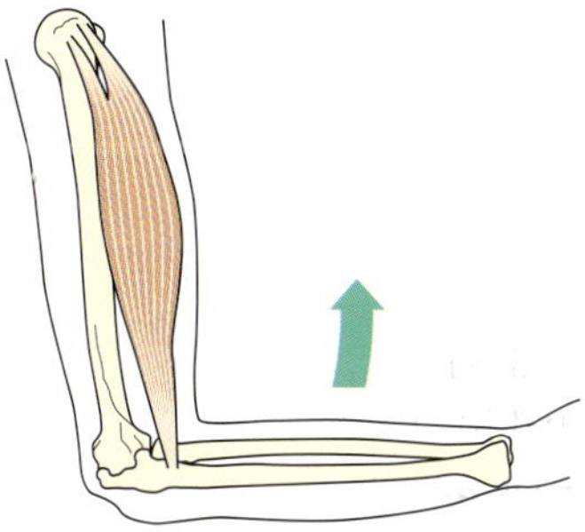

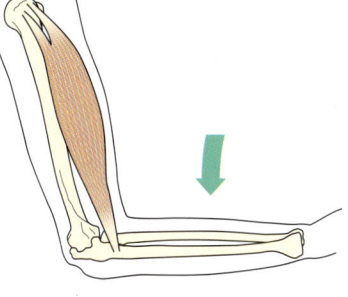

Concentric muscle contraction occurs when a muscle shortens

In eccentric muscle contraction tension is developed in the muscle while it lengthens

ACTIVITY

Concentric and eccentric contraction

Think about the following sporting movements and actions:

- an overhand throw
- kicking a football.

Identify in each of the movements the muscles that are working concentrically (shortening) and the ones that are working eccentrically (lengthening).

Make a list under the headings **Agonist** and **Antagonist** to identify the pairs.

Now complete the task using your own example.

Isometric contraction

Isometric contraction is when the muscle produces tension but does not change in length, so no movement occurs at the joint. In certain sports or activities, there are muscles whose role is to provide a static or stable base for the other muscles to do work.

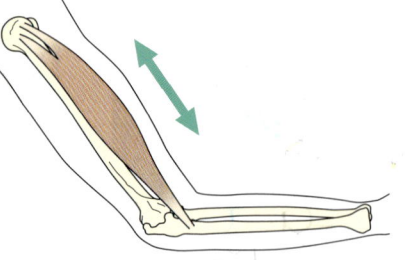

When a muscle contracts isometrically it stays the same length as it contracts. Our shoulder muscles work in this way in a tug of war

For example, in playing a shot at a snooker table, the body needs to be quite still. As the cue is drawn back and then pushed forward through the white ball, it is the biceps and triceps which are making the arm 'work'. The legs, back and shoulders are working to stabilise the body and are under isometric contraction. These muscles are working as **synergists**, enabling the other muscles to work effectively.

Isokinetic contraction

Isokinetic contraction occurs when the speed of movement stays the same throughout the activity. The muscle is changing in length (either shortening or lengthening) but at a constant rate. Isokinetic means 'same speed'.

For instance, in swimming front crawl, the arms are moving at a relatively constant speed, although the forces applied by the arms alter during the stroke.

The arm muscles of a swimmer doing the front crawl are contracting isokinetically

Levers

The bones, the joint and the muscles work together as levers to create movement. All levers have the following characteristics:

◆ a **fulcrum** – the point of movement or pivot

◆ a **load** – the body weight or some external object

◆ an **effort** – a muscular force to move the load.

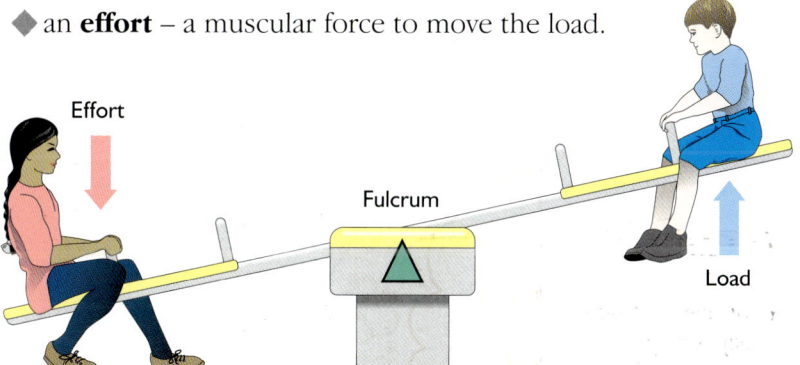

There are three classifications of lever, each of which is capable of producing different types and ranges of movements and different forces.

First-order levers

In a first-order lever the fulcrum or pivot is between the load and the effort – like the arrangement of a crowbar.

This type of system can be found at the joint between the atlas and the skull. The action of raising your head is an example of the work done by a first-order lever. In this example:

◆ the skull acts as the lever

◆ the fulcrum or pivot is the joint between the skull and atlas

◆ the load is the weight of the head and pulls the head forward

◆ the effort is supplied by the trapezius muscle – when it contracts or shortens it pulls the head back.

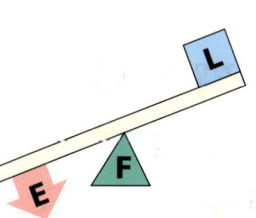
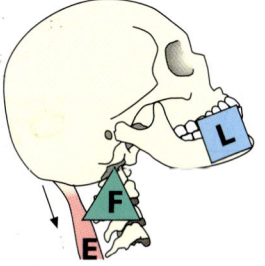

A first-order lever can be found at the joint between the atlas and the skull

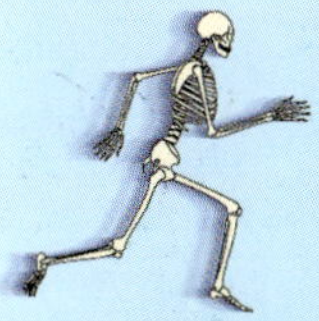

The action of a first-order lever
Locate the trapezius muscle and the joint between the skull and atlas at the back of your neck. If you can't find it, look back at the diagrams of the muscular system and skeletal systems.
Now put your hand against the muscle and then against the joint and raise your head slowly up and down. Can you feel the work being done by this lever?

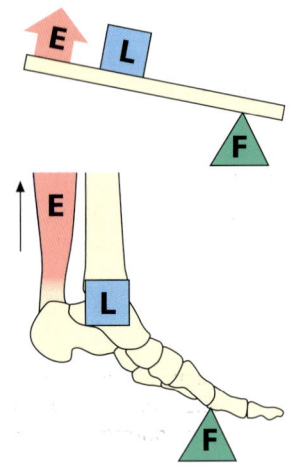

A second-order lever can be likened to the work done by a wheelbarrow. Look at the position of the load between the fulcrum and the effort when standing on your toes

The third-order lever is the most common type of lever found in the human body

Second-order levers

In this lever, the load is between the fulcrum and the effort, similar to a wheelbarrow.

This system can be found at the ankle joint when you are standing on your toes:

◆ your heel is the lever

◆ the fulcrum is the point of contact between your toes and the ground

◆ the load is the weight of your body

◆ the effort is supplied by the gastrocnemius muscle, which pulls on your heel bone.

Third-order levers

In this system, the effort is between the load and the fulcrum. This is the most common type of lever in the human body – an example can be found at the elbow joint.

In this type of lever, the muscle is attached close to the joint, meaning that a small muscular contraction will produce a long lever movement.

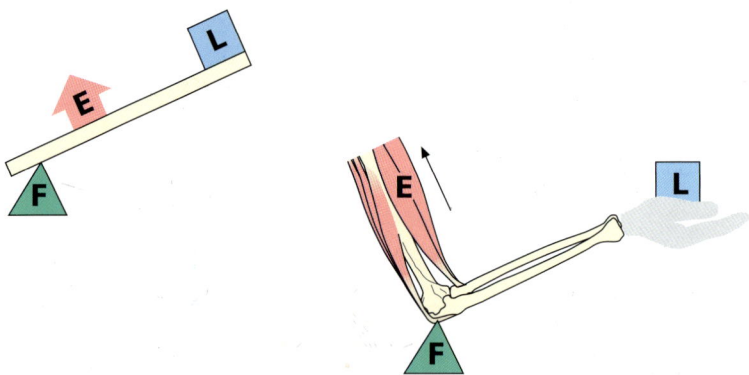

Lifting a weight such as a dumbbell shows a third-order lever in action:

◆ the radius and ulna act as the lever

◆ the fulcrum is your elbow joint

◆ the load is the combined weight of the arm and dumbbell

◆ the effort is supplied by the contraction of your biceps.

ACTIVITY

Levers in the human body

Move other parts of your appendicular skeleton. Try to identify where the fulcrum, load and effort are in the movement.

Identify whether they are acting as first, second or third-order levers.

The respiratory system

In order to function properly, the millions of cells in the human body needs a constant supply of **oxygen** (O_2)

The supply of oxygen is delivered through the process of breathing (**respiration**). The body has a set of breathing equipment – the mouth, nose and lungs – through which oxygen is drawn in and **carbon dioxide** (CO_2) expelled.

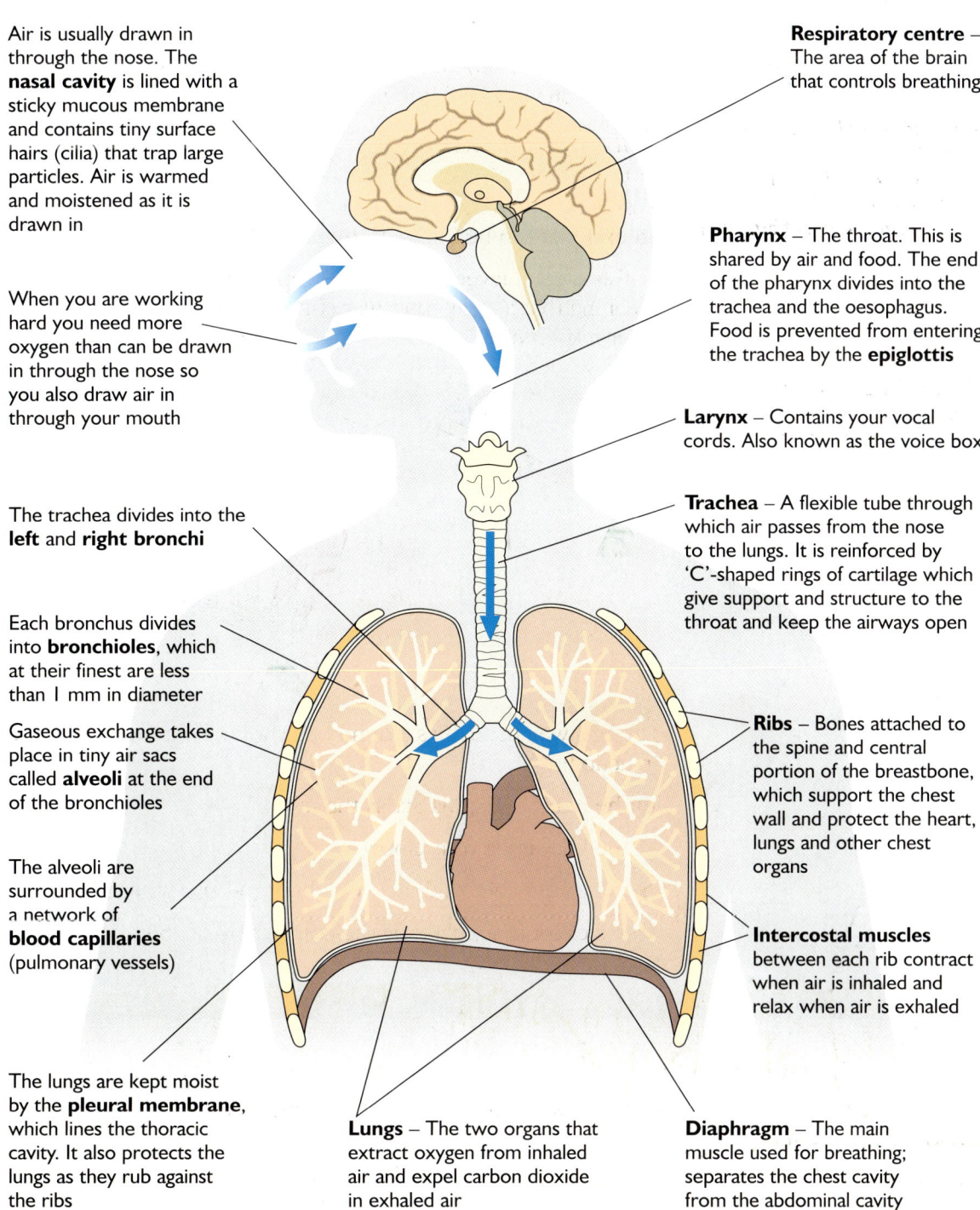

Air is usually drawn in through the nose. The **nasal cavity** is lined with a sticky mucous membrane and contains tiny surface hairs (cilia) that trap large particles. Air is warmed and moistened as it is drawn in

When you are working hard you need more oxygen than can be drawn in through the nose so you also draw air in through your mouth

The trachea divides into the **left** and **right bronchi**

Each bronchus divides into **bronchioles**, which at their finest are less than 1 mm in diameter

Gaseous exchange takes place in tiny air sacs called **alveoli** at the end of the bronchioles

The alveoli are surrounded by a network of **blood capillaries** (pulmonary vessels)

The lungs are kept moist by the **pleural membrane**, which lines the thoracic cavity. It also protects the lungs as they rub against the ribs

Respiratory centre – The area of the brain that controls breathing

Pharynx – The throat. This is shared by air and food. The end of the pharynx divides into the trachea and the oesophagus. Food is prevented from entering the trachea by the **epiglottis**

Larynx – Contains your vocal cords. Also known as the voice box

Trachea – A flexible tube through which air passes from the nose to the lungs. It is reinforced by 'C'-shaped rings of cartilage which give support and structure to the throat and keep the airways open

Ribs – Bones attached to the spine and central portion of the breastbone, which support the chest wall and protect the heart, lungs and other chest organs

Intercostal muscles between each rib contract when air is inhaled and relax when air is exhaled

Lungs – The two organs that extract oxygen from inhaled air and expel carbon dioxide in exhaled air

Diaphragm – The main muscle used for breathing; separates the chest cavity from the abdominal cavity

The mechanics of breathing

There are two breathing phases – in and out. These are also known as **inhalation** (or inspiration) and **exhalation** (or expiration).

Inhalation

When you breathe in, the **intercostal muscles** (which lie between the ribs) contract and draw the rib cage upwards and outwards. At the same time the diaphragm contracts to flatten out. This movement can be seen in the diagram below.

The combined action of the intercostal muscles and the diaphragm means that the volume or space inside the lungs increases and so the pressure inside the lungs decreases. When the pressure inside the lungs becomes lower than the pressure outside air is drawn down the respiratory passages into the lungs.

Exhalation

The intercostals and diaphragm muscles return to their original position. This is known as **elastic recoil** and is a passive action.

When this happens, the space inside the lungs is squeezed. This space is now smaller and the pressure of the air inside the lungs increases and so is higher than the external (atmospheric) pressure. This squeezing effect forces the air out of the lungs and through the nose or mouth – the same route by which air was drawn in.

BREATHING IN

4 The pressure inside the lungs falls as they expand. Air is sucked into the lungs

1 The intercostal muscles contract, pulling the rib cage upwards and outwards, so the chest expands

3 When the chest expands, the lungs also expand because their outside lining clings to the chest lining

2 The diaphragm contracts and flattens, making the chest cavity even larger

BREATHING OUT

3 When the chest gets smaller the lungs are compressed, which pushes air out

1 The intercostal muscles relax, lowering the rib cage and making the chest cavity smaller

2 The diaphragm relaxes and bulges upwards again, making the chest cavity even smaller

→ direction of movement

The mechanics of breathing
Take a really deep breath. Place your hands on your rib cage and feel them moving upwards and outwards.
You will only be able to draw in a certain amount of air until your lungs are full and then you will have to breathe out. Can you feel the changes in the depth of the movements of the rib cage (respiratory movements)?
What do you suppose happens to your breathing – both the breathing rate and respiratory movements – during exercise?

The air you breathe

The air around you contains a number of different gases. The main gas is nitrogen, which makes up 79% of the air you breathe. The proportion of other gases you inhale and exhale are listed in the table below. Notice also the different amounts of water vapour.

GAS	INHALED AIR	EXHALED AIR
Oxygen	21%	17%
Carbon dioxide	0.03%	3%
Nitrogen	79%	79%
Water vapour	a little	a lot

Gaseous exchange in the lungs

The lungs are responsible for taking in and getting rid of two gases – oxygen and carbon dioxide. Oxygen is drawn into the alveoli through the respiratory passages and carbon dioxide is expelled via the same pathway. This **gaseous exchange** takes place in the lungs.

The alveoli (air sacs) at the end of the respiratory tract are completely surrounded by a network of blood capillaries

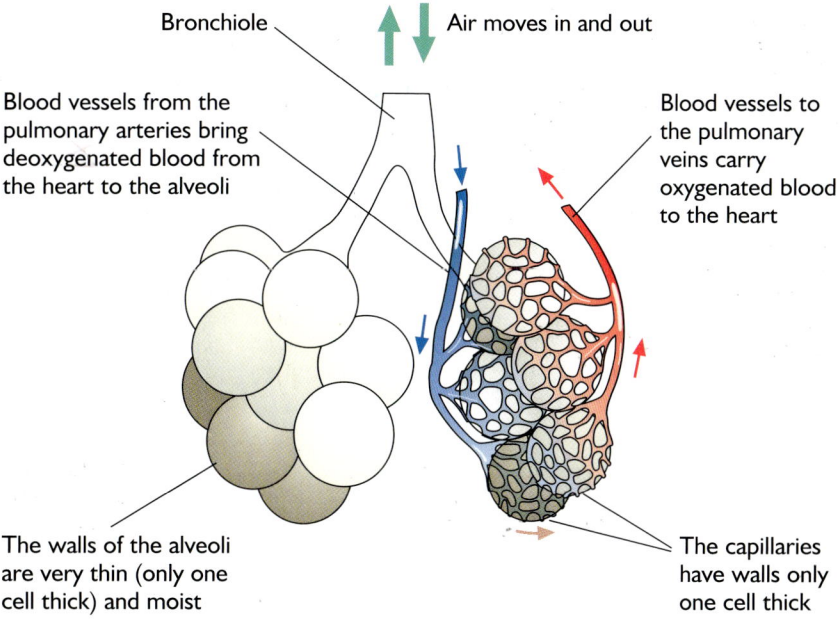

The respiratory system

Gaseous exchange in the alveoli

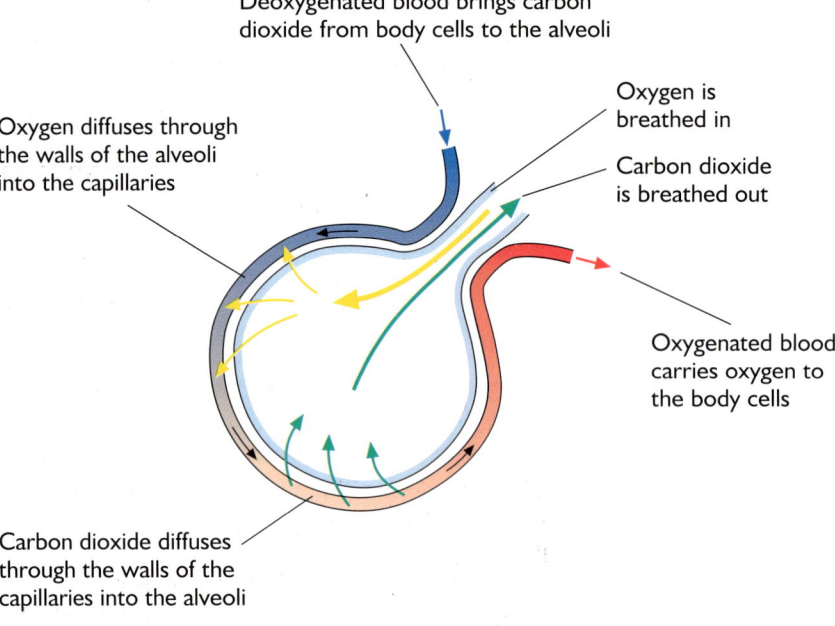

Lung capacity

There are a number of measures that can be taken of the amount of air moving into and out of the lungs:

◆ **Tidal volume** is the amount of air that you can breathe in or out with each breath.

◆ The lungs never completely empty, and the air that is left is the **residual volume**. This is measured after a maximum exhalation and is about 1.5 litres.

◆ **Vital capacity** is the maximum amount of air that you can breathe out after breathing in as deeply as you can. It is usually around 4.5 or 5 litres of air.

◆ The **respiratory rate** is how many breaths you take per minute.

◆ **Minute volume** is the amount of air you breathe in per minute and is calculated from:

Minute volume = Tidal volume ~~minus~~ the respiratory rate

◆ **Total lung capacity = vital capacity + residual volume**

Lung capacity and exercise

When you start to exercise, you put 'increased stress' on your body. The extent of this stress will vary according to what **type** of activity you are performing, how hard you are working (the **intensity**) and how long you are working for (the **duration**).

 the effects of exercise and training p. 81

In order to cope with the increased stress caused by exercise, the body needs more oxygen to release energy in the working muscles. This supply of oxygen is increased by:

◆ increasing the rate of breathing (the respiratory rate)
◆ increasing the amount of air drawn in and expelled with each breath (tidal volume)
◆ increasing the blood supply to and through the lungs
◆ increasing the amount of oxygen taken up by the capillaries at the lungs.

The amount of oxygen used or taken up during exercise increases as the level of exercise increases. The maximum amount of oxygen a person can take up and use within a minute is their $\dot{V}O_2$**max**.

The $\dot{V}O_2$max can be measured to give an indication of a person's fitness levels. It is usually expressed relative to body weight. Typical values are in the range of 30–60 ml kg^{-1} min^{-1}. Most athletes find it impossible to work at their max $\dot{V}O_2$, so they work at a percentage of it.

Professional cyclists like Lance Armstrong have high $\dot{V}O_2$max values

 fitness testing p. 70

The circulatory (cardiovascular) system

The circulatory system is the body's main transport system. It ensures that blood is constantly supplied throughout the body.

This system works with the respiratory system, taking oxygen from the lungs to the rest of the body and carbon dioxide from the cells to the lungs. Carbon dioxide and oxygen transfer from the blood to the lungs or the cells in a process known as **gaseous exchange**. The circulatory system is made up of the heart, a network of blood vessels and the blood. Collectively these components are referred to as the **cardiovascular system**.

The structure of the heart

The heart is a muscular organ about the size of a closed fist. It consists of two side-by-side pumps and has a double pumping action.

Internally the heart is divided into four chambers. The upper chambers are called the **atria**, and the lower chambers the **ventricles** (to remember which chambers are the upper and which are the lower, think **a**tria **a**bove). These chambers regulate the flow of blood through the heart. The right and left sides of the heart are separated by the **septum**.

Notice in the diagram of the heart that the right and left chambers appear to be on the wrong sides. But don't worry – you are seeing the front view of a person facing you.

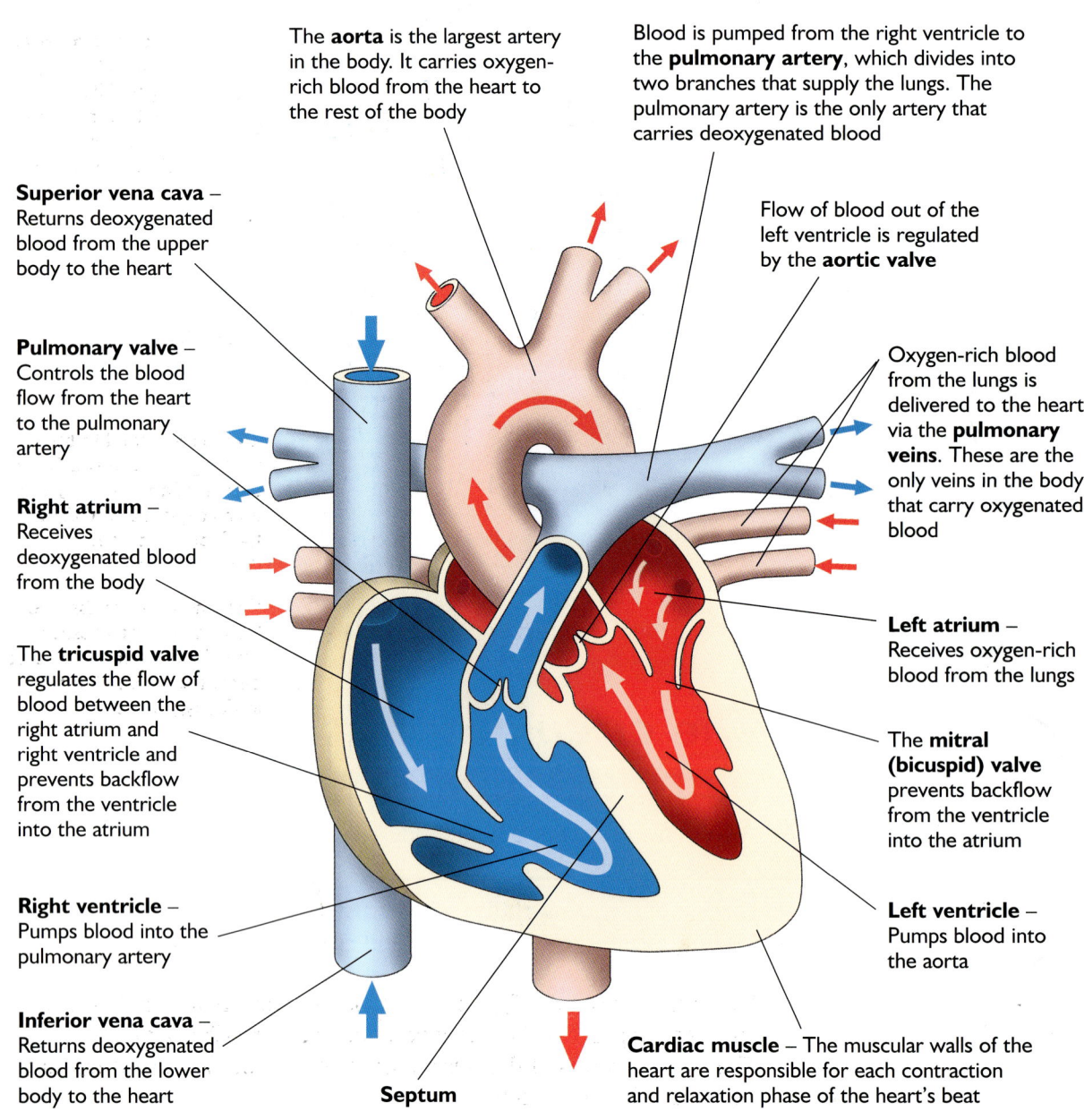

The **aorta** is the largest artery in the body. It carries oxygen-rich blood from the heart to the rest of the body

Blood is pumped from the right ventricle to the **pulmonary artery**, which divides into two branches that supply the lungs. The pulmonary artery is the only artery that carries deoxygenated blood

Flow of blood out of the left ventricle is regulated by the **aortic valve**

Superior vena cava – Returns deoxygenated blood from the upper body to the heart

Oxygen-rich blood from the lungs is delivered to the heart via the **pulmonary veins**. These are the only veins in the body that carry oxygenated blood

Pulmonary valve – Controls the blood flow from the heart to the pulmonary artery

Right atrium – Receives deoxygenated blood from the body

Left atrium – Receives oxygen-rich blood from the lungs

The **tricuspid valve** regulates the flow of blood between the right atrium and right ventricle and prevents backflow from the ventricle into the atrium

The **mitral (bicuspid) valve** prevents backflow from the ventricle into the atrium

Right ventricle – Pumps blood into the pulmonary artery

Left ventricle – Pumps blood into the aorta

Inferior vena cava – Returns deoxygenated blood from the lower body to the heart

Septum

Cardiac muscle – The muscular walls of the heart are responsible for each contraction and relaxation phase of the heart's beat

Circulation of the blood

Blood is circulated around the entire body by a series of arteries, veins and capillaries. Arteries generally carry **oxygenated** blood and veins generally carry **deoxygenated** blood. Blood flow is continuous

The heart pumps oxygenated blood into the **aorta**, the largest artery in the body

Deoxygenated blood is returned to the right side of the heart via the system of **veins**

Deoxygenated blood is pumped to the lungs via the **pulmonary artery**

Oxygen-rich (**oxygenated**) blood is returned to the left side of the heart via the **pulmonary veins**

Gaseous exchange occurs in the lungs – oxygen diffuses into the blood and carbon dioxide diffuses out to be expelled

Oxygen is carried to the working tissues through the system of arteries. By giving up its oxygen to the tissues the blood becomes **deoxygenated**

Carbon dioxide is absorbed from the working tissues. The blood can now be called **carbon dioxide rich** as well as deoxygenated

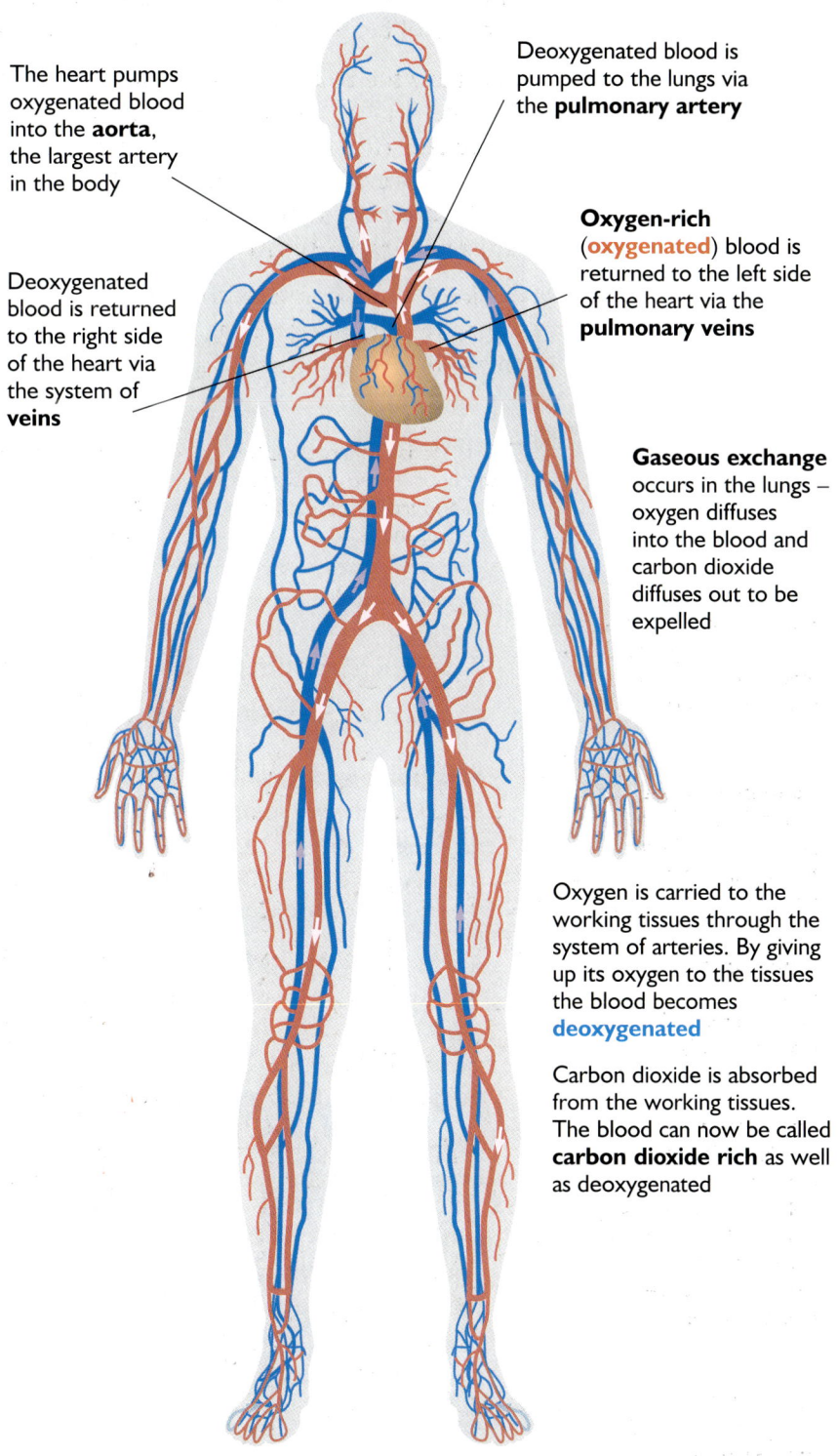

You can see from the figure that blood flow occurs in a cycle – it is an ongoing process. The flow of blood is in **one direction only**. The various valves of the heart ensure that blood flows through the heart in only one direction.

The circulatory (cardiovascular) system

ACTIVITY

The heart and blood circulation

You should be able to identify:

◆ the flow of blood through the heart
◆ which vessels carry blood away from and to the heart
◆ the composition of blood at each stage as it flows through the heart (i.e. whether it is oxygenated or deoxygenated).

If you are not sure of any of these, go back to the diagrams on the earlier pages. Follow the flow of blood in the diagram opposite out of the left atrium around the body and back to the heart.

Which chamber is the blood returned to:

◆ at the end of its cycle around the body?
◆ after it has been re-oxygenated in the lungs?

The blood vessels

Blood is carried around the body by a series of tubes or vessels. They vary in size and function according to their location in the body. There are three types of vessel:

◆ **arteries** ◆ **veins** ◆ **capillaries**.

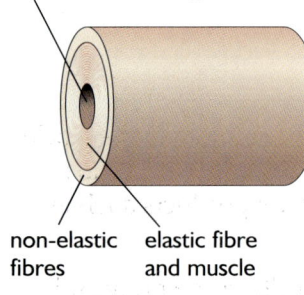

Arteries

Arteries carry oxygenated blood away from the heart (you can remember this by thinking **a**rteries, **a**way). However, the pulmonary artery does not carry oxygenated blood, but carries deoxygenated blood from the heart to the lungs.

The walls of an artery contain elastic tissue. This means that the diameter of the wall can either dilate (expand) or constrict (contract) to allow the flow of blood. During exercise the artery walls will dilate so that they can carry an increased flow of blood from the heart to the working muscles.

Arteries sub-divide greatly into a network of smaller tubes, called **arterioles**, which sub-divide even further into **capillaries**.

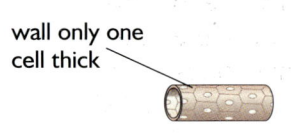

Capillaries

Capillaries are very fine vessels, only one cell thick. Oxygen and nutrients diffuse out of the blood into the cells where they're needed, and carbon dioxide and waste products diffuse out of the cells into the blood to be removed from the body.

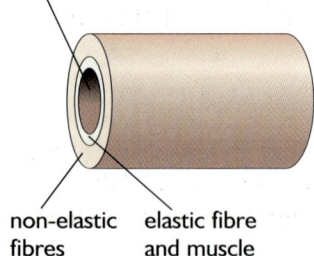

Veins

Carbon dioxide rich blood is then carried away from the capillaries into the **venules**, then veins and back to the heart's right atrium.

Blood travels through the veins at a lower pressure than through the arteries. Veins have a series of valves throughout their length which prevent backflow.

Arteries and veins are part of the network system that carries blood to all parts of the body

Oxygen diffuses from blood into tissues through thin capillary walls. Carbon dioxide diffuses out of the tissues into the blood

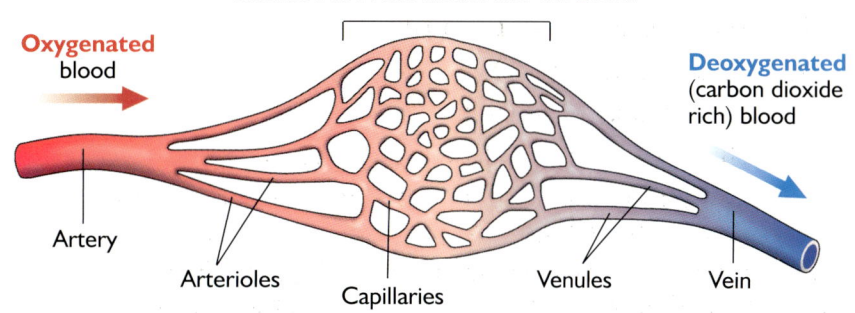

Oxygenated blood

Deoxygenated (carbon dioxide rich) blood

Artery | Arterioles | Capillaries | Venules | Vein

Composition of the blood

The human body contains nearly five litres of blood, though the actual amount may vary according to your size and shape. Men have around one litre more than women and endurance athletes may have more again.

Blood is made up of the following elements:

- **plasma** (the liquid component)
- **red cells** (known as erythrocytes)
- **white cells**
- **platelets**.

Plasma

Blood plasma makes up 55% of the total blood volume and is a pale yellow liquid consisting mainly of water. The remainder contains plasma proteins, glucose, amino acids and waste products such as carbon dioxide and urea.

Proteins and amino acids are transported to cells in the body and used for growth and repair. Glucose is used to supply energy.

Red cells (erythrocytes)

One drop (about 1 mm^3) of healthy blood contains about five million red cells. The erythrocytes make up most of the remaining 45% of blood volume. Their most important function is to carry oxygen. The oxygen-carrying compartment of the cell is called **haemoglobin** and gives the cell its red colour. Iron in the haemoglobin binds oxygen to the red cells to form **oxyhaemoglobin**.

Red blood cells have no nucleus and live about 120 days. They are replaced in vast numbers in the red marrow of bones such as the sternum, ribs and vertebrae.

White blood cells (leukocytes)

White blood cells are larger than the red cells (three times the size) and have a nucleus. Their chief function is to protect the body against disease. They are produced in the bone marrow, the spleen and lymph nodes.

The circulatory (cardiovascular) system

Platelets (thrombocytes)

Platelets are fragments or particles made from special cells in the bone marrow. They appear at the site of a cut and combine to form either a platelet plug (in small blood vessels) or a clot (in larger wounds), in order to stop the bleeding. The clot is known as a **thrombus**.

The blood circulatory systems

The heart is a double pump. It pumps blood around two circulatory circuits, the **systemic** and **pulmonary** circuits.

Systemic circulation

The systemic circuit carries **oxygenated blood** and vital **nutrients** around the body. It begins in the left ventricle where blood is carried to the body via the aorta and the system of arteries. Blood rich in carbon dioxide is returned from the body via the veins and the vena cava into the right atrium.

Pulmonary circulation

The pulmonary circuit carries **deoxygenated blood** from the right ventricle via the pulmonary artery to the lungs. At the lungs, carbon dioxide is exchanged for oxygen. Oxygenated blood is then carried back to the heart via the pulmonary vein to the left atrium.

The pumping action of the heart

The heart is a specialised type of muscle, called **cardiac muscle**, which contracts rhythmically and tirelessly.

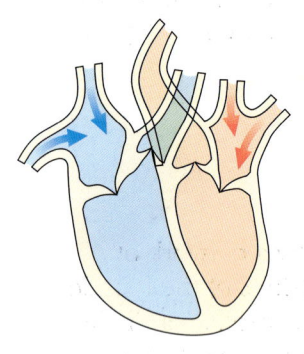

1. When the heart is relaxed between beats, the atria fill with oxygenated blood from the pulmonary vein on the left-hand side and deoxygenated blood from the vena cava on the right

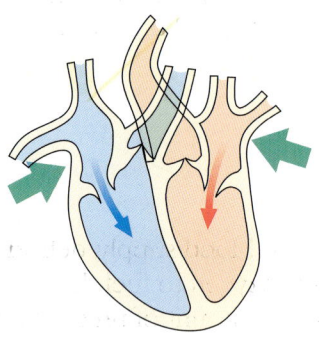

2. The atrium muscles contract and force the blood through the **atrioventricular valves** (bicuspid on the left and tricuspid on the right) into the ventricles

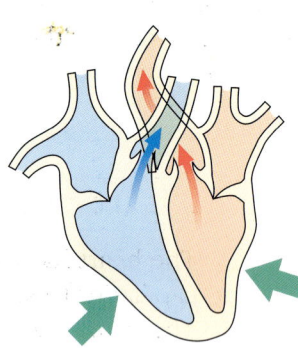

3. The ventricle muscles contract about a tenth of a second later than the atrium muscles. The atrioventricular valves close to prevent backflow. Blood leaves from the left ventricle (via the aorta) for general circulation in the body, and from the right ventricle (via the pulmonary artery) to the lungs for gaseous exchange

4. The heart muscle relaxes again and the stages of contraction are repeated

This cycle of events is called the **cardiac cycle**. One complete cycle of contraction and relaxation is referred to as a **heart beat**.

At rest, your heart beats about 72 times per minute and the blood takes around 20 seconds to go round the body once. Heart rate will vary with many factors, including age and level of fitness. During physical exercise, when the working muscles need more oxygen, heart rate can reach over 200 beats per minute.

ACTIVITY

Measuring your pulse

Find your pulse. There are two places you can do this: the carotid or radial arteries.

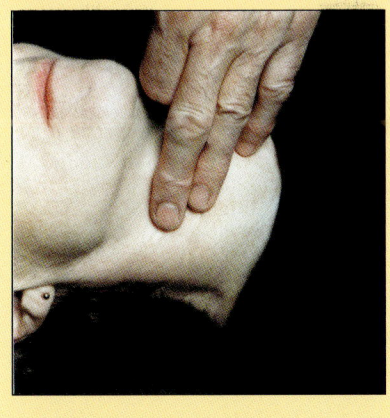

You can take your pulse at either the carotid artery (left) or the radial artery (right)

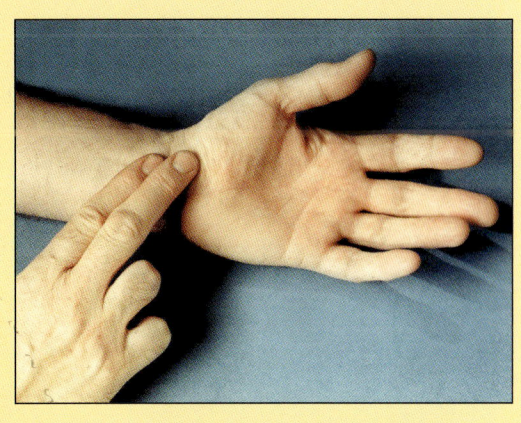

Once you have found your pulse, ask a friend to time 15 seconds on a watch while you count beats. Multiply your score by four to work out your resting heart rate per minute.

Compare your heart rate with the average heart rate of between 50 and 80. Is yours higher or lower? Can you explain why?

Now run on the spot for two minutes. As soon as you stop, take your heart rate again. How high is it now? Do you think it could go even higher? If so, what sort of exercise will you have to do to increase it further?

Heart rate

The heart has its own blood supply, delivered by a network of capillaries to supply oxygen to fuel the contractions of the muscle. The **heart rate** is the amount of times the heart beats in a single minute. It is controlled by the brain in response to the body's needs. The rhythm can be increased or decreased according to the body's demands for oxygen.

Cardiac output

Cardiac output is the measure of the volume of blood that leaves the left ventricle in one minute. It is measured from the left ventricle because it is a measure of the amount of blood required by the body at different times, for example during rest or exercise.

Cardiac output is determined by the heart rate and the **stroke volume**, and is calculated using the following formula:

Cardiac output = stroke volume x heart rate

Stroke volume is the volume of blood ejected from the heart in a single beat. It usually refers to the amount of blood pumped from the left ventricle.

During exercise, your cardiac output increases considerably. For example, an individual at rest may have a stroke volume of 75 ml per beat and a heart rate of 70 beats per minute (bpm).

Cardiac output = 75 ml x 70 bpm
= 5250 ml/min
= 5.250 l/min

During exercise, if their heart rate increases to 150 bpm, and their stroke volume to 150 ml per beat, their cardiac output would increase to over four times the resting rate:

Cardiac output = 150 ml x 150 bpm
= 22500 ml/min
= 22.5 l/min

ACTIVITY

Measuring cardiac output

John is a swimmer. He has a resting heart rate of 60 beats per minute and a stroke volume at rest of 65 ml per beat. During intense or maximal exercise John's heart rate increases to 160 bpm and his stroke volume to 140 ml.

1 Work out John's cardiac output both at rest and during maximal exercise. How much bigger is his exercise value than his resting value?
2 Give three reasons why cardiac output increases during exercise.

Blood pressure

Every time your heart beats it pumps blood through the arteries. The pumping action of the heart creates pressure which can be felt in different parts of the body – most strongly in the arteries.

Blood pressure can be easily measured, by taking the pressure at an artery in the arm. A special instrument is used, called a **sphygmomanometer**. The cuff of this instrument is placed around the upper arm and is inflated with enough pressure to stop the blood flowing (this pressure is measured). The pressure is then reduced and the blood starts to flow again (this pressure is also measured). Modern equipment gives a digital display and print-out of blood pressures.

The two readings are usually taken when you are relaxed and resting.

◆ The pressure needed to stop the blood flowing is known as the **systolic pressure**. It is the maximum reading as the heart contracts and pumps blood into the arteries.

◆ The pressure at which the blood starts to flow again is called the **diastolic pressure**. It is the minimum reading as the heart relaxes and fills with blood.

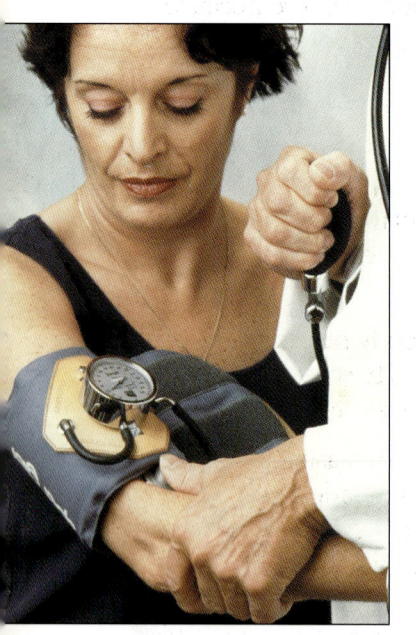

Blood pressure is recorded using a device called a sphygmomanometer

Blood pressure is presented as systolic pressure/diastolic pressure ('over'). The average reading for an adult is 120/80 mmHg (millimetres of mercury). You might have heard this spoken about as 'one hundred and twenty over eighty'.

If a person's blood pressure is consistently greater than 140/90 mmHg, he or she is said to suffer from high blood pressure or **hypertension**. If it is not treated, hypertension can cause untold problems because the heart has to work too hard and will develop cardiovascular disease, which can lead to a stroke or a heart attack.

Factors affecting blood pressure

Blood pressure is an indication of general health. There are a number of factors which affect it.

- **Exercise** Blood pressure increases when you exercise. This is because the heart is working harder to supply your muscles with more oxygen. Regular exercise helps to lower resting and exercise blood pressure and prevent cardiovascular disease.

> NEXT *effects of exercise and training, p. 81*

- **Age** Blood pressure increases as you grow older. This is because the arteries lose their elasticity and do not expand so much when blood is pumped through them.

- **Stress and tension** Both increase blood pressure. This is because hormones are released into the bloodstream when the body becomes stressed.

- **Diet** High levels of fat and salt cause the arteries to stiffen or clog up, leading to an increase in blood pressure.

- **Smoking** Cigarette smoking increases blood pressure because nicotine reduces the efficiency of the capillaries.

Immediate effects of exercise on the oxygen transport systems

Both the respiratory and circulatory systems play a role in the transport of oxygen. These systems are often referred to as the **oxygen transport systems**.

When you take part in sport or exercise, the body places a number of demands on the oxygen transport systems. These demands are also referred to as the **immediate effects of exercise**.

- Even before you start to exercise, your body releases the hormone **adrenaline**, which prepares you for action by stimulating the respiratory and circulatory systems. Most of you will know what the surge of adrenaline feels like if you have ever been nervous about something, say just before a match or race. It is often associated with 'nerves', butterflies in your tummy, rapid breathing, a quickened heart rate and sweating palms – it can even make people feel sick.

◆ During exercise your muscles work harder and the respiration in the muscle cells (called the **internal** or **cell respiration**) increases. This uses up more oxygen and produces more carbon dioxide as waste. Carbon dioxide starts to build up in the blood.

◆ The increased levels of carbon dioxide in the blood are detected by the brain, which sends a message to the lungs to breathe faster and deeper in order to expel the carbon dioxide. So the **respiratory rate** increases.

◆ As a result of the increase in the rate of breathing more carbon dioxide is expelled from the blood and more oxygen is drawn in to supply the muscles.

◆ In order to cope with the working muscles' demand for more oxygen, the brain sends a message to the heart to speed up.

◆ As a response to this message, the heart rate increases. More blood is pumped with each beat of the heart to increase the flow of blood between the muscles and the lungs, and to provide them with more oxygen. The stroke volume increases. If stroke volume and heart rate both increase, then so does the cardiac output.

◀ BACK *cardiac output, p. 37*

◆ Increased cardiac output means that more blood (and therefore oxygen) is being pumped each minute to the working muscles, and more carbon dioxide is being carried away.

◆ The arteries and arterioles **dilate** to accommodate the increased blood flow. Dilation of the blood vessels helps to keep blood pressure low.

◆ Working muscles can receive up to three times the amount of oxygen they receive at rest. Blood flow can be increased up to 30 times the resting rate. The working muscles can therefore receive up to 90 times the resting amount of oxygen.

◆ The need of the working muscles for oxygen means that blood is directed away from areas that need it less at that time. For example, when cycling blood may be redirected from the gut to the legs.

◆ Like any working engine or machine, the body gets hot. To cope with this, more blood is shunted to the skin surface to aid cooling. You can tell when you get hot during exercise because your skin reddens. You also **perspire** (sweat) – sweating cools you by **evaporation**.

The oxygen transport systems work harder during exercise

The nervous system

The nervous system controls and co-ordinates all body movements. During sport, particularly at elite levels, it enables athletes to produce highly complex, sometimes technically difficult movements over and over. Movements such as an overhead scissors kick in football, a lay-up in basketball, a reverse stick sweep in hockey, gymnastic events such as the vault, floor or beam and high-board diving are referred to as **skilful**.

▶ *acquisition of skill, p.143*

The nervous system controls and co-ordinates all human movement, under both our conscious and subconscious control

The central nervous system is made up of the brain and spinal cord

The **brain** is the control centre of the nervous system. It receives information from around the body, interprets this information, makes decisions and sends instructions to the body

Nerves branch out from the spinal cord and extend to all parts of the body. This is the **peripheral nervous system**

The **spinal cord** runs down the spinal column. It contains both sensory and motor nerves to carry messages to and from all parts of the body

Receptor organs throughout the body receive information that is passed to the brain
- sense receptors (eyes, ears, skin, taste buds) sense information about the external environment
- receptors inside the body provide information about the internal organs and positions of your joints and limbs

A huge number of movements are not consciously controlled, such as breathing, heartbeat and digestion. These are under the control of the **autonomic nervous system**

The central nervous system

The brain

The brain controls all the body's actions. It is one of the most delicate organs and is protected by the **cranium**. For extra protection, inside the skull, the brain is suspended in a clear fluid that acts as a shock absorber.

Different parts of the brain have different functions.

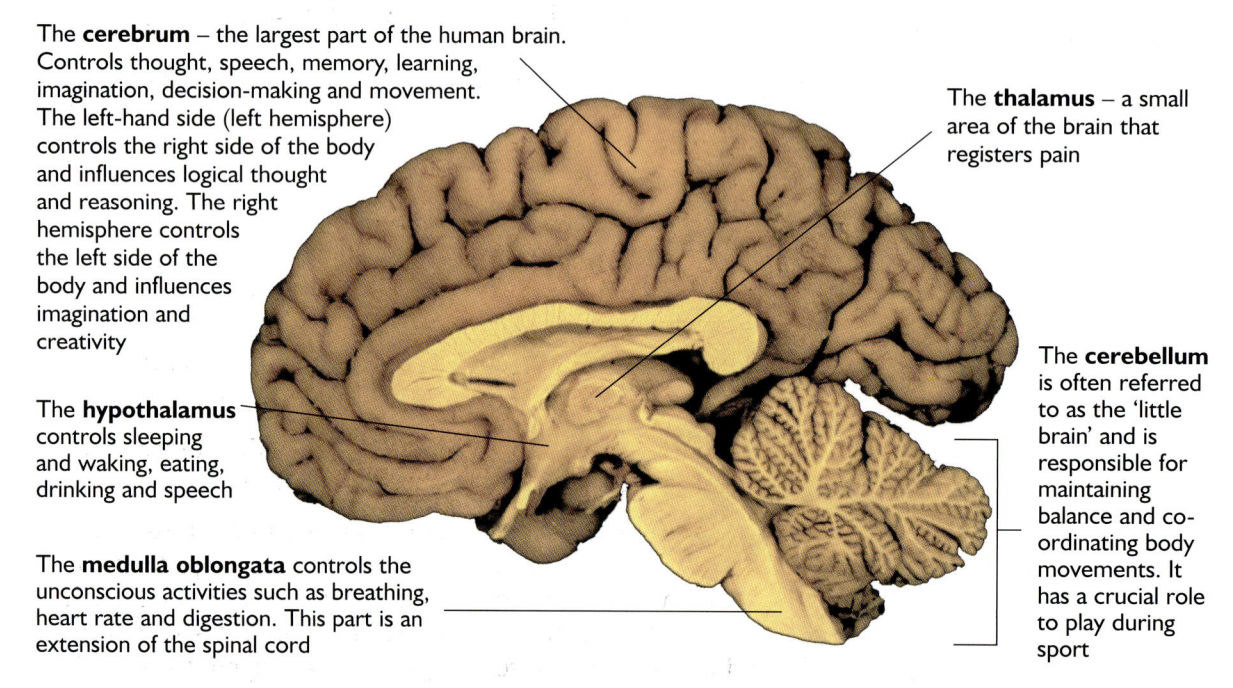

The brain has a number of parts, each of which performs a different and vital function

The **cerebrum** – the largest part of the human brain. Controls thought, speech, memory, learning, imagination, decision-making and movement. The left-hand side (left hemisphere) controls the right side of the body and influences logical thought and reasoning. The right hemisphere controls the left side of the body and influences imagination and creativity

The **hypothalamus** controls sleeping and waking, eating, drinking and speech

The **medulla oblongata** controls the unconscious activities such as breathing, heart rate and digestion. This part is an extension of the spinal cord

The **thalamus** – a small area of the brain that registers pain

The **cerebellum** is often referred to as the 'little brain' and is responsible for maintaining balance and co-ordinating body movements. It has a crucial role to play during sport

The spinal cord

The spinal cord runs from the base of the brain, the medulla oblongata, passes through a space about 1 cm wide and all the way down through the protection of the vertebral column to the base of the spine.

The spinal cord is made up of spinal nerve cells and fibres and carries messages to and from all parts of the body.

The peripheral nervous system

Nerves

Peripheral nerve fibres branch out between gaps in the vertebrae and extend throughout all parts of the body, right to the end of your toes and fingertips.

Nerve fibres are thread-like substances made up of a large number of **neurones**. There are two main types of neurones:

◆ **Motor neurones** transmit impulses from the brain to the receptor organs, where instructions (movements) are carried out.

◆ **Sensory neurones** receive information from the receptor organs and transmit impulses to the brain, where the information is processed.

A neurone provides the pathway through which nerve impulses travel

Nerve **impulses** or messages are carried along neurones, which are not connected directly to each other. Between each is a microscopic gap called a **synapse**. The release of **acetylcholine** allows an impulse to travel through the nervous system at great speed.

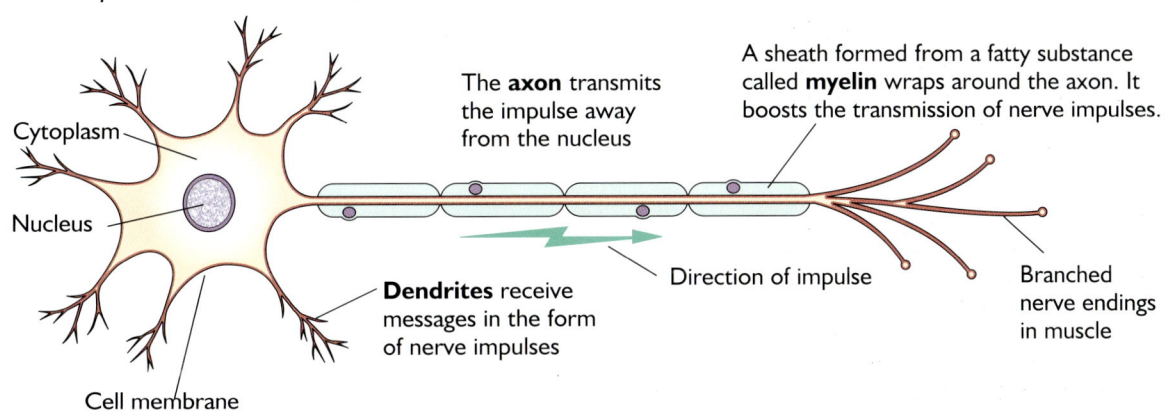

Cytoplasm

Nucleus

Cell membrane

The **axon** transmits the impulse away from the nucleus

A sheath formed from a fatty substance called **myelin** wraps around the axon. It boosts the transmission of nerve impulses.

Dendrites receive messages in the form of nerve impulses

Direction of impulse

Branched nerve endings in muscle

Receptor organs

There are three ways in which your body receives information through your senses:

- **Exteroceptors** pick up information from outside the body through the sense organs of the eyes, ears and skin.

- **Interoceptors** receive information from inside the body about things like chemical changes in the blood, lungs or gut.

- **Proprioceptors** receive information from within the muscles, tendons and joints. The main proprioceptors are **golgi tendon organs**, which detect the amount of stretch in a tendon. **Muscle spindles** detect the amount of stretch in the muscles – they give information about the muscle length and the degree to which it is either shortening or lengthening. **Joint receptors** tell the brain at what angle the joints are positioned. Proprioceptors are essential in all movement. They enable fine body and limb movements and adjustments. These movements do not have to be seen visually to gauge whether they have been successful or not.

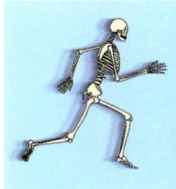

The role of the proprioceptors
Stand on one leg, bend the other, clasp your foot in your hand and pull it up to your bottom as if stretching your quadriceps muscle. Now close your eyes and stand in a balanced position. Some of you may wobble or overbalance but your body will automatically try to correct it, and you will make subconscious adjustments to stay still and upright.
It is your proprioceptors that are working to maintain this balanced position.

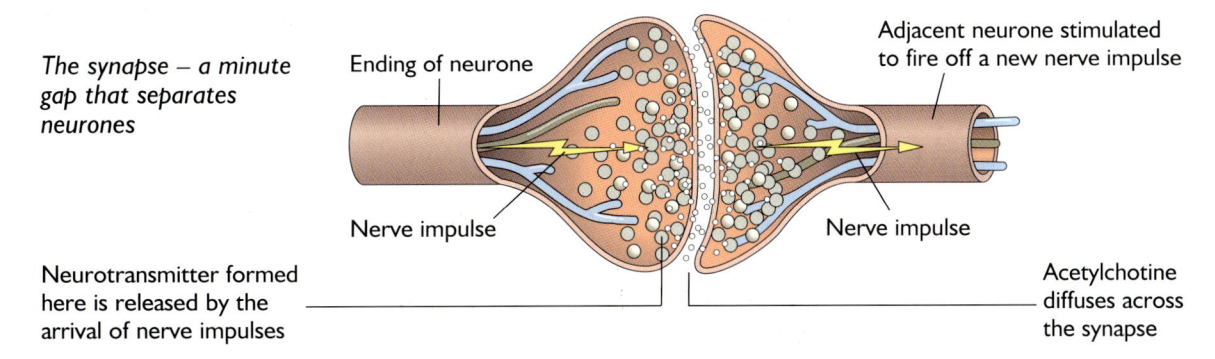

The synapse – a minute gap that separates neurones

Ending of neurone

Adjacent neurone stimulated to fire off a new nerve impulse

Nerve impulse

Nerve impulse

Neurotransmitter formed here is released by the arrival of nerve impulses

Acetylchotine diffuses across the synapse

The nervous system

The autonomic or involuntary nervous system

There are a number of actions in the human body over which you have little or no conscious control, for example your heart beat and digestion. These actions are controlled by the autonomic nervous system, which has as its centre the **medulla oblongata**, an area of the brain at the top of the spinal cord. The system is divided into two sections:

- The **sympathetic nervous system** is responsible for preparing your body for action. It stimulates the adrenal gland to release adrenaline. As a result heart rate increases, your bronchi dilate and your respiratory or breathing rate increases. This is known as the 'fight or flight' response.

- The **parasympathetic nervous system** is responsible for slowing the body down. It has an opposite effect to the sympathetic nervous system.

The autonomic nervous system is also responsible for your **reflex reactions**. Sometimes all or part of your body is forced to react and respond to information immediately without any conscious control. For example, if you touch something very hot your immediate action, without even thinking about it, is to draw your hand away. Reflex reactions help the body to protect itself from possible harm.

In the basic reflex response a nerve impulse is sent from the receptor organs to the spinal cord but, rather than travelling all the way to the brain for processing (and back again), the impulse is returned to the appropriate **effector organs** to take action.

Effector organs are organs and muscles that receive information and instructions from the brain. In producing movement, muscles which receive such impulses are stimulated to perform concentric contractions.

◀ BACK *types of muscle contraction, p.23*

Conditioned reflexes

When you first start to learn a skill, you have to pay a lot of attention to what you're doing. For example, when first learning to ride a bike you spend all your time concentrating on keeping your balance, pedalling, not falling off and so on. As you become better, you pay less attention to these things because you are more competent. Think about each time you get on a bike now: do you think about how to retain your balance and how fast you are pedalling? Your answer will almost certainly be 'no' because this skill has become **automatic**.

Skills that have become automatic are called **conditioned reflexes**.

The nervous system in action

Most of the movements produced in sport are consciously controlled and initiated (started) by you. Any movement occurs as a result of the **concentric** or **eccentric contractions** produced by skeletal muscle. The action or movement itself is under the control of the central nervous system.

◀ BACK **types of muscle contraction, p.23**

Your body is capable of producing a huge range of movements. Some of these movements are very simple, while others are much more complex.

A skill that is performed automatically (a conditioned reflex) is still under the control of the central nervous system, but less conscious thought is given to it. As sports players and athletes become more experienced, they rely more heavily on the information received by their proprioceptors than their exteroceptors.

Freestyle skiers rely heavily on the information received by their proprioceptors to allow them to know where their bodies are in relation to the sky and the ground as they fly through the air

Batsmen have good anticipation and decision-making skills

Reflex actions are incredibly useful and often dominate in sport. For example, a tennis player can return a tennis serve (and can even win the point when the ball is travelling at 150 miles per hour) without really thinking about what they're doing.

The reason that sportspeople are able to make such rapid movements is that they have good anticipation and decision-making skills.

▶ NEXT **skill acquisition, p. 143**

The nervous system

The hormonal system

The nervous system does not control the co-ordination of *all* the body systems or functions. Some are controlled by chemical substances, called **hormones**, that are released into the body. Hormones are the chemical messengers of the body. They are secreted directly into the bloodstream, when they are needed, and carried all round the body to the organs they need to affect.

The organs responsible for producing and releasing hormones (sometimes called **glands**) make up the hormonal or the **endocrine** system. Each gland produces a particular hormone, which affects particular functions or organs of the body.

The hormonal system is responsible for the release of a number of chemical messengers or hormones

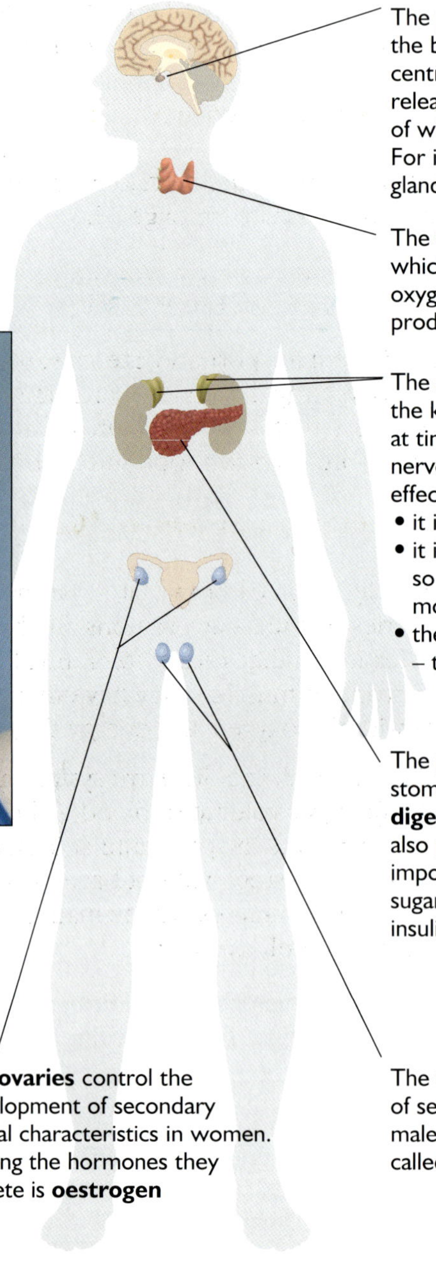

The **pituitary gland** is located under the base of the brain. It is the control centre of the endocrine system, releasing nine different hormones, some of which control other endocrine glands. For instance, it stimulates the thyroid gland to produce thyroxine

The **thyroid gland** produces **thyroxine**, which controls the speed at which oxygen and nutrients are used to produce energy

The **adrenal glands** are located above the kidneys. They produce **adrenaline** at times of stress or when you are nervous. Adrenaline has the following effects:
- it increases heart rate
- it increases the respiration in the cells so they use more oxygen and release more energy
- the body is prepared for instant action – the 'fight or flight' response

Steve Redgrave proves that you can be a top-level athlete even if you have diabetes

The **pancreas** is located beneath the stomach. Its secretions help in the **digestion of food**. The pancreas also produces **insulin**, which is important in controlling the level of sugar in the blood. People lacking in insulin develop **diabetes**

The **ovaries** control the development of secondary sexual characteristics in women. Among the hormones they secrete is **oestrogen**

The **testes** control the development of secondary sexual characteristics in males. They produce a hormone called **testosterone**

46 Anatomy and physiology

The digestive and excretory systems

These systems do not play a major role in human movement but their functions should not be overlooked.

In order to work, to play sport, to take exercise and to remain healthy your body needs a constant supply of food and water. The food you eat is your body's main energy source for producing movement.

Food needs to be broken down or processed so that energy can be released. You need the different nutrients and minerals so that your body and its tissues can grow and repair themselves. Your digestive system breaks down the food you eat into soluble portions so that nutrients can pass easily to the organs that need them.

▶ **diet and nutrition, p. 102**

You can see the structure and functions of the parts of the digestive system in the figure on page 48.

Digestion and exercise

To participate in sport and exercise, the body needs a constant supply of energy. This energy is obtained from the energy-providing foods in our diet – carbohydrates, fats and proteins. The process of digestion breaks down food into nutrients and usable substances.

▶ **diet and nutrition, p. 102**

During digestion carbohydrates, fats and proteins are broken down by a series of chemical reactions and by contraction of **involuntary muscles** in the digestive system. Involuntary muscles are like any other working muscle. They have their own blood supply to provide them with the oxygen and energy they need to do the work.

To digest a meal, the digestive system needs an increased blood supply (a larger volume of blood). This is why the general advice is not to participate in sport until at least two hours after eating – because your system will not have finished digesting food, the blood supply to your muscles will be inadequate, and you may suffer from **cramp** or a **stitch** as a result.

The digestive system is responsible for breaking down the foods you eat into substances your cells can use

Digestion begins in the **mouth**. Food is chewed and mixed with **saliva** (released by the salivary glands). Saliva moistens the food and makes it easier to swallow. It also contains an enzyme called **amylase**, which begins to turn starch into simpler sugars

Salivary glands

The **liver** is located under the diaphragm. It produces **bile**, which aids the digestion of carbohydrates and proteins and neutralises the acid leaving the stomach

The **gall bladder** stores bile

The **pancreas** produces the hormone **insulin**, which is important in the metabolism of sugar. It also produces enzymes that aid the digestion of food

Undigested food travels to the **large intestine** (**colon**). It takes about 12 hours for material to pass through the colon, while most of the water is absorbed and taken to the kidneys for filtering. The waste fluid from the kidneys (now in the form of **urine**) travels to the bladder. The **bladder** stores urine until it is excreted via the **urethra**

The **epiglottis** prevents food from going into the trachea

Food is pushed by the tongue into the **oesophagus** (gullet). The smooth muscles lining the oesophagus contract in a wave-like movement called **peristalsis** and push the food down into the stomach

The muscles of the wall of the **stomach** mix the food with **digestive juices**. These juices contain enzymes that are produced by the **liver** and **pancreas** and begin to break down **fats** into **fatty acids** and **glycerol** and **proteins** into **amino acids**. Starch is broken down in the small intestine. Gastric juices also destroy harmful bacteria. Food can remain in the stomach for up to 4 hours

Food is slowly released into the **small intestine**, which is 4.5–9 m long. Most nutrients are absorbed here. Food takes 4-6 hours to pass through the small intestine

Solid waste from the colon is stored in the **rectum** and excreted through the **anus**

Anatomy and physiology

The energy systems

Your body needs a constant supply of energy for growth, repair and – most importantly, in terms of sports participation and human movement – for muscular contraction.

The main sources of energy in the human diet are carbohydrates, fats and proteins (although proteins are only used for energy if you have *no* other energy supply – i.e. if your body is starving). The energy that these foods release is stored in the body either in the working muscles or in the liver.

Muscles can store only small amounts of energy and use it up very quickly. The body therefore needs to be able to keep producing energy. There is only one usable form of energy in the human body, a chemical substance called **adenosine triphosphate** (**ATP**).

ATP is made up of adenosine and phosphate molecules. It is often represented like this

ATP

The bonds that hold ATP together are a source of quite a lot of energy. ATP can be broken down to **ADP** (**adenosine diphosphate**) in a reaction that releases energy:

ATP → ADP + Pi + Energy

However, there is only a limited supply of ATP in the muscle. In order to continue producing energy, the body needs to be able to resynthesise, or regenerate, ATP from ADP and Pi.

There are three different energy systems that the body can use to resynthesise ATP. These are:

◆ The **creatine phosphate** system.

◆ The **lactic acid** system.

◆ The **oxygen** system.

The energy system used will depend upon a number of factors:

◆ The **type** of activity you are performing.

◆ **How hard** you are working (**intensity**).

◆ **How long** you are working for (**duration**).

When an athlete is working maximally (at 90–100% of their maximum), they are said to be working **anaerobically** (without oxygen). The creatine phosphate and lactic acid systems are anaerobic systems – they produce energy without using oxygen.

If an athlete works submaximally (at 60–80% of their maximum), they can use the third system for producing energy, which needs oxygen. Any activity that needs a constant supply of oxygen to produce energy is called **aerobic** activity, and the oxygen system is also known as the **aerobic energy system**. Using this system an athlete can continue to work for long periods of time.

The creatine phosphate system

Creatine phosphate (**CP**) is stored in the muscles, and the system that breaks it down is an immediate source of energy for the working muscles. However, the supply of energy does not last long because the levels of creatine phosphate stored in the muscles are very small. This system is used to fuel short-burst, high-intensity explosive activity in athletic events like sprinting, hurdling, jumping and throwing.

Creatine phosphate is a naturally occurring high-energy source. It is broken down by the body to release energy but, because stores are small, it gives you enough energy for only a further 20 seconds or so.

During exercise, ATP is broken down to ADP and energy, and the energy released by the breakdown of CP is used to reform ATP:

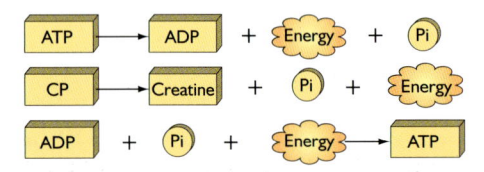

ATP → ADP + Energy + Pi

CP → Creatine + Pi + Energy

ADP + Pi + Energy → ATP

Explosive power athletes rely on the energy made available to them by the creatine phosphate system

After a burst of high-intensity activity, the body needs time to recover and resynthesise ATP to its resting levels. Athletes working at high intensity tire quickly and can't maintain their speed, power or form. This is the reason why athletes would find it impossible to run a marathon in under an hour, for example.

The lactic acid system

The **lactic acid** system also provides short-term energy. If an athlete works beyond the capacity of the CP system – that is, for longer than 20 seconds or so, energy is provided by the lactic acid system. It will produce enough energy for about a minute's extra work.

This system relies on the breakdown of carbohydrates to provide fuel. Carbohydrate in the diet can be broken down to **glucose**, which is stored in the liver and working muscles as glycogen. The process by which glucose is broken down to release energy is called **glycolysis**.

During glycolysis glucose is broken down to **pyruvic acid**. If there is enough oxygen, this is removed, producing more energy. However, if the body can't take on board enough oxygen, the pyruvic acid is converted to **lactic acid**, which starts to build up in the muscles. Lactic acid build up causes pain, makes the limbs feel heavy and as if they are burning. The muscles can't contract fully or properly. As a result the movement stops.

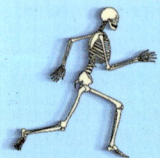

> **Working maximally – the effects of lactic acid build up**
> Try doing some sit ups or push ups – as many as you can until you can do no more. Now write down the physical feelings or symptoms you had. If your muscles felt as though they were burning, this is because lactic acid started to accumulate in them.

Anatomy and physiology

This system resynthesises ATP by the partial breakdown of glucose. The process is also referred to as **anaerobic glycolysis**.

Games players such as footballers, basketballers and squash players work for short periods at a high intensity and rely heavily on the anaerobic systems to provide energy.

Oxygen levels after exercise

All sprint endurance athletes, once they have completed their events, require huge amounts of oxygen – far more than they can take in while performing. Most of this oxygen is therefore taken up after exercise.

The extra oxygen taken up following exercise performs a number of jobs:

- It restores the levels of ATP and CP.
- It removes lactic acid from the muscles.
- It returns heart rate and respiratory (breathing) rate to resting levels.

You can see that athletes are taking up extra oxygen at the end of a race or event by observing them. They will be panting heavily, gasping for breath and often wrap their hands behind their heads to try to open up the airways to take in more oxygen.

Sprint endurance athletes such as 800 metre runners, 400 metre hurdlers and rowers rely on the energy produced by the lactic acid system

The aerobic system

The **aerobic energy system** or **oxygen system** supplies energy to athletes and performers who are working submaximally (60–80% of maximum effort) and can take in a constant supply of oxygen.

This system relies on the complete breakdown of glucose – continuing on from the pyruvic acid step in glycolysis. The breakdown of glucose in the presence of oxygen releases not only energy but carbon dioxide and water – and a lot of heat. The process can be represented in stages, as shown in the figure on the left.

Energy is released by this system much more slowly than the other two systems, too slowly to fuel intense or explosive activity. This system is used to fuel endurance or repetitive activity.

This system could, at a steady state, continue to work indefinitely – or at least, until the energy stores run out.

Glucose
↓
Pyruvic acid + energy
↓ Constant supply of oxygen
Limited oxygen
↓
Lactic acid
$CO_2 + H_2O$ + energy + heat

Using the energy systems in sport

Most sporting events use all of the energy systems in combination. The specific energy system used will depend upon the **type**, the **intensity** and the **duration** of that activity.

Anaerobic activity, which relies on being able to produce short-burst, high-intensity work, uses the first two energy systems. Such events include sprinting, sprint endurance (for example rowing), jumping, throwing and games play.

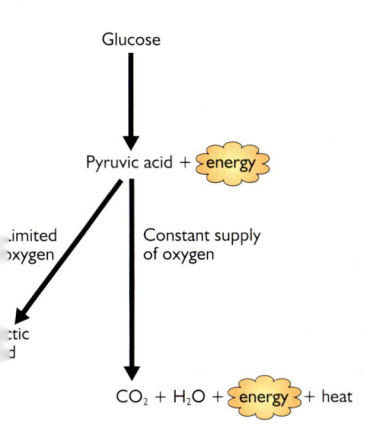

The energy systems

Aerobic activity – long-duration, low-intensity repetitive skill activities such as cycling, swimming, running and walking – relies on the aerobic system as the primary energy source.

Game sports, such as basketball, squash, tennis, soccer and hockey, take place over an extended period of time (one tennis match can last 4–5 hours, for instance). These sports have an aerobic base. However, much of the work is short burst and high intensity, and the athlete has breaks to recover, for example in the time outs, at the change of ends or when the whistle has been blown. These sports are therefore also anaerobic in nature and do rely on the anaerobic systems to produce and provide energy.

It is important to know which energy systems are used in which sport. The table below shows the degree to which sports are either aerobic or anaerobic and also highlights which energy systems are used in each.

Endurance athletes rely on the aerobic system to provide their energy they need to participate over long periods of time

% AEROBIC	EXAMPLES OF EVENTS/ACTIVITIES	PRIMARY ENERGY SOURCE
0	Weightlifting	
	100 metre sprint	
	High, triple and long jumps	
	Javelin, discus and hammer throwing	
10	110 metre hurdles	Creatine phosphate and lactic acid systems
	100 metre swim	
	1 km cycle pursuit	
	Basketball	
20	Squash	
30	Soccer	
	Hockey	
40	800 metre run	
50	Boxing	
60	1500 metre run	Creatine phosphate, lactic acid and oxygen systems
	2 km rowing sculls	
70	800 metre swim	
80	3 km run	
90	Cross-country running	
	Cross-country skiing	Oxygen systems
100	Jogging	
	Golf	

ACTIVITY

Energy pathways in sport

Create your own table using your own examples. Check with your teacher that you have inserted your example in the appropriate box.

Revising anatomy and physiology

This section is designed to help you improve your knowledge and understanding of the anatomy and physiology of the human body.

In order to answer the questions you may well need to look back through the chapter to help you. Completing these questions successfully will help you prepare for your examination.

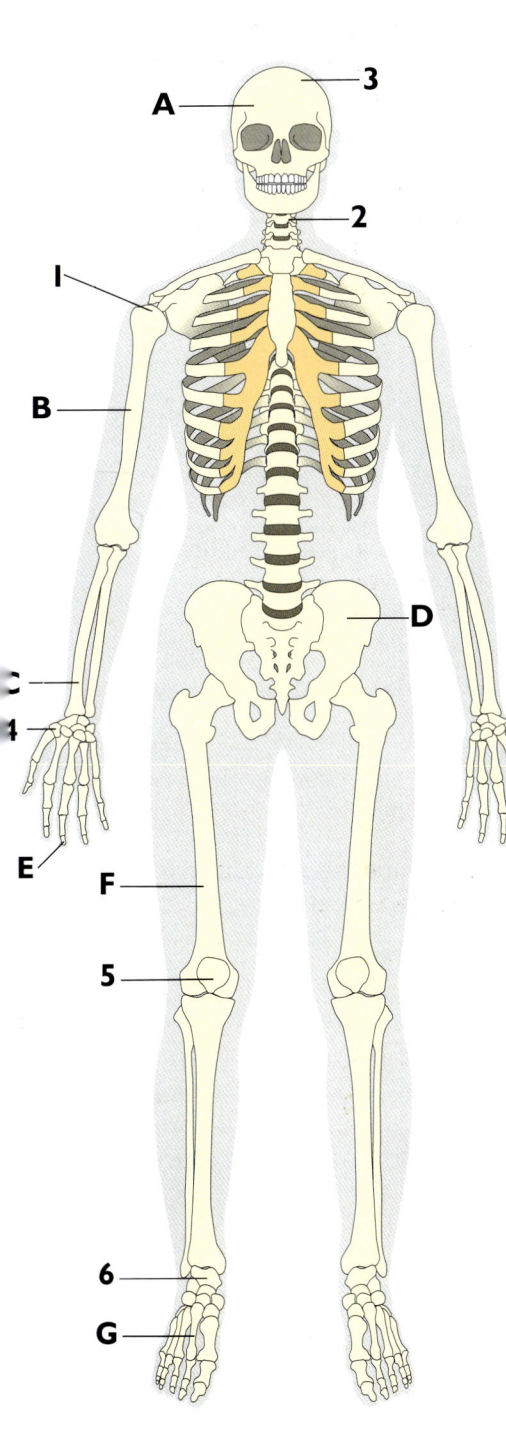

The skeletal system

1. Look at the diagram of the skeleton and write down the names of the bones labelled A–G.

2. Copy and complete the table below, referring to the diagram of the skeleton. One has already been done for you.

NUMBERED JOINT	TYPE OF JOINT
1	Ball and socket
2	
3	
4	
5	
6	

3. For each of the movements listed below, name a type of joint that allows the movement.
   a. Flexion and extension
   b. Rotation
   c. Circumduction
   d. Adduction
   e. Abduction

4. The knee is a synovial joint. Draw a simple diagram of a synovial joint and label it with the following components:

   > synovial membrane
   > synovial fluid   ligament
   > cartilage   bone

5. Copy and complete the following sentence:
   .... attach bone to bone.

6 Draw a diagram of a long bone and use the following terms to label it correctly.

| epiphysis | diaphysis | cartilage | compact bone |
| marrow cavity | periostium | spongy bone |

7 The different types or categories of bone are short, long, flat and irregular. Place each bone in the diagram in the appropriate category.

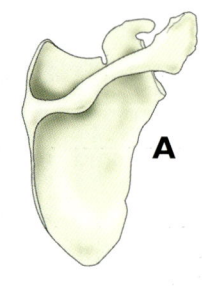

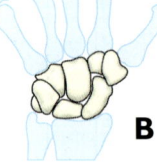

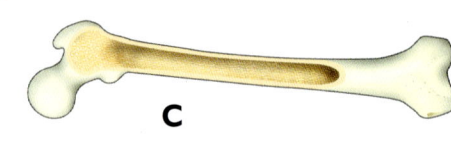

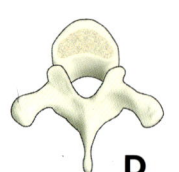

A   B   C   D

8 Give two reasons why bone ends are covered by cartilage.

The muscular system

1 Give the name of one muscle for each of the following categories:

   a Voluntary   b Involuntary   c Cardiac

2 Copy and complete the following sentence:

   Muscles are attached to bones by ....

3 What is the name given to muscles that work in pairs?

4 a Name the muscles shown on the diagram.

   b The action being shown is that of flexion (bending) at the elbow joint. State whether the muscles you have named are shortening or lengthening.

5 Which type of lever (first order, second order or third order) is most common in the human body?

6 Copy out and complete the paragraph using the words in the box. A word might be used more than once.

| explosive   fast   slow   endurance |

Muscles are made up of .... twitch and .... twitch fibres.
.... twitch fibres contract quickly and can be used for .... movements. .... twitch fibres contract slowly and can be used for .... activities.

7 Give a definition for each of these types of muscle contraction:

   a Isotonic

   b Isometric

   c Isokinetic

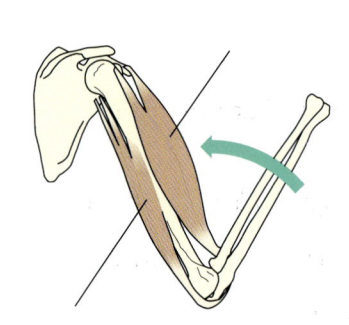

The respiratory system

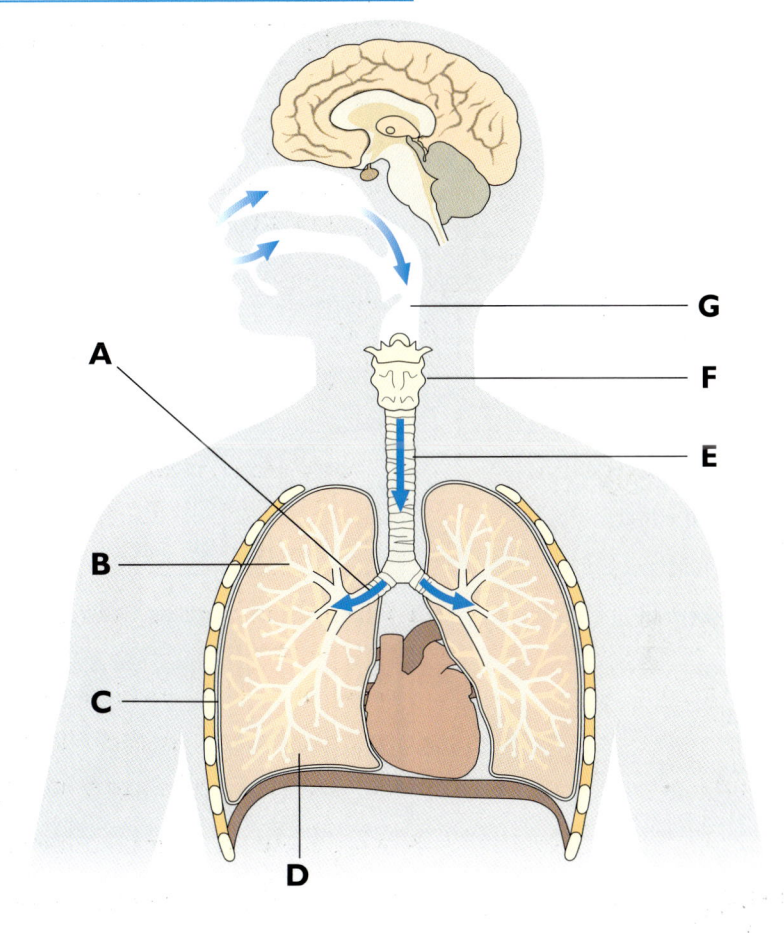

FEATURE	LETTER
bronchioles	
larynx	
lung	
pharynx	
pleura	
trachea	
bronchus	

1. Copy out the table and identify each of the features using a letter from the diagram.

2. When you breathe in, does your diaphragm relax or contract?

3. Name the different gases found in the air that you breathe.

4. Describe how gaseous exchange takes place.

5. What is the amount of air that is breathed in or out with each breath called?

6. Copy and complete this sentence:

    Vital capacity is the .... amount of air you can breathe .... after breathing as deeply as you can.

7. Copy and complete this sentence:

    The number of breaths you take per minute is referred to as the ....

8. When you exercise, you need more oxygen to help release energy to the working muscles. Describe how the body meets this increased need for oxygen.

Revising anatomy and physiology

The circulatory system

1. Look at the diagram of the heart. On a copy of the table identify the structures of the heart using the letters in the diagram.

STRUCTURE	LETTER
left atrium	
right ventricle	
superior vena cava	
pulmonary vein	
right atrium	
pulmonary artery	
tricuspid valve	
pulmonary valve	
left ventricle	
septum	
aorta	
bicuspid valve	

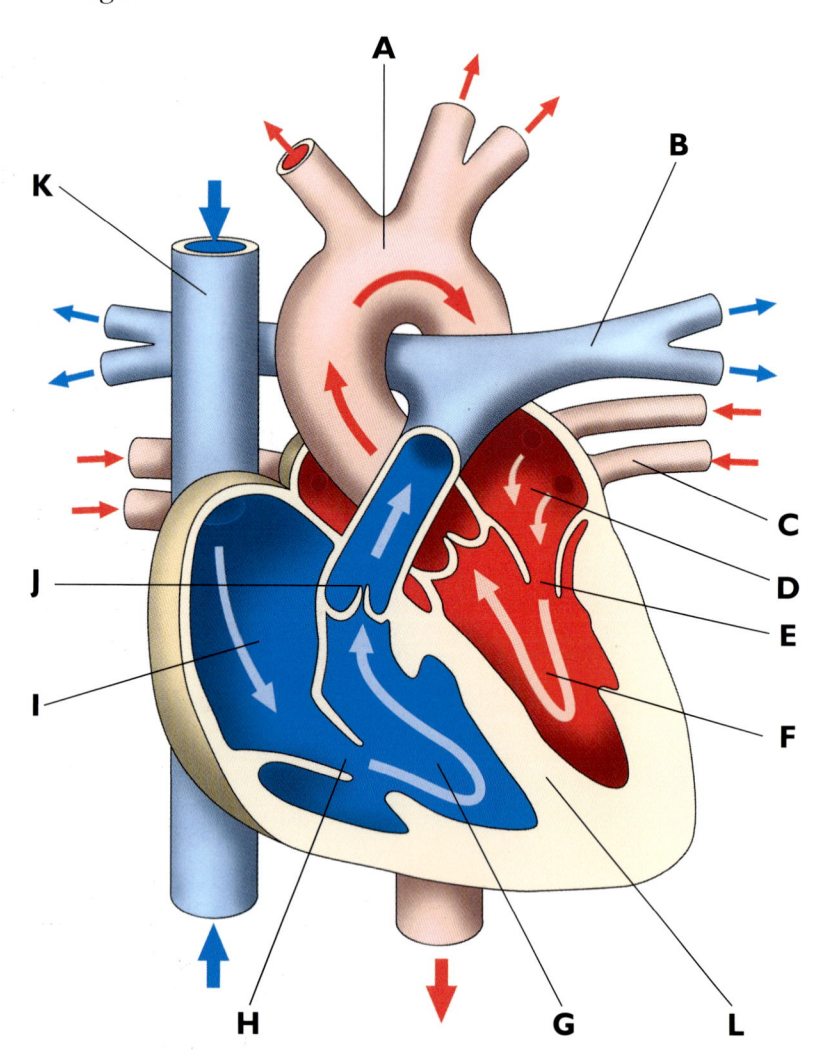

2. Copy and complete this paragraph.

   In all but one case veins carry .... blood .... the heart. Arteries carry .... blood away from the heart. The pulmonary artery carries .... blood from the heart and the pulmonary vein carries .... blood back from the .... to the heart.

3. Copy and complete this sentence:

   Blood consists of red cells, ... cells, ... and ....

4. What cells carry haemoglobin?

5. List three main characteristics of arteries and three of veins.

6 Copy this diagram and label it. Colour the vessels that carry oxygenated blood red and the ones that carry deoxygenated blood blue.

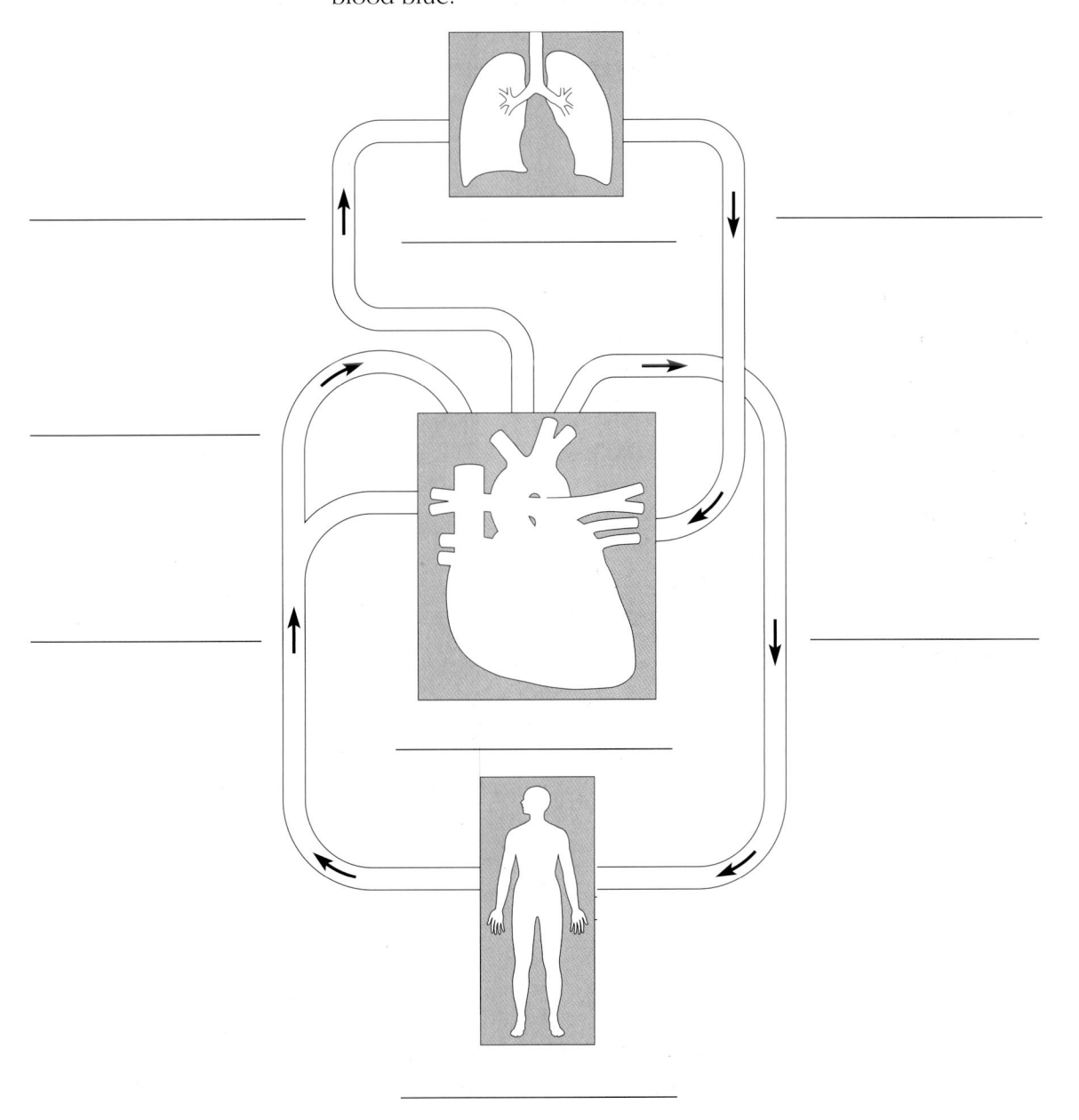

7 Complete the equation:

Cardiac output = ... x ....

8 Using the terms **systolic** and **diastolic**, complete these statements:

  a Minimum reading of the heart as it relaxes and fills with blood is known as .... pressure.

  b Maximum reading of the heart as it contracts and pumps blood into the arteries is the .... pressure.

9 List three factors that could affect a person's blood pressure.

The nervous system

1 List the four main components of the nervous system.

The hormonal system

1 Where is the pituitary gland located, and what is its role within the body?

The digestive system

1 Copy the diagram and label the organs marked.

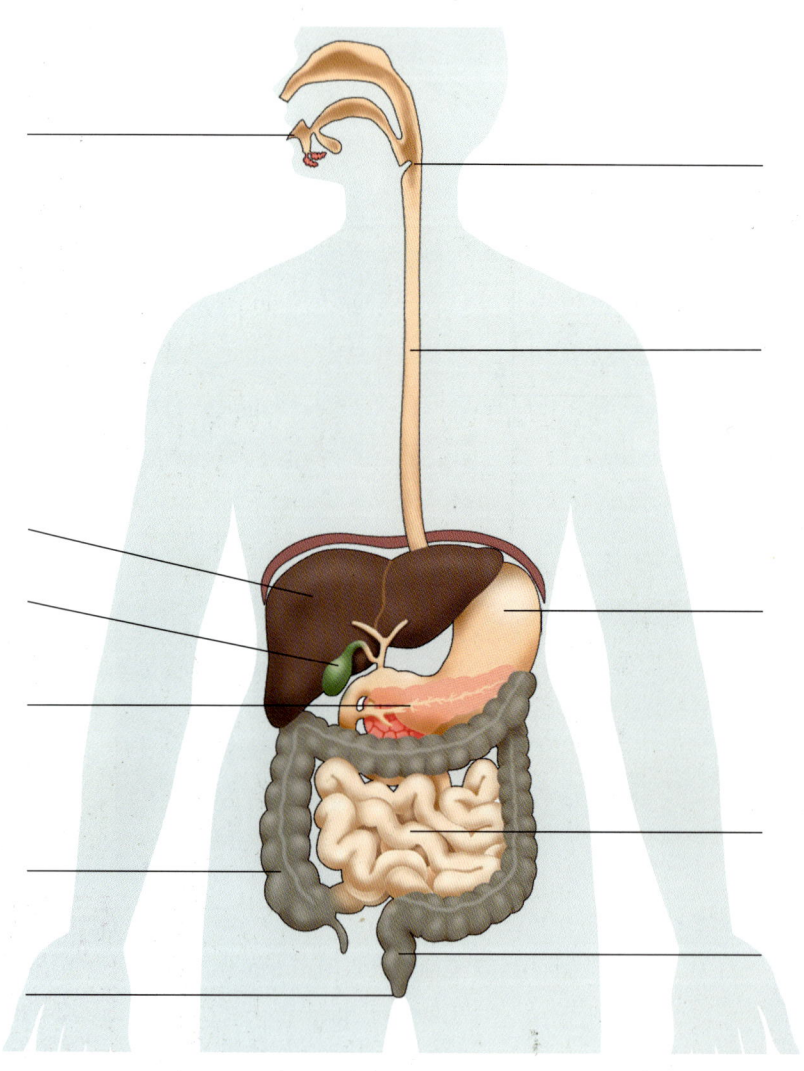

The energy systems

1 Name the three energy systems your body uses during exercise.

2 A sprint and power athlete would use which energy system?

3 A marathon runner would rely on which system to provide the energy required to complete the course?

CHAPTER 2 Fitness, testing and training

The ability to take part in sport and exercise depends on your level of 'fitness' which can be improved by regular exercise or training.

In this chapter you will consider the definition of fitness and learn how to determine levels of fitness using a variety of different fitness tests. You will also learn how the body's fitness levels can be improved by applying the principles of training to an actual physical training programme.

Individuals train in a variety of different ways to improve their fitness levels

CONTENTS

Fitness	60
Body types	67
Testing physical fitness	70
Effects of exercise and training	81
Training and programme design	83
Revising fitness, testing and training	97

Fitness

What is fitness?

The term **fitness** means different things to different people.

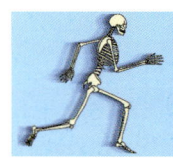

> **What does fitness mean to you?**
> Before you continue reading, think about what the term 'fitness' means to you. Write your definition down now.

Fitness is about your body being able to do what you want and need it to do, without too much effort. How fit you are depends on how active you are. If you walk a mile or two every day, ride a bicycle to school or work or play sport then you are probably basically fit.

One definition of physical fitness is:

> *'the ability of the body to meet the demands of the environment.'*

The environment is constantly changing. It could refer to the school playground, the supermarket or your house. It could mean your workplace, whether it is an office, a building site or a classroom. It might also be, in terms of sport, the running track, the football pitch or the swimming pool.

Being physically fit means that all of your body systems are working properly and are able to cope with a variety of tasks and and movements efficiently and effectively without suffering excessive fatigue. This concept might also be referred to as **health-related fitness**.

Your level of fitness may be determined not just by whether your body systems are functioning effectively but by a number of other factors:

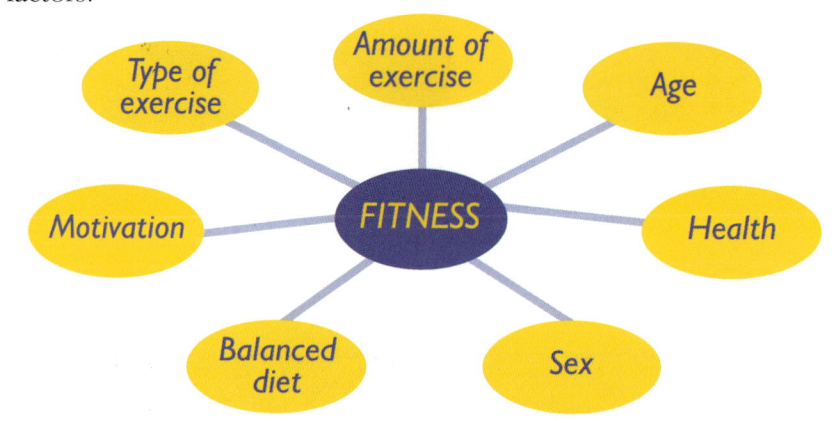

FITNESS
- Type of exercise
- Amount of exercise
- Age
- Health
- Sex
- Balanced diet
- Motivation

Fitness for sport is more specific than just being in a state of good health. For example, a man who is fit for his work as a bus driver may be dangerously unfit for a game of squash. Fitness is at a much higher level than simply good health. Fitness is crucial to success in sport and exercise.

Health and fitness

Health and fitness are two terms that some people think mean the same thing. But there is a difference between them:

Being **fit** is central to your general health and feeling of well-being. Being **healthy** means more than just not being sick or ill. Different parts of your life will contribute to your good health:

◆ **Physical health** If you are in good physical condition your body can cope with the demands of everyday life. You can do activities such as running for a bus, decorating or walking the dog without any real strain or feeling of tiredness.

◆ **Mental health** Being in good mental health helps you to cope with emotional pressures. It will allow you to adapt quickly to the constantly changing world, to make decisions without unnecessary worry and to have a positive outlook on life.

◆ **Social well-being** Being socially healthy will help you to develop good relationships with a wide variety of people from different classes and cultures. It will help you feel that you belong and are valued within society.

Factors affecting health

Your health can be influenced by a number of factors, which can have either a positive or negative effect on your health.

You can significantly improve your levels of health and fitness by taking regular exercise. If you exercise regularly, your body will **adapt** to the demands you make on it, you will get fitter, you will enjoy your favourite sport more, and you will probably get better at it. You will also feel better in yourself.

Factors affecting health

The components of fitness

There are two distinct parts to fitness. One part relates to your health and the ability of your body systems to do work and the other relates to your skill level.

Health-related fitness

If the human body is to work efficiently and effectively, the following components are essential.

- **Cardiovascular endurance** (**aerobic fitness**) – the ability to do moderately strenuous activity over a period of time, at least 30 minutes. It is the ability of your heart and lungs to function together to supply oxygen to your body during exercise.

- **Muscular endurance** – the capacity of a muscle or a group of muscles to exert a force repeatedly, or to hold a fixed or static contraction over a sustained period of time.

- **Muscular strength** – the maximum force that can be exerted by a muscle or muscle group against a resistance during a single repetition (this is the 'one repetition maximum' or 1 RM).

- **Flexibility** – the ability of your limbs to move at the joints through a normal range of movement.

- **Body composition** – the proportion of fat in the body compared to bone and muscle. This does not refer to your weight in pounds or kilograms, but is measured as a percentage.

Skill-related fitness

In order to take part in sport and exercise you will also need:

- **Agility** – the ability to rapidly and accurately change the direction of your entire body in space. One example of such agility is the 'slam-dunk smash' in tennis or the side step in rugby.

- **Balance** – the ability to maintain equilibrium (your balance) while standing and moving. Gymnasts, for example those who perform the beam exercise, have great balance.

- **Co-ordination** – the ability to use your senses and body parts to perform motor skills fluently and accurately. One type of co-ordination you will be aware of is hand–eye co-ordination. Elite-level ball players, for example, squash players and basketball players have excellent hand–eye co-ordination.

- **Power** – the ability to transfer your energy into force. For example, in jumping and throwing events, such as pole vaulting, long jumping and hammer throwing, athletes need to be able to produce powerful or explosive movements.

- **Reaction time** – the ability to respond quickly to stimuli. In sprinting events and competitions it is important to react faster than the other runners to the sound of the gun, so you can leave the blocks first in order to get a 'flyer'.

Pete Sampras is a very agile player who can climb to great heights in performing a 'slam-dunk smash'

Fast reaction time is essential in sprinting. Getting out of the blocks quickly can mean the difference between winning and losing the race

◆ **Speed** – the ability to perform a movement quickly. Cricket batsmen have less than a second to play a delivery that is travelling at over 80 miles an hour.

ACTIVITY

Fitness for sport

In order to understand the fitness requirements of sport, you will have to consider both the health-related and skill-related components of fitness.

It is often easier to understand these requirements if you can see them in action. The photo of Pete Sampras is a good example of agility in sport. The 10,000 metre runner Paula Radcliffe needs cardiovascular endurance in her sport.

Look at newspapers and sports magazines. Find photographs or images that 'best fit' the definition of each component of fitness. Either put them into your file or create a poster to show 'fitness for sport'. Label each image to show which component of fitness is 'in action'.

The four S's of fitness

In order to understand the components of fitness and the role they play in sport, let us now consider some of them in more detail. The main components are often referred to as the 'S' factors.

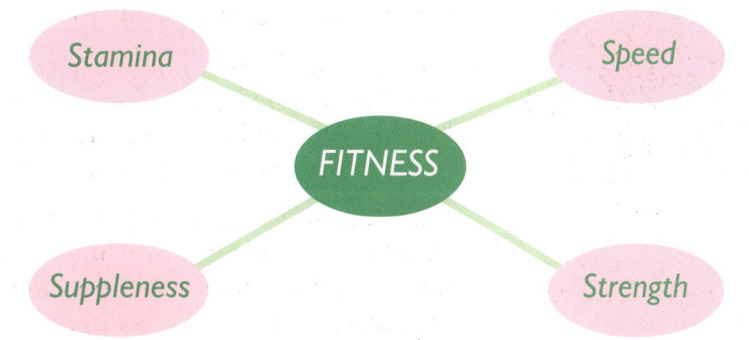

Stamina — Speed — Suppleness — Strength — FITNESS

The four S's of fitness

Speed

Speed can mean two things.

1. **Speed of movement** – how long it takes you to travel a particular distance, for example in running, swimming, skiing, cycling or rowing. The greater an athlete's speed, the less time he or she takes to cover a distance.

2. **Speed of reaction** – for example, a sprinter must react immediately to the starting gun, a goalkeeper must react fast to a penalty kick, and a tennis player has to react to an opponent's serve. If you are fit, your reactions are faster and you respond more quickly.

ACTIVITY

Speed in sport

Copy out the table below. Which type of speed – movement or reaction – do you think is more important in the activities listed? Place a tick in the appropriate box.

In some cases both types of speed are needed, but which is the most important?

SPORT/EXERCISE	SPEED OF MOVEMENT	SPEED OF REACTION
100 metre sprinter starting from the blocks	☐	☐
Running between the wickets in cricket	☐	☐
Long jumper during take off	☐	☐
Tennis player at the net	☐	☐

Stamina

Your **stamina** is your ability to work for long periods of time without tiring. There are two types of stamina:

◆ **Cardiovascular stamina** (**cardiovascular endurance**) relies on the ability of heart and lungs to deliver oxygen to the working muscles. This type of stamina is important for endurance athletes such as marathon runners, road cyclists and cross-country skiers.

◆ **Local muscular stamina** is a particular muscle's ability to go on working without getting tired – for example, being able to perform a number of repetitions of a bench press.

Stamina is more important in some sports than in others. For example, marathon runners need great stamina, high jumpers need much less.

Cardiovascular stamina is essential for sports such as cross-country skiing

ACTIVITY

Stamina

Which type of stamina do you think is more important in the activities given in the table? Copy out the table and place a tick in the appropriate box. The last row has been left blank for you to give your own example.

SPORT/EXERCISE	CARDIOVASCULAR STAMINA	LOCAL MUSCULAR STAMINA
A tri athlete	☐	☐
A weightlifter	☐	☐
An aerobics instructor	☐	☐
	☐	☐

Strength

Strength refers to how much force you can exert when your muscles are contracting or working against some form of resistance. Strength is especially important in weightlifting, climbing and a rugby scrum for example. There are three different types of strength:

- ◆ **Explosive strength** – the energy you use in a single explosive action, such as jumping or throwing.
- ◆ **Dynamic strength** – your muscles being able to move or support your body over a long period of time (a downhill skier needs dynamic strength).
- ◆ **Static strength** – the force you can apply to an object that will not move easily, such as in tug-of-war or weightlifting.

To lift heavy weights you need good static strength

ACTIVITY

Strength

Which types of strength do you think are more important in the activities shown in the table? Copy out the table and place a tick in the appropriate box.

SPORT/EXERCISE	EXPLOSIVE STRENGTH	DYNAMIC STRENGTH	STATIC STRENGTH
Downhill skiing	☐	☐	☐
Javelin throwing	☐	☐	☐
The clean and jerk in weightlifting	☐	☐	☐

Fitness

Suppleness

Suppleness is sometimes called **flexibility**. It refers to the range of movement that can be performed at a joint and how far you can move and bend your body.

You saw the different range of movements that occur at each joint in Chapter 1.

◀ BACK **types of body movement, p.14**

Some sports require more flexibility than others – for example gymnastics would require more flexibility than archery or rifle shooting.

ACTIVITY

Suppleness and flexibility

Some sports require more suppleness than others.

Make a list of sports that you think require performers to be supple.

As you can see, fitness is a blend of a number of physical qualities. We all need these qualities – some more than others – although the amount of each quality needed will depend on the sport you play.

Different activities need different types of fitness. For instance, a marathon runner may be quite unfit for lifting weights and a weightlifter may not be able to run long distances. So, when you are asked the question '*Are you fit?*' you should always answer '*Fit for what?*'.

Gymnastic acts such as those in ice dancing require great suppleness

To perform the Fosbury flop technique a high jumper needs to be very flexible

Body types

The human body comes in a variety of shapes and sizes – and even people who play the same sport will have different heights, weights and builds.

Physique

An individual's size, in terms of their height and weight, is referred to as their **physique**. Physique also refers to the body's composition in terms of muscle and fat.

Your physique will affect the way you produce movements. Your body moves as a result of the combined function of your muscular and skeletal systems. It provides you with a means by which you can move both yourself and objects – for example, on the floor or beam in gymnastics, the pole vault, throwing a javelin, driving a golf ball or performing a clean and jerk in weightlifting.

Players on the same team will have different physiques and be more suited to certain positions

An individual's physique will influence the sports and activities they take part in

A person's physique will influence the sports, and the positions, they play. For example, the ideal height for a basketball player is at least 2 metres (6' 6") but how many gymnasts are this tall? This height is too much for a successful gymnast. An endurance athlete such as a long-distance runner has a very light build so that they can 'carry' their body weight over a long time and distance.

There are three main components of body build or physique:

◆ **Body type** – muscularity, fatness and linearity (limb length).

◆ **Body size** – height compared to weight.

◆ **Body composition** – the percentage of body fat.

ACTIVITY

Sport and physique

Make a list of some famous sportspeople, both men and women. If you can, obtain photograph or images of these athletes.

Now group these athletes into the sports or positions they play. Do the athletes in your groups have similar physiques? Describe their physiques.

Somatotyping

Body size refers to your bone structure (length and density). Everyone inherits a basic body size that no amount of training will change. However, **body shape** *can* be changed by diet, exercise and training.

Sheldon, a scientist in the 1940s, attempted to classify the size and shape of the human body. He identified three body types, which he labelled **somatotypes**.

BODY TYPE	CHARACTERISTICS	SPORTS BODY TYPE IS SUITED TO
Endomorph	• Pear-shaped body • Wide hips and shoulders • A rounded head • A lot of fat on the body, upper arms and thighs • Wider front to back than side to side	Wrestling, Sumo wrestling
Mesomorph	• A wedge-shaped body • Wide shoulders and narrow hips • Broad shoulders and heavily muscled arms and legs • A minimum amount of fat • Narrow front to back • A massive cubical head	Contact sports (e.g. rugby), rowing, swimming, soccer, sprinting
Ectomorph	• Narrow shoulders and hips • Narrow chest and abdomen • Thin arms and legs • A high forehead and receding chin • Little muscle and little fat	High jump, long-distance running, horse-race jockeys

Fitness, testing and training

Somatotyping is a method of description and assessment of the body on three shape and composition scales:

◆ **endomorphy** (relative fatness)

◆ **mesomorphy** (relative musculoskeletal robustness)

◆ **ectomorphy** (relative linearity).

An individual's body shape can change considerably depending on the food they eat, and the amount and type of exercise they do.

▶ NEXT **the effects of exercise and training, p.81**

ACTIVITY

Body types and sports performance

Look at the table on page 68 and make a list of any sports that have players or athletes with that typical build.

Look back to the photographs and images that you collected earlier. Are any of these athletes or players typical examples of that body type?

In game or team sports like rugby do certain positions need players of a certain body type? For example, is there a difference in body type between a full back and a prop in rugby?

Body composition

Your **body composition** is the relative percentage of muscle, fat, bone and other tissues in your body.

Your body tissues can be split into two main groups:

◆ **Body fat** – the amount of fat you have stored in your body. It is found in two main places – around your internal organs and in a layer beneath your skin.

◆ **Lean body mass** – the rest of the weight of the body, including your muscles, internal organs, blood, bones, etc.

The proportion of body fat to lean mass will vary according to a number of factors, including your diet and how much you exercise.

For most sportspeople, the higher the percentage of body fat the worse their performance will be, so they try to keep their body fat low and their fat-free weight high. Long-distance runners need to keep both their fat and non-fat weights low as they have to carry all the extra weight for the length of a race. In some sports a high body fat percentage seems to be a positive advantage (look at Sumo wrestlers!).

You can calculate your percentage of body fat to see if you are overweight. There are also standard charts of height and body weight, but these don't apply to sportspeople because they do not allow for body composition.

▶ NEXT **percentage body fat, p.72**

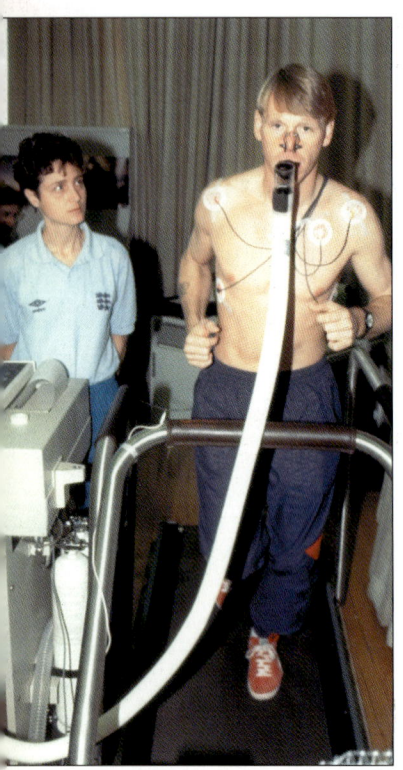

Testing physical fitness

All individuals have a certain level of fitness. This will vary according to a number of factors, primarily how much and what type of exercise they take. In today's society more and more people, not just sportsmen and women, are becoming increasingly aware of their levels of health and fitness. Many people want to know how 'fit' they are. Fitness levels can be determined by **fitness testing**.

Tests of physical fitness can vary from elaborate and expensive laboratory tests to simple and inexpensive field tests. This chapter will identify a variety of physical fitness field tests that can be conducted to determine levels of fitness. The components of fitness to be assessed include:

◆ **body composition**

◆ **stamina**

◆ **strength**

◆ **suppleness**.

Most of the components of fitness that were listed earlier in this chapter can be measured.

◀ BACK **the components of fitness, p.62**

There are a number of benefits to fitness testing and assessment.

◆ The results of fitness tests can provide information about current states of health and fitness.

◆ The results of tests can be used as a baseline measure from which to begin an exercise programme and help to tailor it to meet an individual's specific needs.

◆ Repeat tests carried out at regular intervals during the programme allow progress to be monitored and training patterns to be adjusted according to changes in fitness.

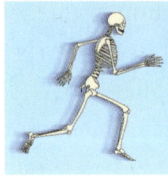

Fitness testing

> **Testing the components of fitness**
> You will have the opportunity take part in these tests to determine your own levels of fitness. You may even learn how to conduct these field tests of physical fitness on other groups of students. If you either undertake or administer these tests to a group of other students you must do so under the direct supervision of your teacher.

Recording results of fitness tests

Some of you may take part in one or more of the fitness tests described in this chapter. You can record the results of these tests in a Fitness Record Chart like the one on page 71 – or you might want to design your own personal fitness record or chart. If you do, then use the one given here as a source of reference and guidelines for your design.

The chart has a column for scores of a second test – for repeat or re-test results. Second (or even third) fitness tests are used during fitness training programmes to evaluate the success of the programme and to identify whether any improvements or adaptations have occurred as a result of training.

You will not be able to fill in any of this chart until you have completed a test and been given a result.

Some of the tests have a **score rating**. The purpose of a score rating is to tell you how fit you are on average or in relation to others taking the test. Not all tests have a score rating.

It is important to record your scores correctly.

In the last column there is room for you to identify at a glance whether there have been any improvements in your score/adaptations to the exercise programme.

FITNESS RECORD CHART					
NAME:					
FITNESS TEST	TEST 1 SCORE	SCORE RATING/ COMPARISON	TEST 2 SCORE	SCORE RATING	FITNESS GAINS
Body composition and health-related fitness					
Height (m)		///		///	
Weight (kg)		///		///	
Body mass index (BMI)		///		///	
Percentage body fat		///		///	
Heart rate (bpm)		///		///	
MHR		///		///	
Stamina					
Harvard step test					
Cooper 12-minute run					
NCF multi-stage fitness test		///		///	
Static strength					
Hand grip					
1 RM		///		///	
Dynamic strength					
Press-up test		///		///	
Abdominal curl					
Explosive strength					
Standing broad jump					
Standing vertical jump					
Suppleness					
Sit and reach test					

Tests of body composition and measures of health-related fitness

There are some basic tests or measures of health-related fitness that should be recorded before any stamina, strength and suppleness tests are conducted.

Height

Record your height (in metres and centimetres) in your bare feet to get an accurate reading.

Weight

When you record your weight you need to make sure that you are consistent from one recording to the next. First thing in the morning is usually the best time, and wear as little as possible, so as to record an accurate and real weight.

Record your weight in kilograms (kg). If your scales read in stones, convert to kg (remember there are 14 pounds to each stone and 2.24 pounds to a kilogram). For example, if you weigh 8 stone your weight in kg is (8 x 14 =) 112 pounds = (112/2.24 =) 50 kg.

Body mass index (BMI)

Using your height and weight measures you can now calculate your **body mass index** (**BMI**).

Your BMI is a measure of your body weight, and an indicator of overall health. Generally, the higher your BMI the higher the percentage of body fat you have – your BMI is therefore a general indicator of how fat you are (although sportspeople with high percentage of lean body mass will have a higher than average BMI because muscle weighs more than fat, so BMI isn't always the best indicator of health for these people).

BMI	STATUS
<20	Underweight
20–25	Normal
25–30	Overweight
30	Obese

Calculating your BMI

The BMI is a simple calculation of your weight-to-height ratio.

$$BMI = \frac{\text{mass (in kg)}}{(\text{Height in metres}) \text{ squared}}$$

In order to calculate your BMI:

1 Measure your weight in kg

2 Divide that answer by your height in metres

3 Now divide that answer by your height again

Percentage body fat

Too much body fat puts a strain on the heart and muscles, which can badly affect performance. By carefully controlling their diet and the amount of exercise they take, athletes can control the amount of fat in their bodies.

To measure your body fat percentage you need to take skin-fold measurements at several sites on the body using skinfold calipers. These sites include:

PERCENTAGE BODY FAT	STATUS
<20% (males) <30% (females)	Normal
>20% (males) >30% (females)	Overweight
>25% (males) >35% (females)	Obese

- triceps
- biceps
- shoulder blade (subscapular)
- waist (supra-iliac).

From these measurements you can calculate the percentage of body fat you have from charts available for the purpose (your teacher should be able to supply these).

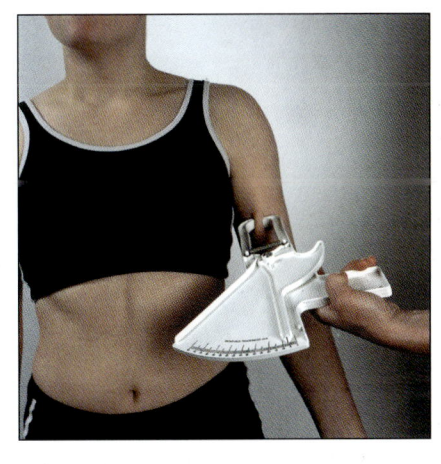

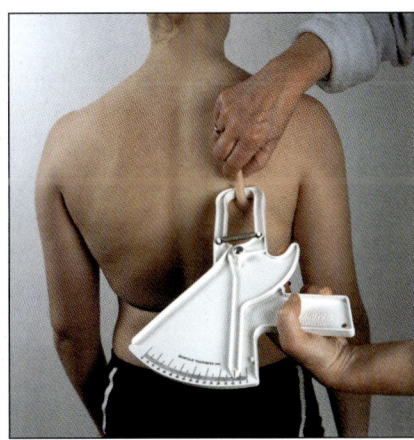

Taking skin-fold measurements over the biceps and the shoulder blades

Heart rate

This is the number of times your heart beats per minute. It can be measured at the pulse points on the carotid and radial arteries. If you cannot remember where these arteries are then look back to the work you did on pulse measurement.

◀ BACK **pulse measurement, p.37**

Press lightly on the pulse point with your first two fingers (*not* your thumb).

When you have found a pulse count the beats for 15 seconds. Now multiply this count by 4 (4 x 15 seconds = heart rate per minute).

Maximum heart rate

You can work out your **maximum heart rate** (MHR) in the following way:

MHR (beats per minute) = 220 minus your age

For example, if you are 20 years old your MHR would be (220 – 20 =) 200 bpm. The MHR of someone who is 58 years old would be 162 (= 220 – 58) bpm.

ACTIVITY

Body composition and health-related measures

Once you have calculated these measures record the scores onto a fitness record chart like the one on page 71.

Testing physical fitness

Testing stamina, strength and suppleness

This section describes a range of tests that can be done to measure stamina, strength and suppleness. There is more than one test for each component of fitness.

Some of these tests have **score ratings**, against which you can compare your own performance. These score ratings show the different levels of fitness.

The tests included in this section are listed in the table below:

STAMINA	STRENGTH	SUPPLENESS
Harvard Step Test Cooper 12 minute run NCF multi-stage fitness (bleep) test	**Static strength:** 　Hand grip dynamometer 　One repetition maximum **Dynamic strength:** 　Press-up test 　Abdominal curl test **Explosive strength:** 　Standing broad jump 　Standing vertical jump	Sit and reach test

Testing stamina

Stamina is also referred to as **aerobic fitness** or **cardiovascular fitness**. The higher your level of aerobic fitness, the longer you will be able to work for (duration) and the harder you will be able to work (intensity).

Harvard step test

This test checks how long it takes your heart rate to return to normal after exercise. This is called the **'recovery rate'**.

Equipment needed
- A step or bench that is 45 cm (about 18 inches) high. Make sure that it is firmly fixed and will not slip. If you cannot find a step of this height, then use one that is as close as possible.
- A stop watch.

Procedure
- First, measure your resting heart rate.
- Next, step on and off the step or bench at a rate of 30 times per minute. You should start with the same foot each time and you must straighten your leg at the top of each step.
- Do this for five minutes (that is, 150 steps in 300 seconds).
- After 5 minutes of exercise stop and rest for 1 minute, then take your pulse.

When stepping on and off the bench your body should be straight, with your arms and hands by your side

◆ Take your pulse again 1 minute later, then after another minute. (You should have three measurements of pulse rate after stopping exercise.)

Record your scores in a table like the one below.

MEASUREMENT	HEART RATE (BPM)
Resting rate	
1 minute after the end of the exercise (minute 6)	
2 minutes after the end of the exercise (minute 7)	
3 minutes after the end of the exercise (minute 8)	
Now add together these three heart rates	
Multiply the total heart rates by 2 (A)	

To get your test score, you need to complete the following calculation:

$$\text{Fitness score} = \frac{\text{number of seconds (300)}}{\text{total heart rates (after exercise)} \times 2 \text{ (A from table)}} \times 100$$

ACTIVITY

If you have taken this test, record your score on your fitness record chart. Now compare your score with the score rating table below and record your score rating.

	HIGH SCORE	ABOVE AVERAGE	AVERAGE	BELOW AVERAGE	LOW SCORE
Males	above 90	90–80	79–65	64–55	less than 55
Females	above 86	86–76	75–61	60–50	less than 50

Harvard step test score ratings

Cooper 12-minute run

In this test, the distance you cover in 12 minutes is used as a measure of your aerobic fitness. **You must perform this test at your own pace**. You can walk, jog or run, but the important thing is that you keep moving for 12 minutes and record the distance that you cover.

It would be easiest to measure the distance you cover if you have access to a treadmill, an athletics track or a marked area such as a pitch (where you would run around the edge). If you don't have access to any of these, you could run along the road and note how far you have travelled after 12 minutes.

The further you go, the fitter you are – that is, the higher your level of stamina.

ACTIVITY

After your run, record your score on your fitness record chart. Compare this distance with the table below to find your score rating, and record that on your chart.

	HIGH	ABOVE AVERAGE	AVERAGE	BELOW AVERAGE	LOW
Males	>2800 m	2799–2500 m	2499–2300 m	2299–2200 m	<2200 m
Females	>2300 m	2299–2000 m	1999–1900 m	1899–1800 m	<1800 m

Cooper 12-minute run score ratings

NCF multi-stage fitness test

This test has been developed by the National Coaching Foundation (NCF – now Sports Coach UK) to determine an individual's maximum oxygen uptake or $\dot{V}O_2$max. Your $\dot{V}O_2$max is a measure of your aerobic endurance.

The test is a stamina-based running test. It is one of progressive and increasing intensity, that is it gets harder the longer you work for. Running speed and therefore the intensity of the exercise is dictated by a series of beeps recorded onto the tape.

◀ BACK $\dot{V}O_2$max, p.31

Equipment
- The NCF's tape and tables for determining $\dot{V}O_2$max values.
- A tape recorder.
- A flat surface 20 m long. The end lines must be clearly marked.

Procedure
You will perform a number of 20-m shuttle runs in time to beeps on the tape.

- At the beginning you will be almost at a walking pace. You must hit the end line on or at the beep.
- There are 25 levels in the test. At the end of each level the time distance between each beep gets shorter, so you will have to run faster to keep the pace up.
- The test is a maximal test so you should run to exhaustion – until you cannot physically keep in time with the beeps.
- Record the level at which you had to stop.

ACTIVITY

You can check your score with the table to work out your $\dot{V}O_2$max. Record this in the score rating column on your fitness record chart.

Testing strength

Strength is the ability of a muscle or a group of muscles to apply force or overcome resistance. There are three types of strength that are important for health-related fitness and sport:

◆ **Static or maximum strength**.

◆ **Dynamic strength**.

◆ **Explosive strength**.

All three of these can be measured using different tests.

Static strength (maximum strength)

Static strength is the force you can apply to an object that will not move easily, for example, in a rugby scrum or weightlifting.

It can be measured in several ways.

Hand grip dynamometer

A hand grip dynamometer (strength measuring device) is used to measure static or maximum strength.

◆ First adjust the grip to suit the size of your hand.

◆ Squeeze the handle as hard as you can for about two seconds.

◆ Repeat this three times and record the highest of your three scores on your fitness record chart.

Repeat the exercise with your other hand. If you are right-handed, is this your stronger hand?

A handgrip dynamometer is used to measure static strength

ACTIVITY

Don't forget to add your score rating to your fitness record chart.

	HIGH	ABOVE AVERAGE	AVERAGE	BELOW AVERAGE	LOW
Males	>53 kg	53–50 kg	49–45 kg	44–41 kg	<41 kg
Females	>30 kg	30–27 kg	26–25 kg	24–22 kg	<21 kg

Hand grip dynamometer score ratings

One repetition maximum (1RM) test

You can try this test on one muscle or on a group of muscles, for example legs, arms or pectorals (chest muscles). You should only do this test under supervision.

The test can be conducted using either a piece of resistance machinery in a multi-gym or free weights.

In either case, you should start with a weight that you can lift fairly easily.

◆ Raise the weight once and take a short rest. Add more weight. Raise the new weight once. Take another rest.

◆ Carry on gradually increasing the weight until you cannot lift it.

You must have a rest between each lift to give yourself time to recover. The last weight you lifted is your measure of 1RM.

You could conduct a 1RM test on several different muscle groups to establish a set of measures of your strength.

Dynamic strength (muscular endurance)

Dynamic strength is the ability of your muscles to move or support your body over a long period of time. There are two tests that are commonly used to measure muscular endurance:

Press-up test

- Lie flat on the floor, face downwards.
- Place the palms of your hands flat on the floor underneath your shoulders.
- Straighten your arms and push your entire body upwards from the floor. Make sure that your body is held flat and rigid.
- Only your hands and your toes should be in contact with the floor.
- When you have fully extended your arms, lower yourself again until your arms are at right angles at the elbow joint. Then straighten your arms again.

ACTIVITY

Complete as many press-ups as you can in 60 seconds. Record your score. You can use this score as a base measure, against which you can try to improve.

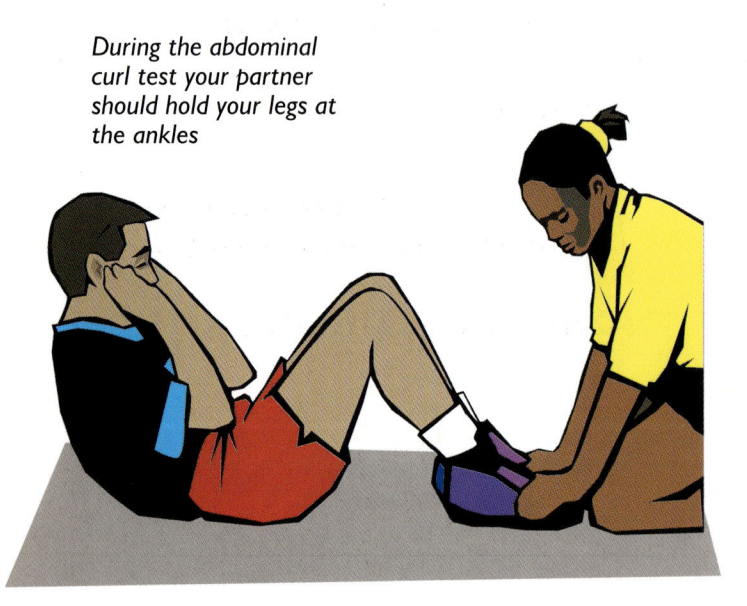

During the abdominal curl test your partner should hold your legs at the ankles

There is a second method for performing this test. It is basically the same as the first, except that you keep your knees in contact with the floor instead of your toes. This method is more often suited to women, older people and anyone recovering from injury.

Abdominal curl test

Work with a partner.

- Lie flat on your back on a mat, with your knees bent at right angles. Ask your partner to hold your ankles so that your feet stay on the floor.
- Fold your arms across your chest. Sit up until your body is upright.

ACTIVITY

Sit up as many times as you can in 30 seconds. Make a note of your score on your chart and record your score ratings from the table on the next page.

Fitness, testing and training

	HIGH	ABOVE AVERAGE	AVERAGE	BELOW AVERAGE	LOW
Males	> 27	26–25	24–23	22–21	< 21
Females	> 24	23–21	20–19	18–17	< 17

Abdominal curl score ratings

Explosive strength (muscular power)

Explosive strength is the energy you use in a single explosive action. For example, in jumping or throwing activities, the aim of the performer is to move themselves or an object as far and as fast as possible.

> **Before doing these tests, make sure that you warm up thoroughly and complete a stretch routine. Your muscles are more likely to tear in explosive actions if you haven't warmed up.**

There are two simple ways to measure explosive strength.

Standing broad jump

- Find a flat area of ground at least four metres long. An open indoor area would be ideal, but a space in your garden or on your driveway would do.
- Draw a line on the ground at one end of the area you have chosen.
- Stand behind this line with your feet about shoulder-width apart.
- Bending your knees a little and swinging your arms, jump forwards with your feet together.
- Mark where your heels strike the ground.
- Do this three times.
- Measure the distance (in metres and centimetres) between the start line and where your heels first landed in the best of your three attempts.
- Record your best score onto your fitness record chart.

Performing the standing broad jump

ACTIVITY

The table below gives some scores that you can compare with your own to give your score rating. Record your score rating on your chart.

Standing broad jump score ratings

	HIGH	ABOVE AVERAGE	AVERAGE	BELOW AVERAGE	LOW
Males	>2.01 m	2.00–1.86 m	1.85–1.76 m	1.75–1.65 m	<1.65 m
Females	>1.66 m	1.65–1.56 m	1.55–1.46 m	1.45–1.35 m	<1.35 m

Standing vertical jump

This is a good test as it takes your height into account, which may make it fairer than the standing broad jump.

You will need to have access to a high wall with some space in front of it.

◆ Stand sideways on to the wall.

◆ Keeping your feet flat on the ground, reach up as far as you can with the arm nearest the wall.

◆ Mark the highest point, perhaps with a piece of chalk.

◆ Rub some chalk onto your finger-tips.

◆ With a slight flex of the knees and a swing of the arms, leap upwards against the wall and touch it as high as you can, leaving a chalk mark. Take care to jump straight up in the air and not towards the wall.

◆ Do this three times.

◆ Measure the distance between the first mark and the highest of your three jump marks.

The standing vertical jump

Standing vertical jump score ratings

ACTIVITY

Record your score on your chart. Also record your score rating, which you can find from the table below.

	HIGH	ABOVE AVERAGE	AVERAGE	BELOW AVERAGE	LOW
Males	>65 cm	65–56 cm	55–50 cm	49–40 cm	<40 cm
Females	>60 cm	60–51 cm	50–41 cm	40–35 cm	<35 cm

Testing suppleness (flexibility)

The terms 'suppleness' and 'flexibility' refer to how far you can move and bend your body at the joints. Although you can bend and twist your body in many ways, there are only a few ways to measure flexibility. The hip joint is probably the easiest to measure.

Sit and reach test

This test measures the flexibility of your hip joint. The movement of this joint is restricted by the hamstrings in the back of your upper legs. You do not need specialised equipment. You could use a small footstool, a low bench, or a sturdy box. You will also need a measuring tape or a ruler. You will need to work with a partner to help you record your scores.

Complete the test using the following procedure:

◆ Place the box or bench firmly against the bottom of a wall.

You should reach slowly with outstretched fingers to push the marker away. Do not bounce to gain extra distance – you could tear or strain a muscle

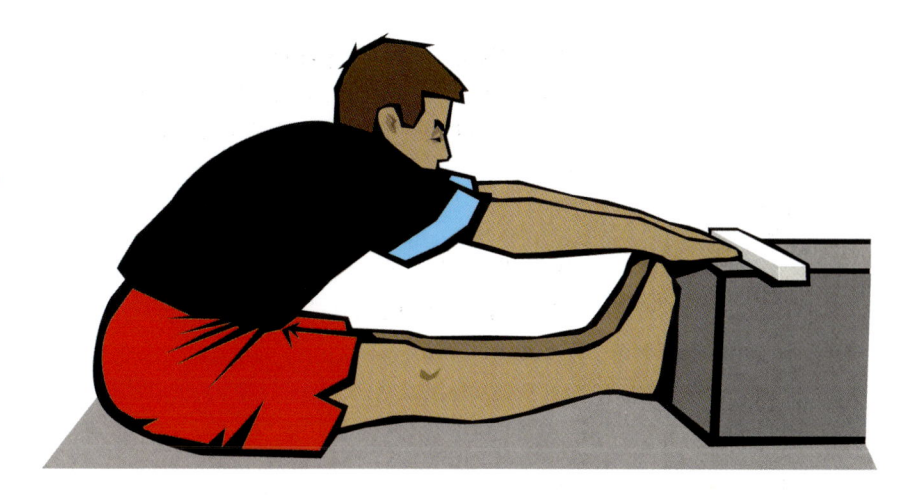

◆ Put a marker, ideally a ruler or a small flat object, at the front edge of the top of the box.

◆ Sit flat on the floor with your bare feet against the side of the box, keeping the back of your legs in contact with the floor.

◆ Reach slowly towards the box with both hands, fingers outstretched.

◆ With your finger-tips, push the marker as far away from you as you can.

◆ Do this three times.

◆ Measure the distance from the edge of the box to the position reached by your fingertips, as indicated by the marker. Record this in centimetres onto your chart.

◆ Compare your result with those in the table to give your score rating. A person who can just reach their toes will score 0 cm.

Sit and reach test score ratings

	HIGH	ABOVE AVERAGE	AVERAGE	BELOW AVERAGE	LOW
Males	>7 cm	7–3 cm	+2 to –2 cm	–3 to –6 cm	< –7 cm
Females	9 cm	9–4 cm	3–0 cm	–1 to –5 cm	< –5 cm

Effects of exercise and training

When you put greater stress on your body, or make it work harder, your body systems respond. These responses are called the **effects of exercise**. The effects of exercise are both immediate and long term.

We considered the immediate effects of exercise Chapter 1 when we looked at the role of the oxygen transport systems in exercise. If you cannot remember have a look back at this section to remind you.

◀ BACK *immediate effects of exercise on the oxygen transport systems, p.40*

Long-term effects of exercise

When the body is placed under repeated bouts of stress (exercise and training) it starts to **adapt** to the increased workload and becomes more efficient. Individuals keep training until they have achieved their exercise goals. It may also be repeated until they can no longer improve or adapt to training – but only the very elite athletes have hit their 'personal performance ceiling'.

Long-term adaptations to exercise are gradual. There are changes in the body's physical capacity to do work both aerobically and anaerobically depending upon the emphasis of the training programme.

As a result of training there are noticeable changes to the circulatory, respiratory and muscular systems, as shown below.

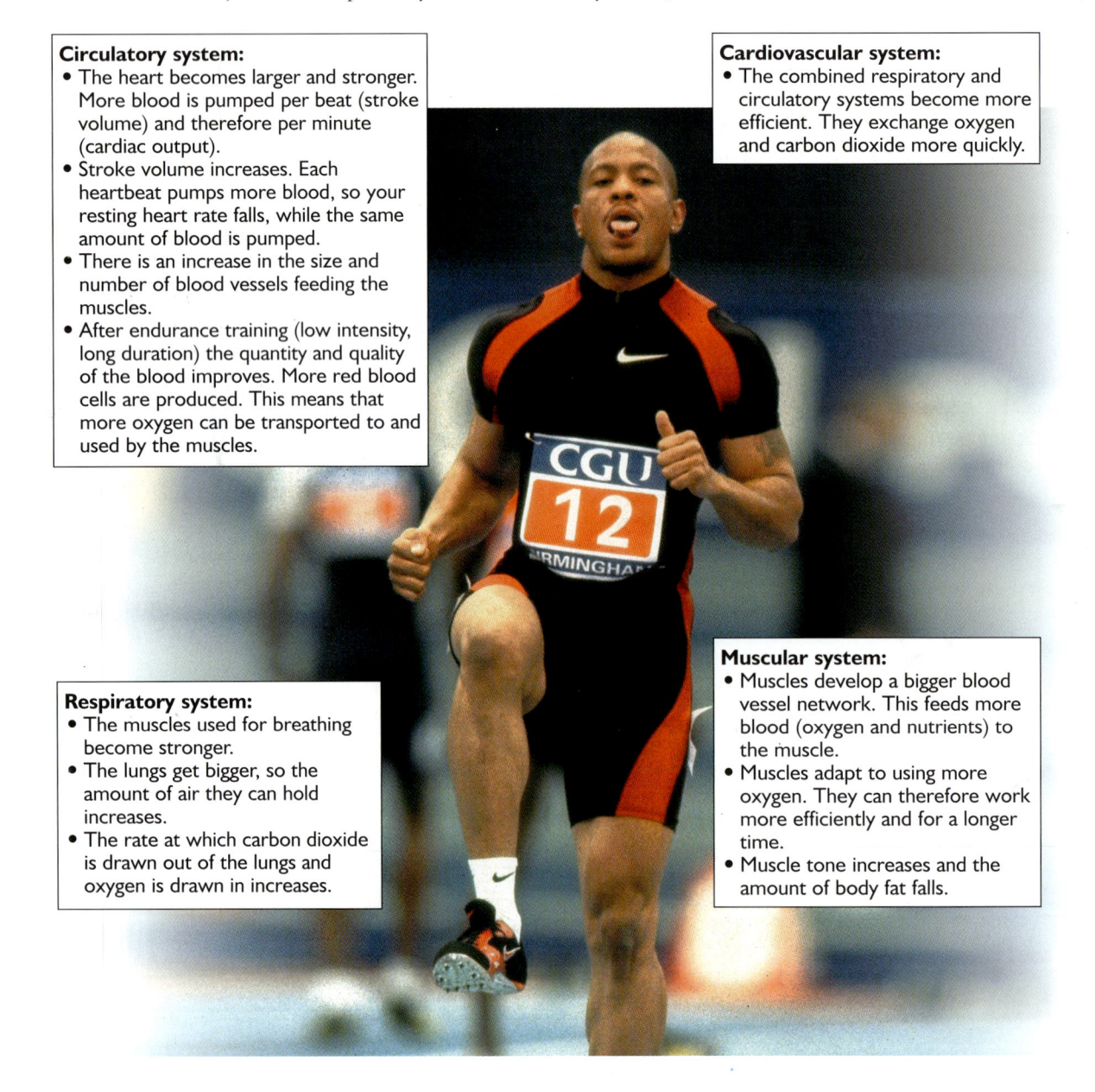

The long-term effects of exercise on the body

Circulatory system:
- The heart becomes larger and stronger. More blood is pumped per beat (stroke volume) and therefore per minute (cardiac output).
- Stroke volume increases. Each heartbeat pumps more blood, so your resting heart rate falls, while the same amount of blood is pumped.
- There is an increase in the size and number of blood vessels feeding the muscles.
- After endurance training (low intensity, long duration) the quantity and quality of the blood improves. More red blood cells are produced. This means that more oxygen can be transported to and used by the muscles.

Cardiovascular system:
- The combined respiratory and circulatory systems become more efficient. They exchange oxygen and carbon dioxide more quickly.

Respiratory system:
- The muscles used for breathing become stronger.
- The lungs get bigger, so the amount of air they can hold increases.
- The rate at which carbon dioxide is drawn out of the lungs and oxygen is drawn in increases.

Muscular system:
- Muscles develop a bigger blood vessel network. This feeds more blood (oxygen and nutrients) to the muscle.
- Muscles adapt to using more oxygen. They can therefore work more efficiently and for a longer time.
- Muscle tone increases and the amount of body fat falls.

Fitness, testing and training

Training and programme design

Why people train

People undertake an exercise or training programme:

- To train for a specific sport, that is to be more successful.
- To manage their weight (reduce or slim, tone and trim, although some people need to gain weight).
- Muscle development or body-building.
- To increase general fitness.
- Rehabilitation or recovery from illness or injury.
- For social, physical and mental reasons.

ACTIVITY

Participation in sport and exercise

If you exercise regularly or train write down the reasons why you do it.

Ask other people you know who train why they undertake their specific programme. You may well find a variety of different reasons have been noted.

Exercise or training programmes are tailored (designed) to meet the specific needs of the individual. Before designing any form of training programme the individual should know what they want to achieve from the programme. What an individual wants to achieve is sometimes referred to as their **exercise goal**.

Designing an exercise or training programme

Most training programmes are designed to improve aspects of an individual's fitness.

In order to design an exercise or training programme, you will need to understand:

- **the exercise goal**
- **the principles of training**
- **how to plan a training programme**
- **training methods**
- **how to complete a training plan**.

The principles of training

The training threshold

There is a minimum amount of exercise or training that an individual is required to do in order to produce significant improvements in aspect of their physical fitness and to achieve their 'exercise goal'. This is called the **training threshold**.

How hard you train (the intensity), the length of time you spend in each training session (the duration) and the number of sessions you undertake (the frequency) should be above your training threshold.

As your body gradually gets used to each workload and adapts to the demands placed upon it by training then the intensity, duration and frequency should be gradually but progressively increased. As your fitness levels improve, so your training threshold will be raised.

Your training threshold will rise as your fitness increase – this means you will have to work harder!

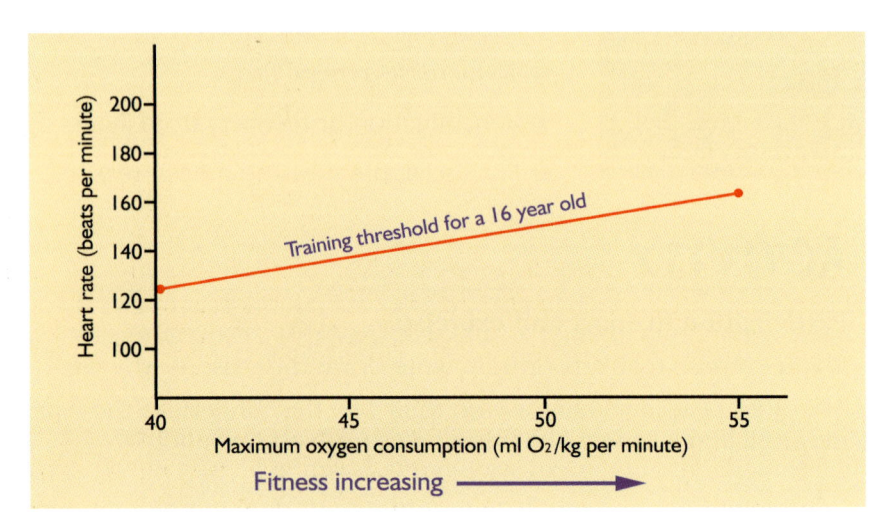

[Graph: Training threshold for a 16 year old. Heart rate (beats per minute) on y-axis from 100 to 200; Maximum oxygen consumption (ml O₂/kg per minute) on x-axis from 40 to 55. Fitness increasing →]

NEXT *training zones, p.88*

The exact nature of any exercise or training workload must be accurately determined. Accuracy is required in order to ensure that adaptations occur, improvements in specific areas of fitness are made and that illness or injury is prevented.

The type, intensity and duration of training are therefore subject to a range of principles or guidelines. These guidelines are referred to as the **principles of training**.

There are five principles of effective training:('SPORT")

◆ **S**pecificity

◆ **P**rogression

◆ **O**verload

◆ **R**eversibility

◆ **T**edium

Specificity

The effects of training need to be specific for the exercise or to the muscle group you're working. For example, if your objective is to develop strength in your quadriceps (front thigh) muscle, then you will need an exercise that focuses on that muscle. If you want to improve your stamina, you will have to do endurance-type activity

Fitness, testing and training

Hockey players need speed, endurance and agility, so their training sessions should include shuttle runs, sprinting and agility work

on a regular basis. If you want to improve a specific aspect of your skill or ability, you will have to find a way of placing it under a stress that is most like the actual movements that you want to perform.

Progression

As you increase the amount of exercise you do, you put more stress on your body systems. You must make sure that this stress builds up gradually (progressively) during your training programme.

This increase must be realistic and create a workload that you can cope with. If the increases are too small, you may get bored and there will be no improvements. On the other hand, if you increase the workload too quickly you will easily become de-motivated because it is too difficult.

You will probably find that your fitness and skill improve quickly at the beginning of your training programme. As your body adapts, the improvements will become more gradual. You may find that there are times when you seem to be making little progress and you seem to stay at the same level for a while. This is known as the 'plateau'. Everybody experiences it and you should not get discouraged by these 'slow' periods.

Overload

If you overload your body systems with higher work rates and increased loads or stresses, your body will adapt to the extra demands being made on it. As a result your performance improves.

You can increase the load in three ways.

- ◆ By increasing the **frequency** of the exercise. Train more often and allow less time for recovery between training sessions.
- ◆ By increasing the **intensity** of the exercise. Increase the workload or work rate. You could increase the number of repetitions, the weight, the distance or the level.

Progressively building up the workload will increase fitness

Training and programme design

◆ By increasing the **duration** of the exercise. Train for longer periods of time. If you are untrained or unfit, you will only be able to work for very short periods of time to begin with.

Reversibility

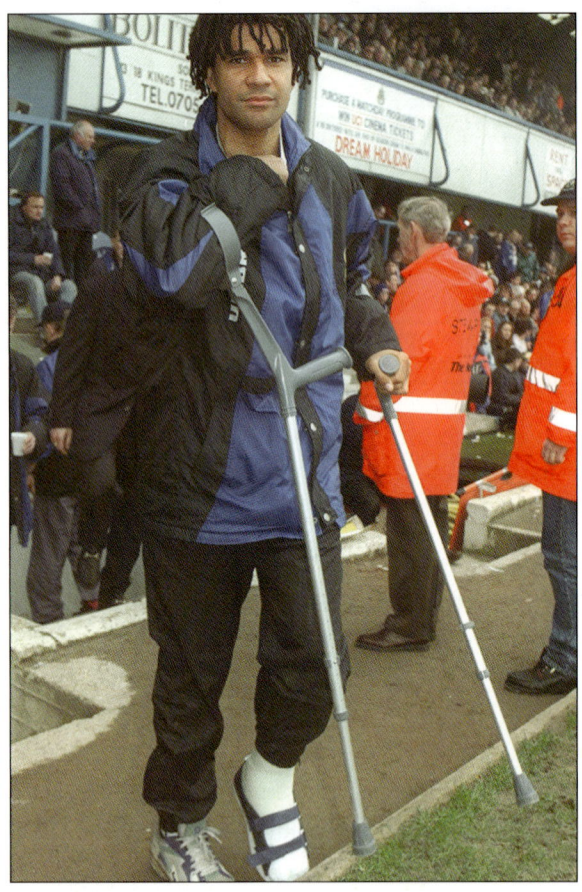

You may have heard the expression 'if you don't use it, you lose it.' If you reduce or stop your training, your body will soon adapt to the reduced workload. **It takes only three or four weeks to get out of condition**. There will be a significant reduction in fitness after 2 weeks of inactivity. Approximately 50% of fitness will be lost after 4–12 weeks of inactivity and 100% after 10–30 weeks.

Aerobic fitness levels deteriorate most quickly, as the cardiovascular system becomes less efficient. At the same time, muscles lose their ability to use oxygen. If muscles are not used they waste away. Generally, you will lose strength at about one-third of the rate that you gained it.

If you lose fitness, your skill levels may be less affected than your muscle power, but your performance will be reduced. For example, a long jumper might improve their technique through specific training but, if they stop practising actual jumps, the distance they jump might be reduced because they will have less muscle power.

If you have been training three times a week for four weeks to improve your leg muscles, and then you stop, all the strength you have gained will disappear relatively quickly

Tedium

You should avoid boredom in training. **To keep your enthusiasm for training, you should use a variety of different training methods or types of activity**. For example, if you want to improve your aerobic endurance, use a variety of different activities such as running, cycling, rowing machines and step machines. This is called 'cross training'.

How to plan a training programme

When you are planning your fitness training programme, you will need to think about the four 'FITT' principles.

Frequency
Intensity
Time
Type

The four 'FITT' principles

Frequency

This is **how often** you need to train each week if you want to improve your fitness. You should try to train at least three times each week. These sessions should be spaced out over the week, maybe every other day, so that your body has enough time to recover between each session.

Fitness, testing and training

Intensity

This is **how hard** you need to work during your exercise session. You can work it out by monitoring your heart rate. You should train at a level that will bring about changes in your body systems – at least 60% of MHR at the start and getting higher as you get more fit.

◀ BACK *maximum heart rate, p.73*

Time

This is the amount of time you need to spend training in each session. If you are going to achieve any benefit, you should train for at least 20 minutes per session.

Type

Your training programme must include the type of **activities that will develop the fitness and skills** that you need. Your training programme should be designed to help you meet your exercise goal. They should be the same as or very similar to your particular sport or activity.

The type of exercise you do will also depend on what you enjoy, your interests, where you live, the facilities that are available and perhaps the cost involved.

ACTIVITY

Designing your own training programme

The following questions might help you start to plan your exercise programme.
- What time do I have during my working day and at weekends to spend doing exercise?
- How often can I find time to exercise each week?
- How much time can I spend working during each session?
- How hard can I work?
- Do I have enough energy or the right level of fitness to do that type of activity?
- What type of activities do I like?
- Which activities/exercises do I want to include in my exercise programme?

Improving stamina, strength and suppleness

There are many different training methods that can be followed to improve aspects of fitness. They are all based on an understanding of how the body adapts to exercise. In this chapter you looked in detail at the long-term effects of exercise and training.

◀ BACK *long-term effects of training, p.82*

Any type of training must always include a warm-up and cool-down phase. There is more information about the structure and content of these phases in Chapter 6.

Heart rate, maximum heart rate and training

Heart rate and maximum heart rate (MHR) are important guides to how much training you should do. You learnt how to calculate your MHR earlier in this chapter.

◀ **maximum heart rate, p.73**

To gain aerobic fitness you should train above a minimum heart rate (usually worked out as a percentage of your MHR), which will depend on how fit you are and what you are training for. You should also work below an upper limit – once your heart rate reaches a certain point you are doing **anaerobic work**. For **aerobic training** you must therefore work within a range of heart rates – your **aerobic training zone**. You reach this zone and stay in it by adjusting the intensity at which you work.

◀ **energy systems, p.49**

The diagram below shows the effects of working in the various training zones.

The training zones

Percentage of MHR (beats per minute)

Over 95% of MHR – the speed training zone
This is training flat out to improve speed and recovery time.
You should take long recovery periods after each bout of work.

90–95% of MHR – the anaerobic training zone
Training at this level improves anaerobic fitness – your strength in terms of speed and power. It is important to include recovery periods between each bout of work.

80–90% of MHR – the anaerobic threshold
As you approach 90%, your training time will get shorter and your recovery time will get longer. This is because more of the exercise is anaerobic and lactic acid will start to build up in the muscles.

60–80% of MHR – the aerobic training zone
Training at this level will improve your stamina or aerobic fitness.

Below 60% of MHR – the recovery zone
You may work at this level when you are recovering between activities. For example, in a sprint workout (4 x 100 metre sprints), recovery between each sprint should be active but at MHR of less than 60%.

- If you are trying to improve your **stamina** (aerobic endurance) you will work for **longer periods at lower percentages of MHR**.
- If you want to improve your **strength** then you will work at **higher percentages of MHR for shorter periods**.

For example, the MHR of a 40-year-old is 180 beats per minute, and to work at 60–80% of their MHR (in their aerobic training zone) this person's heart rate should be 108–144 beats per minute. Someone of 25 years old has a MHR of 195 beats per minute and 60–80% of this would be 117–156 beats per minute, so this is that person's aerobic training zone.

This is a useful guide when you are deciding how hard you need to work during exercise or training.

Stamina training

There are several kinds of training that you can use to improve your stamina. These include:

- **continuous training**
- **fartlek**
- **interval training**.

Continuous training

In continuous training there are no rest periods or recovery intervals. Training relies on the work done by the heart and lungs (cardiovascular system) and improves your stamina. The work or training you do should be continuous and at a steady pace. Examples are cycling, running, swimming – even using aerobic conditioning machines such as the stepper will help improve your stamina.

The fitter you are the higher the level (intensity) you can work at. Remember the intensity of this type of work is calculated as a percentage of your MHR. **You should try to work for at least 20 minutes at a time to achieve the benefits**. The fitter you become, the longer you will be able to work.

If you want to exercise to lose weight, you will need to perform long, slow distance training. You will need to take part in whole-body activities such as running, swimming, cycling, rowing, or working on the stepper. You will need to work at about 60% of your MHR and for at least 40 minutes. You lose weight doing this type of activity because after a certain period of time your carbohydrate stores 'run out'. The body needs another supply of energy to keep working and so starts to use the body's fat stores instead. Fat is the energy fuel for this type of exercise, so it is called 'fat-burning exercise'.

Other forms of continuous training include aerobics classes, which are ideal forms of continuous training. They are usually done to music and involve the use of the legs, arms and co-ordinated whole body movements. There are classes designed to cater for all standards and levels of fitness.

Training and programme design

- **Step aerobics** – This is similar to aerobics but a step is used to increase the effort needed. The height of the step can be varied for different levels of fitness.
- **Aquarobics** – This is performed in water. The water acts as a resistance against which you have to move. This increases your work rate or effort. The buoyancy of the water relieves stress on joints, especially knees and hips. This form of exercise is ideal for older people, pregnant women and people recovering from injury.
- **Chair aerobics** – You can do aerobics while sitting in a chair. This way of keeping fit is good for older people and wheelchair-users.

Fartlek training

The word 'fartlek' is derived from the Swedish term meaning '**speed play**'. It means that you vary what you are doing, the speed at which you do it, and how long you do it for. Running is the most commonly used exercise for fartlek training – but you could walk, swim, cycle or row to train in this way.

In fartlek training, you can work both anaerobically (short burst, high intensity, no oxygen) and aerobically (low intensity, long duration, using oxygen). If you are working anaerobically then the intensity of each play will be harder and the duration of each speed play shorter than when working aerobically.

Fartlek can be varied to suit the fitness level of each individual (aerobic and anaerobic) and the time you have available to train.

Fartlek is a valuable method of training because the variety helps to keep you motivated and avoids boredom. There are no fixed amounts of time for each activity.

To make the best use of this kind of training you will need to plan a session. A typical fartlek session designed to improve your **stamina** might look like this:

Aerobics classes are excellent for improving your stamina

TIME (IN MINUTES)	TYPE OF EXERCISE
10–15	Jog at normal pace
5	Fast walk
10	Normal jog with a sprint every 2 minutes. Each sprint to be between 75 and 100 metres
Time spent will vary according to how fit you are and the level you can work at	Uphill sprint: 150–200 m
Time spent will vary according to how fit you are and the level you can work at	1 mile jog at normal pace, with frequent 5–10-m bursts
10	Fast walk
Varies	1–5 sprints of 150 m
5	Slow walk; cool down
5	Stretching exercises
Total – at least 60 minutes	

Interval training

Interval training means that you alternate periods of strenuous exercise with periods of rest or light activity. The rest periods allow you to recover from each bout of heavy exercise.

If you want to develop your aerobic fitness, you should work at about 85% of your MHR. Equal periods of work and recovery, each lasting between two and five minutes, seem to produce the greatest aerobic improvements.

You should plan interval training carefully. How long you train, how hard you work, and how much rest you take must all be carefully matched to your level of fitness.

In order to suit your own training needs you can vary:

- **total length** of each training session
- **type of activity** or exercise done in each period
- **number** of exercise and recovery periods in each session
- **length of rest** between each period of strenuous exercise
- **length of each bout** of strenuous exercise
- amount of effort (**intensity**) put into each period of strenuous exercise
- **distance** covered in each period of strenuous exercise.

Strength training

Strength is the force that your muscles can exert. There are several different ways in which you can improve your strength.

There are three different types of strength that can be developed. If you can not remember the different types then look back to the work done earlier in this chapter to remind you.

◀ BACK **muscular strength, p.65**

Weight training

Weight training is a good way of improving muscle strength.

The type of strength you develop will depend on the type of weights that you work with:

- **a heavy weight moved a few times will increase your static or maximum strength**
- **a light weight moved repeatedly will increase your dynamic strength or muscular endurance**
- **a medium weight moved fast will increase your explosive strength or muscular power**.

In weight training, you can use either free weights (barbells and dumbbells) or weight-training machines.

Training using weights and resistance machinery can improve your muscular strength

Repetitions and sets

When you are planning a weight-training programme, you will need to figure out how many **repetitions** ('reps') and **sets** you will do.

◆ 'Sets' are the number of times an activity is done in a training session. In weight-training sessions you usually perform three sets.

◆ 'Reps' are the number of times you perform a movement in a set. This might vary from three or four to 30, depending on the type of strength you are trying to improve.

The table shows what sets, reps and weights you should use in order to improve your strength.

	SETS	REPS	WEIGHT (% OF 1RM)
Static strength	3	6	90
Dynamic strength	3	20–30	40–60
Explosive strength	3	10–15 at speed	60–80

Circuit training

In a 'circuit', you follow a sequence of exercises, performing each at a different 'work station'.

You do each exercise for a specified number of times or for a prescribed length of time before you move on to the next exercise. You rest for a short time between each work station. If you do more than one circuit, each circuit is separated by a rest period.

The type of fitness that you improve will depend on:

◆ **what activities** you include in the circuit

◆ **how long** you spend on each activity

◆ **how many** circuits you complete.

The number of circuits you do in a training session may vary from two to six, depending on:

◆ your **training level** (beginner, intermediate, advanced)

◆ the **stage of your training** (are you preparing or competing?)

◆ your **exercise goal**.

The table below shows a range of exercises that can be done to train specific muscle groups of the different parts of the body.

BODY PART/MUSCLE GROUP	EXERCISE
Arm	Press-ups, bench dips, triceps dips, pull-ups
Abdominals	Sit ups (lower abdominals), stomach crunch (upper abdominals)
Lower back	Back extension, chest raise
Legs	Shuttle run, squat jumps, compass jumps, astride jumps, step ups
Arms and legs	Burpees, star jumps, squat thrusts, skipping

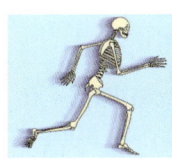

Working muscles in circuit training
Try each type of exercise listed in the table. When performing it think about which muscles are working to enable you to perform that exercise.

You should not exercise the same muscle group in two consecutive exercises in a circuit. For example, don't follow press-ups by pull-ups.

Sequence of exercises

- *Step-ups, press-ups, star jumps, sit-ups, skipping, triceps dips, shuttle run, pull-ups*

Duration

- *30 seconds work on each exercise with a 30 second recovery between each exercise*
- *Three circuits with a 2 minute recovery between each circuit*

Exercises that could be included in a circuit training session

As your fitness improves you can make the circuit more difficult by increasing:

◆ the number of work stations

◆ the time you spend at each station

◆ the number of repetitions at each station

◆ the number of complete circuits.

If you do increase any aspect, you will be using the 'overload' training principle.

overload, p.85

Neck
Shoulders
and arms

Quadriceps
(front of thigh)

Groin and inner thigh

Back and hips

Hamstrings (back of thigh)

Calf and Achilles tendon
(muscles on back of
lower leg)

Buttocks
(backside)

Stretching from top to toe

Improving your flexibility

Maintaining and improving **flexibility** is an essential part of fitness. You can maintain and improve your suppleness by stretching.

Stretching should also be part of your warm-up and cool-down phases of any exercise session. Hold the stretches (for 10–15 seconds in warm up and 20–30 seconds in the cool down) and repeat them at least twice for each muscle group.

If you don't stretch, you lose suppleness very quickly. You may like to perform your stretch routine every day, regardless of whether it is your training day.

> **Stretching**
> The next time you are taking part in a warm-up before a match or training session try and remember the different types of stretching that are done to prepare you for the competition. You could include some of these in your own stretching routine.

Completing your training plan

You can now start planning your own exercise programme. If you have decided to undertake a training programme a good length of time to begin with would be six weeks.

When planning a training programme you should draw up a schedule which shows the content of each session and the number of sessions across a given time period.

Do not forget to include a thorough **warm-up** and **cool-down** as part of each session. You do not need to record the content of these but make sure that time is set aside to complete them.

▶ NEXT *warming up and cooling down, p.128*

The chart below is an example of a schedule you could use each week as part of your training diary. The exercise goal should be written in at the top of the form to act as a reminder – and possibly as an incentive to train.

Once you have completed each session, take time to review your programme. In the third column of the chart record whether the training was undertaken and completed, and note any changes you made to the content of the session. The last column is for you to record how you felt during the training session itself. These comments form a critical part of the training review.

TRAINING GOAL:			
	Planning section		**Review section**
Day/Time	Training session details	Session completion	Comments
Sunday			
Monday			
Tuesday			
Wednesday			
Thursday			
Friday			
Saturday			

Designing an exercise or training programme

Work in pairs when designing your plan and training. This may provide you with some motivation to undertake the training and achieve your exercise goals.

Once you have identified your exercise goal and considered how you will achieve it (that is, the structure and content of the programme) you should be able to see your exercise and training commitments for each session clearly laid out.

It is your responsibility to design a plan that identifies:

- your **exercise goal**
- **when** each session is
- **where** it will take place
- the **exercise session details** in terms of details of time/intensity/distance/repetitions
- whether these details were **completed**
- your **comments and feelings**.

Reviewing your training

After you have completed the first week of your training you should review the progress you have made.

You might want to ask yourself the following questions:

- Did I complete all the planned sessions?
- Was the amount of exercise right?
- Which sessions did I enjoy and would want to do again next week?
- Which sessions didn't go well and why? How can I change them or make them better?
- How was each session? Were any too hard or too easy?
- Can I do the same again for next week or shall I change it slightly?
- Can I achieve my exercise goal using this plan?

The answers to these questions should help you plan the next week of your training and make decisions about the content of the next phase. Reviewing training also helps you to avoid wasting time on a training programme that you are not enjoying or which is not helping you meet your goal.

You will find as your progress through the training programme that your body starts to adapt and change as a result of the training. You should note these changes down. To see and feel your fitness levels improve can be a big motivating factor.

Revising fitness, testing and training

This section is designed to help you improve your knowledge and understanding of fitness, testing and training.

In order to answer the questions you may well need to look back through the chapter to help you. Completing these questions successfully will help you prepare for your examination.

Fitness

1. Define the following terms:
   a. fitness
   b. health
   c. social well-being

2. Name the five components of health-related fitness.

3. Define the term cardiovascular fitness. Give an example of a sport in which cardiovascular fitness is essential.

4. What is the difference between muscular strength and muscular endurance? Use examples of sport and exercise in your explanation.

5. Name the six components of skill-related fitness. Copy the table below and identify which component is the most important in the sports listed.

SPORT	SKILL-RELATED FITNESS COMPONENT
Sprint hurdling	
Weight lifting	
Receiving a tennis serve	

6. In sport the four S's (speed, stamina, strength and suppleness) make up some of the components of fitness.

   a. There are two types of speed. What are they? Give examples of sports in your answer.

   b. Marathon runners require which types of stamina? Explain why.

7. Complete the definitions below using the key terms listed.

   static strength   dynamic strength   explosive strength

   a. .... refers to when your muscles are able to move or support your body over a long period of time.

   b. .... is the energy you use in a single explosive action.

   c. .... is the force you can apply to an object that will not move easily.

8 Suppleness can also be referred to as flexibility. Explain the term suppleness using examples of sport and activity to help you.

Body types

1 There are three main components of the human physique – body type, body size and body composition. Match each component correctly in the definitions below:

   a .... is height compared to weight.

   b .... is the amount of fat in the body.

   c .... is the muscularity, fatness and linearity of the body.

2 Somatotyping is the classification and assessment of body type. Some body types are particularly suited to certain types of sport and activity. Copy the table below and complete it by giving examples of sport that match each body type.

BODY TYPE	SPORT
Ectomorph	
Mesomorph	
Endomorph	

Testing physical fitness

1 Calculate the body mass index for an athlete who is 1.7 m tall and weighs 63 kg.

2 A person is 27 years old. What would be his maximum heart rate?

3 Copy and complete the table below by identifying a fitness test that would measure each component listed.

COMPONENT OF FITNESS	TEST
Cardiovascular endurance	
Dynamic strength	
Suppleness	

Effects of exercise and training

1. As a result of training there are noticeable changes to the body systems. These are also known as the long-term effects of training. Copy and complete the table below.

BODY SYSTEM	LONG-TERM EFFECTS
Circulatory	
Respiratory	
Muscular	

Methods of training and programme design

1. There are five principles that need to be followed for effective training. Copy the table below and identify the principles. Explain each in a single sentence.

PRINCIPLE	EXPLANATION
1	
2	
3	
4	
5	

2. Rhys plays rugby for his local club. He does general fitness and skill training with the team once a week, but feels he needs to improve his stamina and dynamic strength.

Copy the chart below and use it to design week 1 of a training schedule for Rhys. You should show the intensity, duration and type of activity that Rhys needs to undertake in that first week.

DAY	ACTIVITY	EXERCISE TYPE	INTENSITY (WEIGHT/DISTANCE)	FREQUENCY (REPS/SPEED)

Revising fitness, testing and training

3. What activity must Rhys undertake at the beginning and end of each training session?

4. Give three reasons why people may undertake an exercise training programme.

5. Fatima is a shot putter and needs to improve her explosive strength in order to throw further. She has decided to include weight training in her fitness programme.

   What percentage of her 1RM should Fatima lift, and how many reps should she perform per set?

6. Matthew is training for a rowing competition. His coach has told him to increase his workload during training.

   Name three ways in which Matthew can overload his body, and explain why he should do this.

7. Denise injured her hamstring during a hurdle event. She has been told to rest from training and competition for 3 weeks.

   What will happen to her cardiovascular fitness during this rest period?

8. Naseem is a 22-year-old hockey player who runs on a treadmill to help maintain his stamina. He has been advised to run at 80% of his MHR.

   What level should he aim to raise his heart rate to when training? Make sure you show all your calculations in your answer.

9. Caz is a javelin thrower who needs to improve her flexibility. She has been advised to stretch at least twice a week as part of her training programme.

   How long should Caz hold each stretch, and how many times should she stretch each muscle group?

CHAPTER 3
Factors affecting performance

Your health and fitness and ultimately your performance in sport and exercise can be affected by a number of factors. In this chapter you will consider each of these factors in more detail.

CONTENTS

Diet and nutrition	102
Physiological factors	112
Drug use and abuse	117
Safe practice in sport, activity and competition	126
Prevention of injury	128
Sports injuries	131
Revising factors affecting performance	140

Controlling the factors that might have a negative effect on your lifestyle and your performance is your own responsibility

Diet and nutrition

Your **diet** – the amount and type of food that you eat on a daily basis – is important. A good diet helps to keep your body healthy and gives you the energy you need for exercise. Your body, much like a car, relies on the fuel that is put into its tank. Food and drink are the fuels your body needs. A good diet, on its own, will not make you more fit or more skilful, but it will help you make the most of your abilities.

Participation in sport, exercise and activity requires energy. This energy comes from the food you eat. In order to fuel and optimise performance it is important that you have an appropriate diet.

Nutrition is the science of feeding the body with the right foodstuffs or **nutrients**. It is important that you understand what the different nutrients are and the specific function of each one in your diet.

Food, diet and nutrients

We need food for a number of different reasons:

- **energy** to do work
- **growth and repair** of body tissues
- general **good health** – warding off disease and illness.

All foods and drinks contain nutrients. All of the nutrients in the diet have a specific role to play. In terms of participation in sport, exercise and training the most important nutrients are those that provide us with energy. They are the **carbohydrates**, **fats** and **proteins**.

Carbohydrates

Carbohydrates are the body's main source of energy. They are broken down into glucose. Glucose is stored as glycogen in the liver and working muscles and is an immediate energy source.

◀ BACK **energy systems, p.49**

Carbohydrates are found especially in foods such as bread, potatoes, pasta (these are the **starches** or **complex carbohydrates**) and sweet and sugary foods (**simple sugars**).

Eating carbohydrates regularly helps to build up your reserves of energy and to replace them when they have been partly used up. If you have an active lifestyle or take part in exercise and training carbohydrates should make up at least half of your food intake.

Carbohydrates are the body's main energy source

Factors affecting performance

Fats

Fats provide:

◆ a source of energy when you are resting, sleeping or gently exercising (such as walking)

◆ a layer beneath your skin which keeps you warm and protects your vital organs.

Like carbohydrates, fats are a source of energy. However, energy is released only slowly from fat and high levels of oxygen are needed to release this energy. Fats supply the energy we need for endurance activities, whereas carbohydrates supply energy that we need immediately. Fats should account for about one third of our food intake.

There are two main kinds of fats.

◆ **Saturated fats** are found in animal products such as milk, meat, butter and cheese. These keep their shape when they are in a normal room temperature (though they may melt if it gets very hot).

◆ **Polyunsaturated fats** are found in fish oils and cooking oils such as sunflower seed oil. These stay liquid at normal room temperature (though they can thicken if they get very cold). These fats are also found in nuts and seeds.

Sources of dietary fats

Proteins

Proteins are used to generate energy only when the body has used up its stores of carbohydrates and fats.

Proteins are made from amino acids. Your body cannot make most of these, so you have to take them in through the food you eat. Your body uses the amino acids in proteins to build cells, make blood and repair and replace body tissue.

Fish, eggs and meat are all rich in proteins. People have specific needs in their diet, for instance those with food allergies or vegetarians look for meat alternatives to make sure they take in the proteins they need.

Sources of protein in the diet

Diet and nutrition

ACTIVITY

Types of energy foods

Draw a table with three columns in it. Label the first column 'carbohydrate', the second 'fats' and the third 'proteins'. In each column write down the names and/or types of food that are the major providers. Try to identify at least five of each.

To do this you will need to have a few packets and tins of food, so that you can read the labels. The label will tell you how much carbohydrate, fat or protein is in it. If you are eating chocolate, crisps or any other food at this moment look at their food contents and write them in the table.

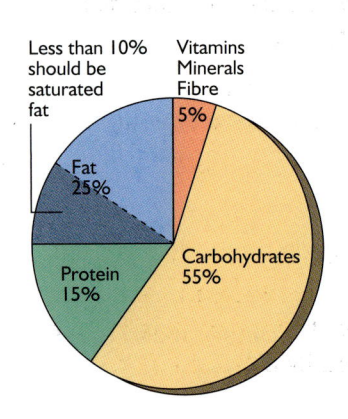

A balanced diet

Everybody, whether they are involved in sport or not, should aim to eat a **balanced** diet (sometimes called a 'healthy diet').

A balanced diet will give you the energy to take part in exercise and recover from it quickly.

The pie chart shows the recommended proportions in which the energy providers should be taken in a balanced diet:

◆ **Carbohydrates** are the body's primary energy provider (50%).

◆ **Fats** supply the energy we need for endurance activities (35%).

◆ **Proteins** supply energy only when our body has used up its stores of carbohydrates and fats (15%).

A balanced and healthy diet should contain, in addition to the energy providers, all the essential items that you need – nutrients, vitamins, minerals, fibre and water. But it is important not to take in too much of any one constituent, particularly fats.

Other essential nutrients

There are other foodstuffs or 'essential nutrients' that do not provide you with energy to do work, but have other important jobs to do in the body.

Vitamins

You need vitamins to help your body to work normally. They:

◆ help work on the food you eat in order to release its **energy**

◆ help with the **growth and repair** of tissues.

◆ help you to **resist infections** and disease

◆ **regulate the chemical reactions** that are going on in your body.

The table at the top of page 105 shows a range of vitamins that you should include in your diet.

VITAMIN	FOUND IN	WHY IT IS NEEDED
A – Carotene or retinol	Cheese, eggs, green vegetables, liver	For eyesight and healthy skin
B_1 – Thiamine	Beans, cereals, meat, nuts	Helps turn carbohydrates into energy. Health of the nerves
B_2 – Riboflavin	Eggs, green vegetables, milk, yeast extract	Same as B_1 and for the health of the nose and throat
B_6 – Pyridoxine	Cereals, fish, green vegetables, meat	Health of blood and nerves
Folic acid	Green vegetables, liver	When taken with B_{12} it helps form new blood and cells
B_{12} – Cobalamin	Dairy products, fish, meat	Health of the nerves
Niacin	Cereals, fish, liver, peanuts	Helps turn carbohydrates into energy
C – Ascorbic acid	Citrus fruits, green vegetables, potatoes	Healthy teeth and gums. Helps to extract iron from foods
D – Calciferol	Dairy products. Made in the body when the sun shines on the skin	Helps to take in calcium and phosphorus
E – Tocopherol	Green vegetables Liver, oily fish, vegetable oils	Helps take waste products away from mucus
K	Green vegetables, liver	Helps to mend cuts

Vitamins can now be bought 'over the counter' in the form of pills, which people use to supplement their diet, to ensure that they get their recommended daily doses of vitamins. However, most people do not need supplements if they eat a healthily balanced diet.

Minerals

Minerals are basic elements found in the soil and in the air. They carry out particular jobs in the body to keep you healthy.

The table below shows the range of minerals, their function and the foodstuffs in which they are found.

MINERAL	FOUND IN	WHY IT IS NEEDED
Calcium	Beans, broccoli, dairy products, peas, sardines, turnips	To keep our teeth and bones hard
Iron	Dark green leafy vegetables, heart, kidney, liver, red meat	To help produce the oxygen-carrying compartments in the blood
Iodine	Dairy products, seafood	To help maintain the thyroid gland, which controls and regulates the body's functions
Sodium	Salt, cheese, bread	To make the muscles work (contract)
Potassium	Milk, oranges, bananas	To make the muscles work and prevent cramps

Fibre

Fibre is found in whole-grain cereals and bread, fruit and vegetables.

Fibre does not contain any nutrients. It cannot be digested but it is needed to keep your digestive system working smoothly. Without fibre food would stay in the gut too long and cause illness. Fibre helps to prevent constipation. Fibre can make you feel full and therefore also reduces your appetite.

Water

Water is the main component of cells and blood. About 66% of an adult's weight and 80% of a child's is made up of water.

Water plays an important part in regulating your temperature when you are exercising. As perspiration (sweat), it helps cool you down during exercise and activity. Even when you are not actually sweating, you are losing water all the time, just through breathing (that's why glass mists up when you breathe on it).

The more active you are, the more water you lose. If you lose too much water, you become **dehydrated**, which can cause illness and eventually death. It is therefore important to take in water frequently during the day but especially during exercise.

Drinking plenty of water during sport and activity can prevent dehydration

ACTIVITY

Analysing your diet

Write down all of the foods that you eat in your next meal then comment on their nutritional value – what energy providers and nutrients the foods contain. You may have to look at the label on the packet to identify those values.

Now analyse the balance of this meal. Ask yourself some key questions that relate to the balance of the energy providers in that meal:

◆ Have the foods I have eaten been in the right proportions?

◆ Does my diet reflect a balance of all of the nutrients and energy providers I need?

◆ If not, what should I change in my diet?

Adults and children have different dietary requirements, and this should be reflected in the food they eat

Health and diet

A good diet is important to maintain healthy body systems and to ensure that the body functions effectively.

Children and adults have different needs from their diet. Diet should reflect an individual's age and their stage of development.

It is important to understand how you can get the most out of the food that you eat. Exercise can place significant additional demands upon the body and your body's ability to meet these demands depends upon the ability of the energy systems to convert the foods digested into fuel.

◀ BACK **energy systems, p.49**

Any physical recreation, training or competition requires some degree of energy expenditure. The amount of energy required will depend upon the type of sport or exercise, its duration (how long it will go on for) and its intensity (how hard you are working).

There is a link between diet, nutrition and exercise. An individual must eat the correct amount of appropriate foodstuffs at the right time so that their body has enough fuel to work.

The energy you need

Different kinds of people have different amounts and require different amounts of energy. This may be because of their

- **age** – for example, small children usually have lots of energy
- **gender** – males tend to use more energy than females
- **lifestyle** – people with active jobs, and people who take regular exercise, need more energy.

When you are thinking about your own diet, the first thing to do is to work out how much energy you need. As well as your age and gender, this will be affected by:

- the job that you do
- the amount of exercise or activity that you take part in.

FOOD	ENERGY (kJ/g)
Butter	31.2
Peanuts	24.5
Milk chocolate	24.2
White sugar	16.5
Rice	15
Pork sausages	15.5
White bread	10.6
Chips	9.9
Roast chicken	7.7
Eggs	6.6
Boiled potatoes	3.3
Milk	2.7
Apple	1.9
Beer	1.2

The amounts of energy available in a range of foods

All food contains energy, measured in kilojoules (kJ). The amount of energy you take in from your food will depend on the type of food you are eating and the size of the portion.

The exact amount of energy available in food is usually marked on the packet or listed in food or cookery books. It is usually given as the number of kilojoules per 100 g of the food type. We can use these values to compare the amount of energy in different foods.

ACTIVITY

Energy intake in your diet

Write down the energy contents of all of the foodstuffs that you might eat during the course of an average day. Look at the labels or use a reference book to identify the food value.

It might be interesting to cut the food value chart from the packet so that you can contrast one food to another. Ask permission before you start to cut food packets.

The energy equation

Everyday energy

You need a certain amount of energy just to keep you alive, healthy and 'ticking over'. This rate is called your **basal metabolic rate** and is often referred to simply as your **BMR**. An individual's BMR will vary according to their age, gender and body size.

The table below gives examples of the energy needed each day (BMR) by a range of different individuals.

	ENERGY (kJ) NEEDED FOR BMR	
	Male	Female
8 year old	8,200	7,300
15 year old	11,500	8,800
Adult office worker	10,500	9,000
Adult labourer	14,000	10,500
Retired adult	9,000	7,000

Energy for exercise and sport

Everyday activities such as walking, gardening and performing household chores all require extra energy. Taking part in sport, exercise and training will require even more energy.

This extra demand is called your **physical activity level** or **PAL**. The greater your PAL, the more energy you will need to get from your diet.

The table on page 109 outlines the energy requirements of certain activities.

ACTIVITY	ENERGY NEEDED (kJ) PER HOUR (PAL)
Walking	380
Golf	560
Housework	560
Badminton	710
Gardening	880
Gymnastics	880
Tennis	1,000
Rugby	1,130
Squash	1,254
Jogging	1,320
Cycling	1,380
Swimming	1,500

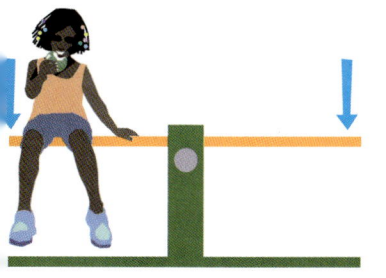

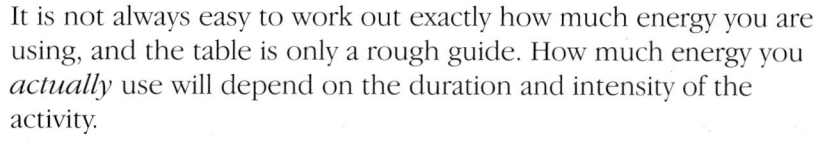

It is not always easy to work out exactly how much energy you are using, and the table is only a rough guide. How much energy you *actually* use will depend on the duration and intensity of the activity.

Working out the energy equation

To ensure a healthy diet, you need to find the balance that is right for you, at your age and with your lifestyle. The energy equation is a simple guide to managing your weight.

Look at the balances to the left.

To identify which balance you fit into you need to compare your total energy expenditure with the amount of energy you take in through your diet.

To calculate your total energy expenditure you will need to work out your BMR and the PAL values for the exercise you're doing. Add these two values together.

Compare this value (the total energy expenditure) with the amount of kJ that you eat each day. In order to do this you will need to track the foodstuffs you eat in a typical day. You can use the figure you obtained from the task on page 108.

◀ BACK *energy intake in your diet, p.102*

To work out your place in the energy equation compare the energy you eat (kJ) and the energy you need (BMR + PAL).

Now answer the following questions:

◆ Which total is the biggest?

◆ What is the difference between them?

◆ Where do you fall in the energy equation?

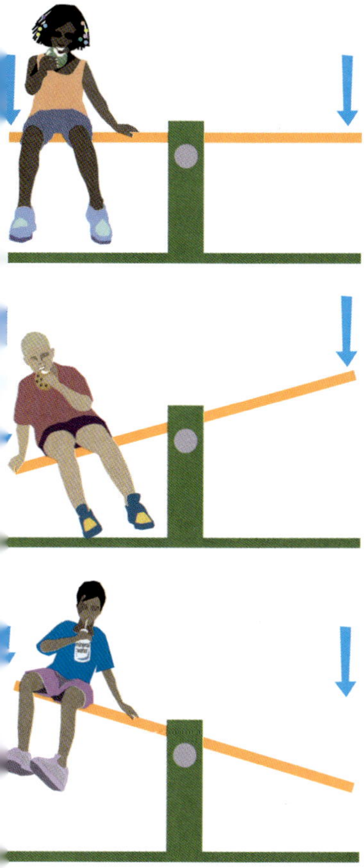

The energy balances

Diet for sport and exercise

There is a direct relationship between diet and performance during activity.

The point at which you begin to tire during exercise will depend upon how hard you are working and the amount of energy you have available to continue working at that intensity. When you get tired you slow down, your recovery periods are longer, your limbs will start to feel heavy, and you may think less clearly and make mistakes.

Eating the right foodstuffs in the appropriate quantities will give you sufficient energy to delay these feelings, and you will be able to work harder for longer. Increasing your energy is not just a matter of eating more food. You have to eat the right *kinds* of food. **To help increase your energy, you should increase your carbohydrate intake, not the amount of fat and protein that you eat.** You should be able to get as much as 60–70% of your total energy from carbohydrate, more than you need for an everyday healthy diet.

Carbohydrates are the body's immediate energy source as energy can be released from carbohydrate up to three times as quickly as from fat. When carbohydrate is broken down it is stored in the body as glycogen, either in the muscle or liver. The only way to replenish empty carbohydrate stores is to eat more carbohydrate. The body can convert excess carbohydrate to fat, but fat cannot be converted to carbohydrate. That is why a good diet all the time, containing plenty of carbohydrates, is important for an athlete.

Carbohydrates are the main fuel for high-intensity activities, maximal activities such as sprint and power activities. They are also the primary energy source for people who engage in repetitive exercise at a fairly high intensity, for example runners, swimmers during training sessions and games players (squash, rugby, hockey).

◀ BACK **energy systems, p.49**

The energy from fat is burned far more slowly and is therefore the main fuel for low-intensity endurance activity such as walking.

Athletes need to eat high proportions of energy-providing foods

ACTIVITY

Energy foods for sport

Copy the table and complete it by identifying the energy source for that particular activity.

SPORT/ACTIVITY	CARBOHYDRATE OR FAT?
Interval sprint training session	
Golf (an 18-hole round)	
A mini triathlon (400 m swim, 20 km cycle and a 5 km run)	
A three-set tennis match	

Factors affecting performance

Eating before sport and exercise

◆ A full meal should be eaten no less than 4 hours before and a snack meal no less than 2 hours before so that that you have time to digest your food and avoid cramps, stitches and vomiting.

◆ Include starches such as bread, cereal, pasta and fruit to give a slow steady release of energy.

◆ Avoid simple sugars (sweets, biscuits, cakes and sugar) because they reduce insulin levels, which in turn reduce blood glucose levels and you may feel tired and sluggish.

◆ Avoid foods high in fat and protein as they take longer to digest.

◆ Include plenty of drinks to avoid dehydration.

Drinks for sport and exercise

Exercising makes you feel thirsty. **Drink plenty of water**.

There are a number of reasons why your body needs water:

◆ During exercise your body gets hot. You need water to help you sweat to cool down.

◆ Water is one of the main components of the blood, which is used in the transport of oxygen and glucose to the working muscles and carbon dioxide away from them.

◆ Water, in urine, helps remove other waste products from the body.

Waiting until you feel thirsty before you take a drink can be dangerous because by the time you are thirsty you are already becoming dehydrated. It can lead to a significant loss in performance, symptoms such as fainting, nausea, tiredness and cramp and you can dehydrate. It is important therefore that you are fully hydrated before you start and that you take plenty fluids on board during and immediately after activity.

Often during sport and activity athletes will drink energy drinks to take in energy quickly

Sports drinks

Sports drinks (often called 'isotonic' drinks) contain energy-giving carbohydrates. Gatorade and Lucozade Sport are just two examples. They are usually used in sports that last for more than half an hour, such as games and lengthy endurance-type activity such as half marathons or triathlons.

These drinks are effective for rehydration during exercise, where there is more emphasis on fluid replacement than on restoring carbohydrates.

Diet and nutrition

Physiological factors

Age

Participation in sport is often determined on the basis of age. You may be familiar with the terms 'junior', 'senior', 'veteran'. You may also be aware that junior sport is further categorised into different age groups, such as Under 11, Under 14, Under 16, Under 18 and Under 21. The most significant difference between the age groups is their stage of physical growth and development, which is particularly obvious if you compare juniors and seniors.

A player's ability to perform physical skills will be influenced by their stage of physical and mental development. Their balance, agility and co-ordination increase as their nervous system grows and they become familiar with complex tasks and progress though the early stages of learning. As the body systems develop, children have more control over their movements. Their ability to perform will increase as they approach physical maturity. However, as a person ages further, their performance will fall off.

The growth and development of children

Your physical capacity and ability to do work or perform are influenced by your **growth** or stage of **development.**

◆ **Growth** is increase in size – which can be measured by recording weight, height, limb length and bone age over a period of time.

◆ **Development** refers to the way the mind and body's structure and function change (in terms of physical and mental abilities) to cope with increasingly complex tasks.

In the first two years of life the growth stage is immense. The rate of growth then slows down until you reach puberty. Individuals then grow very rapidly, with girls usually reaching full height at about 16.5 years and boys at about 18.

Regular physical exercise during childhood and adolescence establishes a healthy pattern of activity for the rest of a person's life. Exercise ensures that their bones grow properly. However, care must be taken to ensure that no damage is done to the growth areas at the end of the long bones because that will stunt growth.

Up to the end of puberty, an individual improves more due to the fact that they are growing and developing than as a result of training. Training has more effect as you mature physically and mentally.

Some young people reach the top of their sport very quickly and are able to compete with athletes and players much older than themselves. They have reached physical maturity early and progressed very quickly through the early stages of learning to world-class performance.

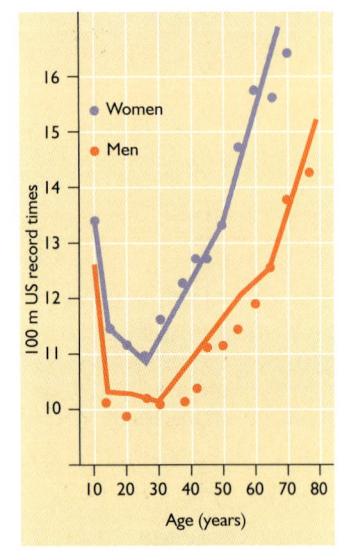

Performance reaches a peak in your 20s and 30s and then falls off with age

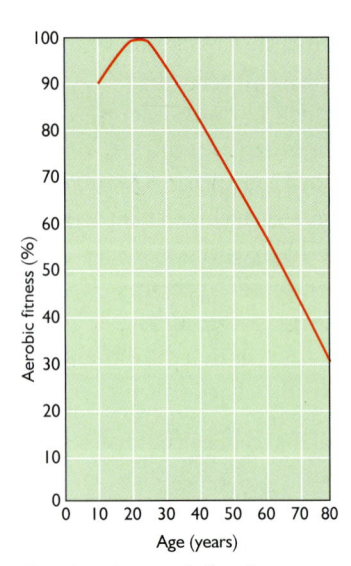

Aerobic fitness falls after peaking in your 20s

Factors affecting performance

Players like Jennifer Capriati, Martina Hingis and Venus Williams competed with much older players when they were still technically 'juniors'

The effects of ageing

Sports records suggest that you are in your prime during your late 20s and early 30s, although this will vary according to the sport that you compete in. Gymnasts and swimmers reach their prime at about 16 and 25 years old respectively. For some sports it may be later: Nick Faldo and Greg Norman, for example, are in their 40s and they are still competing at the highest level.

From your mid-twenties there are a number of reductions in your physiological capacities:

◆ Your arteries will gradually lose their elasticity. This will increase your blood pressure and reduce the blood flow to your working muscles.

◆ Your maximum stroke volume (the amount of blood pumped in a single beat) and vital capacity of your lungs (the maximum amount of air that can be breathed out in one breath) will steadily decrease. These changes mean that less oxygen is carried to your working muscles and that your ability to take up oxygen ($\dot{V}O_2$max) will decrease. Your endurance abilities will gradually decrease, your times will become slower and distances gradually shorter.

◆ Body fat steadily increases due to decreased physical activity, increased food intake and reduced ability to make use of fat for energy.

Other non-physiological changes include:

◆ a gradual drop in the efficiency of the sensory systems

◆ a slowing of reactions

◆ greater risk of injury

◆ slower powers of recovery.

Nick Faldo is in his 40s, but still competing at the highest level

Physiological factors

The changes that occur in your body because of increasing age cannot be prevented. This steady decline in physical ability is also due largely to a reduction in the amount of endurance activity that is undertaken on a regular basis.

Training can help lessen the effects of ageing by keeping the body systems as fit as possible. If you continue to exercise and train correctly all parts of your body (including the heart, lungs, muscles and joints) will benefit.

Gender differences

Children grow and mature at very different rates. Maturity refers not only to physiological growth but to psychological growth. It is at this point that gender differences should be considered.

Physical development

The muscle composition of an adult male totals about 40% of his total body mass. For women it is about 24% but for a child it is quite different. At birth a baby will possess all of the muscle fibres they're going to have but these are small and watery. They will develop and thicken as the child grows.

The gain in strength is most dramatic between the ages of 11 and 17. During and after puberty boys will become much stronger than girls, largely due to the male hormone testosterone. This is produced naturally in the body by both males and females but is more prolific in males and gives them increased strength, aggression and competitive urge.

Up until the age of 11 it is not unusual for boys and girls to compete together. However, when the strength gains start to become evident boys and girls should be separated, particularly where practice and competition involves body contact.

Exercise at all ages is beneficial to your health

Until puberty boys and girls often compete together

After puberty boys become physically stronger than girls and it is no longer possible to compete equally in some sports and activities

Male cross-country skiers are on average 30% better than women of the same level. This is because they have a much better oxygen-carrying capacity

It also during this time that girls will start their periods (menstruating). The physical effects of this can affect ability to do physical work. Young women may suffer from abdominal cramps, headaches and general lethargy.

The body fat levels differ between the sexes, with boys generally storing less fat than girls. This can be affected by exercise and training – for example, an athletic girl will possess fat levels similar to those of an average boy. Body fat levels will vary throughout life.

Up to the age of 10 girls and boys have an equal oxygen-transporting capacity. The boys' capacity tends to increase throughout puberty but that of girls tends to level off (or even decrease) at the age of 12. However, female athletes will have a better oxygen-carrying capacity than inactive men. The best male athletes in endurance sports such as speed skating, cross country skiing and orienteering are better than the best females in the sport by at least 30%. This is because women have smaller hearts and lungs. They also have 30% less haemoglobin (the oxygen-carrying compartment of the red blood cells), which accounts for the difference in aerobic capacity.

Stress

You have probably heard the saying 'A healthy mind in a healthy body', which suggests that there is a link between the mind and the body. If your body is physically fit then your mind will be in good working order. On the other hand, if either your body or your mind becomes stressed, you will feel the effect in both.

Your body will suffer physical stress when you are ill, when you are hurt, or when you are very tired. Mental stress may be caused by work, family relationships, love-life, financial situation, whether you are taking an exam – or innumerable other things. The problem really starts if several of these happen at once or if they go on for a long time.

It is well known that physical activity is a good way to reduce stress levels, and to help you deal better with stress when it happens. But when you are suffering from stress, you just don't feel like taking part in exercise: you lack **motivation**. And so the stress continues.

Rest

Adults need about eight hours' sleep per night. Children need even more. You can probably manage on less sleep than this but if you carry on like this for long, you are likely to suffer from **sleep deprivation**. Your work may suffer, you may show signs of tension or stress, you may become irritable and impatient with other people.

This is why rest is an important part of a good fitness and training programme. Your programme must include the right amount of rest to give your body a chance to recover from and get used to the extra demands that exercise is making on it. If you don't take enough rest, you are more likely to have an injury or to damage yourself. There will be no more improvements in your ability or fitness and your performance may even deteriorate.

Exercise

The amount and the type of exercise that you do will influence your level of fitness. The more exercise you do the better your level of fitness.

Fitness is an active state. You cannot get fit by reading about exercise, talking about exercise or watching other people work out. You have to do something about it. You can only get fit through movement and effort. The more physically active you are, the more fit you will be.

fitness training, p.83

Drug use and abuse

Drugs are chemical substances that affect the body's functioning. Drugs are used across the world, mostly to treat a variety of illnesses, which range from mild afflictions to terminal illnesses.

Drugs have a number of beneficial effects, such as relieving pain, removing anxiety, inducing sleep, fending off sleep, controlling weight.

To reduce pain or to treat illness and disease doctors use **medicinal drugs**. But medicinal drugs can also be used wrongly – they can be abused.

Some drugs, such as alcohol and nicotine, are called **social drugs**.

Alcohol

If someone drinks too much alcohol, they will:

- be less able to co-ordinate their movements
- lose their balance
- begin to slur their speech
- find that their hearing is affected
- find that their muscles don't work as well as they should
- have a 'hangover' (caused by losing fluid from the body and becoming dehydrated).

Abuse of alcohol over a long period of time leads to kidney and liver damage. Athletes who drink too much lose their drive to train and to compete.

Smoking

If somebody smokes they will breathe in carbon monoxide. This is a poisonous gas, which binds to haemoglobin more readily than oxygen and so prevents oxygen getting to the tissues.
The nicotine in tobacco causes a rise in both heart rate and blood pressure. This in turn puts a strain on the heart and can lead to heart disease, heart attacks and even sometimes death.

Smokers find it hard to breathe as the tar in cigarettes collects in their lungs and blocks the tubes that carry air. The higher the levels of tar and nicotine in a cigarette, the more smokers put themselves at risk.

Doping and performance-enhancing drugs

Doping means taking drugs to improve sports performance.

The International Olympic Committee (IOC) have identified the following methods of doping:

◆ blood doping

◆ pharmacological, chemical or physical manipulation.

As drug testing becomes more precise, athletes are continually seeking new ways to avoid being caught, and seem to keep one step ahead of the governing bodies.

Manufacturers are producing drugs that are increasingly difficult to detect. Drugs are now being made to resemble natural body hormones, and some are almost impossible to detect.

Human growth hormone (HGH) is the major hormone influencing growth and development. There has been a synthetic version of this drug on the market for over a decade. It increases lean body mass and may improve muscle strength and the body's ability to cope with fatigue – makes it able to tolerate higher levels of lactate.

Most elite-level sportspeople, like these British rowers, achieve greatness without having to use performance-enhancing drugs

Drug use is most evident in elite-level sport, where the difference between winning or losing may only be a thousandth of a second, less than a hair's breadth or the blink of an eye. However, the difference in terms of recognition and reward (especially financial) can be significant. Some athletes use drugs to make up this difference.

Using performance-enhancing drugs can be an effective means of gaining the upper hand against an opponent. It is not as blatant as other tactics and is often the hardest to detect.

Drugs have been used widely to improve sports performance. Notorious examples have occurred in swimming, athletics, cycling and weightlifting.

The reasons put forward by athletes for taking performance-enhancing drugs are many:

◆ to be the best in the world

◆ the financial reward for being the best

◆ to build muscles faster or reduce the pain of an injury so that they can keep on working

◆ to calm themselves before big events

◆ because of the pressure to be the best

◆ because 'everyone else is doing it'

◆ because they believe they will not get caught.

Andreea Raducan of Romania tested positive for drugs at the 2000 Olympics

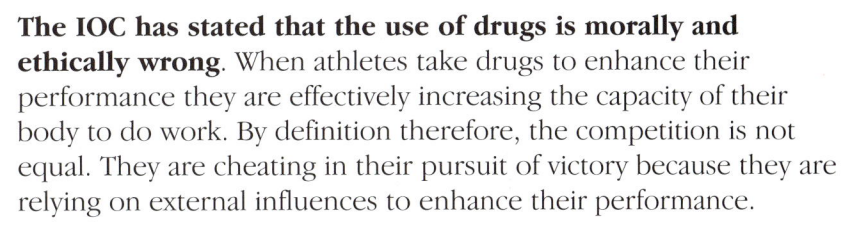

The IOC has stated that the use of drugs is morally and ethically wrong. When athletes take drugs to enhance their performance they are effectively increasing the capacity of their body to do work. By definition therefore, the competition is not equal. They are cheating in their pursuit of victory because they are relying on external influences to enhance their performance.

Drugs that improve sports performance are banned because they are harmful to health, damage the image of the sport and are a way of cheating. If an athlete is caught using drugs, he or she could be banned from their sport for a fixed period or even forever.

Types of performance-enhancing drugs

The IOC has categorised a range of drugs according to type:

- stimulants
- narcotic analgesics
- beta blockers
- diuretics
- anabolic steroids.

Stimulants

These raise heart rate and stimulate the nervous system. They improve reactions and the user is said to feel more alert and have increased confidence in their abilities. It has been reported that the user can maintain increasingly high levels of work for longer periods of time without feeling fatigue.

Examples
- Caffeine – found in tea and coffee and some soda drinks.
- Amphetamines – such as ephedrine, dexedrine and benzedrine.

Possible side-effects
- Heavy use can lead to high blood pressure, liver and brain damage.
- Sensory feelings such as pain and fatigue are masked or suppressed, and so the athlete is more prone to injury and accidents as they will be unaware that they are doing themselves some damage.
- Can cause aggressive behaviour and hostility.
- The athlete may feel mentally low or depressed after the immediate effects have worn off.

In the 1967 Tour de France, the British cyclist Tommy Simpson died of heart failure due to heat exhaustion. He had been taking amphetamines, which had hidden his growing exhaustion.

Narcotic analgesics

Narcotics cause drowsiness and analgesics are painkillers. These drugs suppress pain and enable athletes to perform even with an injury. After competition or a hard training session they induce sleep, enabling the body to recover.

Cyclists who have to perform at a high level for days on end have been found to use these drugs.

Tommy Simpson

Drug use and abuse

Examples
- Morphine – medical painkiller.
- Heroin – medical painkiller, although now abused by individuals seeking a sensory stimulation.
- Codeine – available over the counter as a painkiller and sometimes found in medicines for diarrhoea.

Possible side-effects
- Highly addictive – therefore illegal in most countries.
- Constipation and low blood pressure.
- Mental apathy.
- Withdrawal symptoms are particularly unpleasant.

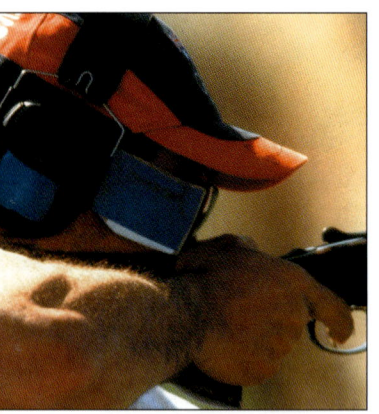

Beta blockers

These block the action of adrenaline, slowing heart rate and breathing rate and reducing feelings of anxiety and nerves. They are used to treat heart disease and high blood pressure.

Some athletes take beta blockers to calm their nerves before big events.

Beta blocker use in sports requiring great accuracy (such as snooker, golf and rifle shooting) is not uncommon.

Examples
- Propranolol.
- Tranquillisers such as diazepam (Valium).

Possible side-effects
- Drowsiness.
- Insomnia.
- Depression.
- Poor performance during prolonged events.

Diuretics

These increase the amount of water passed out in the urine, reducing body weight very quickly. Fighters who need to be at an optimum weight before a weigh-in misuse them. Athletes also use them when they need to flush banned substances from their body.

Examples
- Frusemide.
- Probenecid.

Possible side-effects
- Rashes.
- Nausea.
- Loss of sodium and potassium salts.
- Muscle weakness and heart damage.

Anabolic steroids

These are the drugs most commonly abused by sportspeople. They were developed in the 1940s to help build up patients suffering from loss of muscle and bone. The natural male hormone testosterone is responsible for the developing male characteristics such as deep voice, hair growth and increased muscle mass.

The anabolic steroid drugs were developed to perform the same function. The advantages of these are that they result in increased strength, weight, muscle growth and endurance when combined with training. Some athletes misuse these drugs to increase the size and strength of their muscles and speed their recovery time after training.

In 1988 at the Seoul Olympics Ben Johnson was tested positive for a banned anabolic steroid and was stripped of his gold medal and banned for two years.

The male hormone testosterone is responsible for building up muscle

Examples
- Nandrolone.
- Stanozol.
- Artificial testosterone.
- Clenbuterol.

Possible side-effects
- Heart disease and high blood pressure.
- Bone, tendon and ligament weakness.
- Infertility and cancer.
- Facial hair growth and deepening voice in women.
- Liver disorders.
- Aggressive behaviour.

ACTIVITY

The banned athletes

Identify banned athletes from the world of sport who were tested positive for banned substances. You may well have to refer to textbooks, newspaper articles and the Internet.

Identify when and where they were tested and state what penalty they received.

In class discuss the question 'Does the punishment fit the crime?'

ACTIVITY

Drugs in sport

Copy the table and fill in the gaps.

DRUG TYPE	USE	EXAMPLE	SIDE-EFFECTS
Beta blockers			
			Highly addictive; constipation and low blood pressure; mental apathy; withdrawal symptoms unpleasant
Diuretics			
			Increases strength, weight, muscle growth and endurance when combined with training
		Caffeine, amphetamines	

Blood doping

In this method blood is injected into the body to increase the number of red blood cells. It is usually the athlete's own blood that has been removed earlier and 'stored' for this specific reason.

By increasing the number of red blood cells the blood can carry more oxygen to the working muscles and increase an athlete's endurance abilities.

There are, however, risks associated with this method of doping, such as the possible transmission of HIV and hepatitis. Kidney damage may result if the blood used is not a match.

It is difficult to test accurately for blood doping.

Dope testing procedures

The IOC, World Federations and National Governing Bodies all agree that the use of drugs to improve performance is cheating.

In the UK the UK Sports Council is responsible for monitoring and implementing drug testing standards, procedures and protocol. The flow chart opposite shows the standard procedures that must be followed when testing for drugs.

Testing for drugs

1 Competitors are chosen for testing
- Competitors can be tested while training or after the event.
- Competition rules usually state who will be tested.
- Competitors tested in competition are informed immediately after the event that they will be tested.
- Competitors to be tested are usually informed in writing.

2 Competitor reports to the doping control centre
- An official will accompany the competitor.
- All identity documents are checked.
- The competitor will declare any medication being used.

3 Competitor produces a urine sample
- The competitor selects a numbered sample bottle.
- Competitors are supervised the whole time and must remove enough of their clothing for it to be possible to observe the sample being given.
- Only the competitor is allowed to handle the sample bottle.
- Sealed drinks are available for competitors who are dehydrated.

4 Sample is split
- The sample is divided equally between two sealed containers that have been chosen by the competitor.
- The competitor then seals the containers. One is labelled A, the other B.

5 The procedure is checked
- The competitor certifies that the procedure has been carried out correctly.

6 Laboratory analysis
- Both samples are sent to an approved laboratory.
- The technicians at the lab are not told who the sample belongs to.

7 Testing
- Sample A is tested.
- If this sample is negative both samples are destroyed and the competitor is informed of the result.
- If sample A is positive then the governing body is informed, the competitor is told and is usually suspended.
- The competitor is asked for an explanation, and (if requested) Sample B is tested.

8 Post test
- If there is no doubt that drugs have been used the governing body arranges a hearing.
- The competitor presents his or her case.
- If they are found guilty then a punishment will be decided. It could be short ban or even a lifetime suspension.
- The competitor may appeal.

Drug use and abuse

Drug testing is not a foolproof method; mistakes can occur and sometimes an innocent competitor is charged with using drugs.

Dope test procedures are not foolproof. Some athletes have been found guilty when new evidence has proved otherwise. Diane Modahl was one such athlete

Avoiding detection

Athletes who take drugs have to use a number of different methods to avoid detection.

One common method is to use 'clean' urine, provided by another person hidden in a bag and released into a sample bottle through a tube. Some athletes have sent another athlete in their place when told they have to be tested. In extreme cases athletes have had clean urine put through a small tube into their bladder, so that their sample is clean.

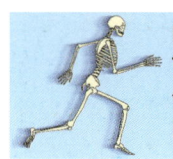

Drugs in sport – worth the risk?
The use of drugs in sport is becoming even more widespread. The manufacturers are continually trying to make 'undetectable' drugs and the chemists are trying to catch them.
Discuss with your classmates the advantages and disadvantages of drug taking in sport.

Consequences of drug taking

Drug taking in sport has become more widespread as the emphasis on winning and the financial rewards associated with it have increased. Taking drugs can cause untold damage to an athlete's physical and mental well-being and can cause permanent damage to their physical, personal and professional lives.

The table opposite highlights incidents and examples of drug use over the last 50 years and identifies some of the repercussions that athletes have faced.

DATE	OCCASION	INCIDENT
1952	Winter Olympics	Doping cases involving amphetamines. Several speed skaters became ill and needed medical attention
1960	Olympics	Danish cyclist Kurt Jenson collapsed and died from an amphetamine overdose
1967	Tour de France	Tommy Simpson died as a result of taking stimulants
1972	Munich Olympics	Full drug testing took place for the first time. US swimmer Rick DeMont tested positive for ephedrine and was stripped of his gold medal. The drug was part of his asthma medication
1976	Montreal Olympics	Seven out of eight weightlifters found guilty of taking steroids
1984	Los Angeles Olympics	Marti Viano was the first track athlete to be stripped of a medal in the 10,000 metre race. The winner Alberto Cova admitted to having engaged in the now illegal practise of blood doping
1988	Seoul Olympics	Ben Johnson tested positive for a banned anabolic steroid, was stripped of the 100 m gold medal and banned for 2 years. He was tested again in 1993, failed and has since been banned for life
1989		British runner David Jenkins was jailed in California for importing steroids from Mexico. He also admitted to using the drug during his career
1990		Butch Reynolds (world 400 m record holder) and Randy Barnes (world record holder shot put) tested positive for anabolic steroids
1994	Commonwealth Games	Diane Modahl and Paul Edwards were sent home after failing drugs tests. Modahl was later cleared but Edwards faces a life ban after failing another test
1994	Asian Games	11 Chinese swimmers and athletes tested positive for dihydrotestosterone
1997		Evidence uncovered identified a state-sponsored doping programme during East Germany's 20-year participation in the Olympics. Only their yachtsmen did not receive drugs
1998	World Swimming Championships	Chinese swimmer Yuan Yuan caught trying to smuggle human growth hormone into the event
1999	Tour de France	Several teams and individual cyclists disqualified from the race because of drug taking
2000	Sydney Olympics	Some athletes, including medal winners, found guilty of using drugs, although overall the organisers felt that the Sydney games were largely 'clean'

Safe practice in sport, activity and competition

Physical activities, because of their physical nature, involve some degree of physical risk for the participants.

The exercise environment

One of your most important considerations, in terms of planning for safe practice, must be the **exercise environment**. The exercise environment is made up of three components:

◆ size and space

◆ clothing

◆ equipment.

Size and space

To keep the physical environment safe you should be aware of the potential hazards. You can then take steps to control these hazards, or at least make participants aware of them so that you can ensure safe and effective exercise.

◆ Indoor facilities may be damaged by wear and tear. Damp patches may appear, caused by sweat, or standing water from condensation or leaking roofs. Dance and gymnastics sessions need a very smooth surface and a sprung floor.

◆ Outdoor surfaces may be affected by the weather. If a field is hard and dry falling on it can cause injuries. Synthetic surfaces (all-weather and astro-turf) can cause injuries to joints and ligaments because of the hardness of the surface. Outdoor surfaces should be checked for any broken glass or discarded rubbish.

Having enough space for performers to move freely in during competition and training is essential

The temperature, humidity and lighting should also be considered. When performing under floodlights you need to make sure that there is sufficient light to work safely.

The space available is very important. If the numbers in the group are too large for the space then the exercise or activity could be quite dangerous. On no account should any practice or drill take place where people could collide with or trip over each other. Neither should they have to concentrate on avoiding walls, bags or equipment at the sides of the activity area.

Some sports require athletes to wear protective sports clothing and use safety equipment

Clothing

It is important to be dressed appropriately for the exercise you are taking. Clothes for general exercise need to be clean, comfortable and warm enough (yet also cool enough) to work in.

'Clothing' also refers to the accessories worn by participants. All jewellery, especially rings and earrings, should be removed before commencing.

Some sports require specific clothing to be worn for protection or safety. Examples of safe clothing and equipment include:

- knee pads (volleyball)
- a helmet (cycling)
- a luminous band or vest (a road runner at night)
- shoulder padding or a scrum cap (rugby)
- mouth guard and face mask for the goalkeeper (hockey)
- helmets, shoulder pads and gloves (lacrosse)
- head guard and gloves (all amateur boxers).

Equipment

The equipment being used should be suitable for the activity and well maintained. Records of safety checks and maintenance should be kept. If equipment is damaged, is faulty in operation or parts are missing then it should not be used.

Having enough equipment for all players and competitors is very important. If there is sufficient equipment all of the group can be active during a session. When participants are waiting for their turns or for a piece of equipment they could become bored and disruptive or cold and more prone to injury.

Manufacturers' guidelines on the use of equipment

All equipment should be used correctly following the manufacturer's guidelines.

Maintenance

If any equipment or apparatus has not been well maintained or is faulty the problem should be reported to the person responsible for the maintenance of the equipment.

A trampoline, if not properly maintained, can be a dangerous piece of equipment

Safe practice in sport, activity and competition

Prevention of injury

Sports injuries happen often. Many injures can be prevented by following the guidelines in the previous section. Other injuries can be prevented through the use of effective warm-up and cool-down phases of the game, exercise or training session.

Any session, whether it is a training session, friendly game or competition, should incorporate the following stages:

◆ warm-up ◆ main exercise/activity session ◆ cool-down.

Warming up

The warm up prepares both your body and your mind for the exercise that is to come. Your body is taken gradually from its non-active state to a state of being ready for the exercise. Your mind is calmed down and focused on what you are about to do, so that you can concentrate properly.

How long it takes to warm up varies from one person to another. It will also be affected by the weather (warm, cold, wet or dry). Often when it is cold more time will be spent in the warm-up phase to thoroughly prepare the athlete for activity and competition. The warm-up may be longer for some activities than for others.

A good warm-up has four parts:

1 Activities that **increase your pulse rate**.
2 Activities that help you move more easily and **loosen up your joints** (mobility).
3 Exercises that **warm up and stretch** your muscles and tendons.
4 Final preparation.

Warming up is an essential part of any sport, activity or exercise session

Pulse-raising activities

These are rhythmic movements of your whole body. They use the large groups of muscles.

These activities make your heart beat faster. This sends the blood round your body more quickly so that it can carry oxygen to your muscles and warm them up. Exercises include:

◆ walking
◆ marching (lifting your knees high)
◆ gentle jogging
◆ stepping from side to side
◆ swinging your arms
◆ bending your knees (but only half way)
◆ skipping.

Mobility exercises

These are all ways of moving your main joints to prepare them for the movements they will be making in your activity. They also help with the general warming of your body. Examples are:

- rolling your shoulders
- swinging your arms in circles
- reaching your arms out to each side
- bending to each side
- twisting from the waist
- circling your hips
- raising your knees
- bending your knees (but only half way)
- circling your ankles.

You should prepare for the exercise you will be taking by doing mobility exercises

Stretching

All your stretching movements should be slow and well balanced. You should be standing in one place as you do them. You should not stretch until you've done the pulse-raising part of the warm-up and your muscles are warm – stretching cold muscles can cause injury.

Stretching your muscles helps them to be ready for the movements you will be doing in the main part of the exercise session. And, if you slip or fall, your muscles will be more ready to react.

Stretching is also an important part of your cool-down routine.

Guidelines for safe stretching

- Complete the pulse raising section of the warm-up first.
- Only stretch the muscle to the point **before** it begins to feel uncomfortable.
- Hold the stretch steadily for 8–10 seconds.

Stretching muscles in the warm-up helps prepare them for action

Prevention of injury

- ◆ **Do not bounce**.
- ◆ Try to relax the muscle as it is stretched.
- ◆ Keep a good balance.
- ◆ Release the stretch slowly.
- ◆ Repeat the stretch so that you can make a slightly greater movement.

It is useful to follow a standard routine for your stretching, whether as part of your warm-up or your cool-down.

If you can not remember the structure of a stretching routine, then refer back to the work done in Chapter 2.

◀ BACK *training suppleness, p.66*

Cooling down

Cooling down is as important as warming up. When you have finished exercising, your body has to get back to its resting state. It needs time to do this.

The aims of cooling down are:

- ◆ to slowly reduce the warmth of your body
- ◆ to slowly reduce your pulse and heart rate
- ◆ to bring your breathing back to normal
- ◆ to keep your joints and muscles loose.

You can make yourself ill if you don't take time to cool down. Blood will go on flowing to your muscles rather than to your brain. Less oxygen will reach your brain, so you may feel dizzy and even faint.

A cool-down should include:

- ◆ **A full stretching routine**. This should be the same as the warm-up routine but you should hold each stretch for longer (20–30 seconds).
- ◆ **Gentle rhythmic exercises**. These can be the same pulse-raisers as you used in your warm-up.
- ◆ **Simple mobility exercises**. Again, the same ones as you used in the warm-up are fine.
- ◆ **Gentle shaking of the arms and legs** will help the blood return from the ends of your arms and legs and leave you feeling relaxed. You can do this on your own but it is better if you lie down and relax and a partner lifts and shakes your arms and legs for you.

People often don't bother with the cool-down part of an exercise session. They may be in a hurry, or think it doesn't matter, or even feel too tired to do it. This is a mistake – the cool-down is an essential part of any training, exercise or sports programme.

Sports injuries

In any physical activity there is always the chance that injuries and accidents will occur. The type of activity being engaged in, the level at which it is being played and the fitness and skill level of the performers are all factors in the cause of injury.

Participants will slip, trip, fall, collide and bump into somebody or could be hit by an object or piece of equipment. The weather conditions might result in injury, if it is too hot or too cold, if it is too wet or icy. As the level of activity and competition increases the higher the risk of injury and accidents.

Types of injury

There are two types of injury that you need to be aware of.

- **Acute** injuries are the result of a sudden stress on the body. These injuries are more common in contact sports where players come into contact with each other. These stresses happen as a result of tackles, fouls and collisions. For example, a collision of heads during a header in football could give one player a broken nose.

Some players have collisions that can cause horrific injuries

- **Chronic** or **overuse** injuries are caused by a number of factors, including over-training, insufficient recovery time, poor technique or badly designed footwear or equipment. For example, long-distance runners can get pain at the front of their shins ('shin splints').

The table on page 132 identifies examples of injuries that could occur during a hockey training session or a match.

	INJURY	HOW IT COULD OCCUR
Acute injury (sudden stress)	Broken nose	Stick swung into the face
	Split lip/teeth knocked out	A stick or ball in the face
	Broken fingers	Being hit by a rising ball or a stick
	Dislocated shoulder	Collision with a goalkeeper
	Torn knee ligaments	Turning, twisting or falling awkwardly
Chronic (overuse)	Cartilage trouble	Constant twisting and turning places stress on the knee joint
	Achilles tendonitis	Turf shoes or grass boots do not cushion the foot as well as a normal running shoe

ACTIVITY

Injuries in your sport

Draw a table like the one above, listing the injuries that could occur in your sport. If your sport is hockey use another sport.

Recognising injuries and how to deal with them

- Dealing with sports injuries is a specialised business.
- Do not attempt to diagnose the injury.
- Keep calm, isolate the injured player and make them comfortable.
- Just because an injury is not visible it does not mean that it is not serious.
- If you are in doubt about the nature of the injury do nothing until the emergency services arrive.
- In the event of a serious injury remember exactly what happened, how and when. The paramedics will need to know everything.

Many types of injury can occur during training and competition. You should be able to recognise the injury and know how to deal with it.

Soft-tissue injuries

Soft-tissue injuries include damage to muscles, ligaments, tendons and cartilage. When soft tissues are injured they become inflamed. Treatment aims to reduce the swelling, prevent further damage and ease the pain.

Athletes can damage their muscles internally by applying too much force in moving their own body or an external object. In sprinting towards a ball, chasing back to defend a player or in sprinting to the net from the rear of the court a player is trying to accelerate as quickly as possible to maximum speed. This means that considerable forces are being applied to the body, mainly through the legs. Under

Rest
Keep the participant still, as movement encourages increased blood flow. Using the injured body part can cause permanent damage.

Ice
Apply ice to the injured area. Ice causes the blood vessels and surrounding tissues to contract and reduce blood flow to the area. The result of this is to reduce inflammation and swelling and so reduce pain. Remove the ice pack after 10–12 minutes but repeat every 3 hours.

Compression
To keep the swelling to a minimum secure the ice pack with an elastic bandage, however, do not wrap it so tightly that you cut off the blood supply.

Elevation
Raise the injured body part above the level of the heart. The force of gravity will help to drain excess fluid from the damaged area and reduce swelling.

The RICE routine for treating minor soft-tissue injuries

this pressure, some of the muscle fibres can tear or rupture, causing localised pain.

Signs and symptoms:
- Sudden pain, followed by
- swelling, stiffness and perhaps cramp.
- The participant will find it difficult to stand and will not be able to put any weight on the injured part.

Treatment:
- For minor muscle tears, strains and pulls use the **RICE** (**R**est, **I**ce, **C**ompression, **E**levation) routine to reduce pain, swelling and bruising around an injured part and speed up the healing process.

Someone with a serious strain should be taken to hospital as bones may be broken and tendons and ligaments damaged.

Skin injuries
Abrasions or grazes
Abrasions are usually the result of sliding or falling on a rough or hard surface. The skin layers are scraped off or there is a friction burn.

Treatment:
- Clean the wound with warm water, then with antiseptic wipe.
- If it is still bleeding, allow it to clot.
- Let the wound dry naturally if possible.
- If there is danger of an infection, cover the wound with a plaster.

Cuts
In a cut the skin and blood vessels are damaged and blood flows freely out of the body. The aim of the treatment is to stop the blood flowing as quickly as possible.

Treatment:
- **You should wear plastic gloves**, if possible, to avoid the possibility of infection.
- Remove any splinters, dirt or gravel from the cut by gently washing with clean water, or using tweezers if necessary.
- Cover the cut with a clean pad or cloth and press down firmly to stop the bleeding.
- If the cut is severe and blood is flowing freely then lie the patient down and raise the injured part to reduce blood flow to it.
- Continue to apply pressure until the bleeding stops.
- If blood seeps through the pad, change it.
- For severe bleeding call for an ambulance – the wound may need stitching.

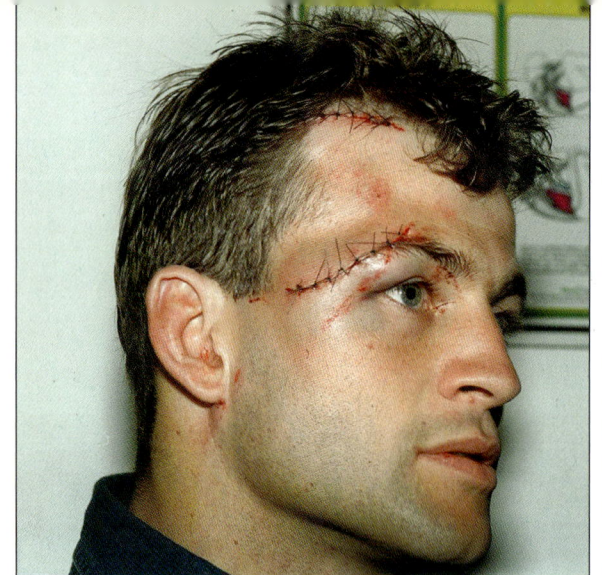

Players often receive open cuts and wounds as a result of the physical contact. Some of these cuts will be stitched and the player can often return to the field

All serious cuts or abrasions should be reported to a doctor so your participant can receive an anti-tetanus injection.

Blisters

Repeated friction against the skin causes separation of the skin layers. The gap formed by this is filled by a tissue fluid (serum), which forms a thin bubble or blister. Blisters can occur on the heel and foot when wearing new shoes and on the palms of the hand during sports in which you use an implement – rowing, golf and tennis are but a few examples

Treatment:

- Small blisters can be covered with an adhesive dressing.
- Blisters do heal more quickly if the fluid is drained from them. Large blisters can be punctured with a sterile needle and the fluid removed by exerting gentle pressure against the bubble. Then cover the blister with a plaster.
- Blisters can become infected. If they do further medical advice will be necessary.

Bruises

Bruises are a sign that blood is leaking from damaged vessels underneath the skin surface.

- Use the RICE treatment.

Hard tissue (bone and joint) injuries

Fractures

A fracture is a crack or break in bone. There are two types of fractures.

- In a **simple** or **closed** fracture the skin surface is not damaged or penetrated.
- In an **open** or **compound** fracture the skin layer is punctured by the bone.

Direct blows from another person or piece of equipment, an awkward fall or a collision can break bones. Fractures can also occur from pulls or as a result of too much stress on a body part.

Simple and compound fractures

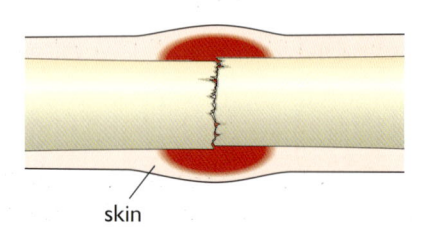

skin

In a **simple** or **closed** fracture the bone is broken but the skin surface is not damaged

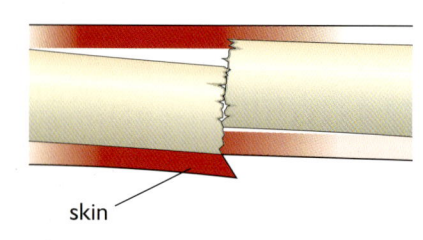

skin

In an **open** or **compound** fracture the skin is damaged and the bone may stick out

Signs and symptoms
- A crack or snap might have been heard.
- Pain and tenderness around the injury.
- The limb may look deformed or twisted.
- Difficulty in moving the body part.
- Bones and nerves contain blood vessels, which means pain and bleeding. The area will swell and bruising will occur when the blood seeps into surrounding tissue.

Treatment
- Call for an ambulance.
- Do not move the casualty and do not try to straighten the limb.
- Make the injured person as comfortable as possible. Prevent any movement at the site of injury.
- If you have to wait for the ambulance immobilise the injured limb by bandaging it to a sound part of the body.
- A sling made from a towel or bandage can be used to support a fractured arm bone.
- If you suspect a leg bone might be fractured, tie the leg gently to a splint (for example to the other leg or a hockey stick) to prevent movement.
- Do not attempt to use a sling or a splint unless you have passed a first aid course.

Stress fractures

These are small cracks in a bone and are often overuse injuries. Stress fractures can be caused by a running on hard surfaces and are known as 'shin splints'. Abruptly stopping, twisting and turning on hard surfaces can also cause stress fractures.

Signs and symptoms
- Pain, which gets gradually worse in a particular part of the limb.
- There will also be signs of swelling and tenderness in the area.

Treatment
- Use RICE to reduce inflammation.
- Get immediate rest.
- Keep fit doing other activities.
- Check running action and footwear – is it appropriate for the activity?

Dislocation

Dislocations occur when one or more of the bones at a joint are forced out of their normal position. This can happen as a result of an external force or through a sudden muscular contraction. Shoulder dislocations are common in contact sports like rugby, football and judo. Netball players and cricketers tend to suffer from finger and thumb dislocations. Dislocations have a tendency to recur, because the ligaments protecting the joint become stretched and the whole joint is less stable.

> ***Signs and symptoms***
> ◆ Severe pain at or near the joint.
> ◆ The joint appears deformed and the participant can not move it.
> ◆ The joint will appear fixed with no movement possible,
> ◆ There will be swelling around the joint, followed by bruising.
>
> ***Treatment***
> ◆ Call for an ambulance.
> ◆ Support the injured part in the most comfortable position, using bandages or slings.
> ◆ If you in any doubt as to the nature of the injury, then treat it as a fracture.
> ◆ Do not attempt to manipulate the joint back into place.

Unconsciousness

If a player is knocked out, he or she could have a fractured skull, bleeding from the vessels within the skull or bruising to the brain. They could have a spinal injury.

> **If you think there is any possibility that your participant has a neck or spinal injury, do not move them. Dial for an ambulance immediately.**

Even if the unconscious person 'comes to' within a few seconds and insists that they are all right, do *not* let them continue playing.

Treatment – the DR ABC routine

Read the instructions in the flow chart opposite.

Other conditions

A number of other conditions are not classed as sports injuries but you should be able to recognise and respond to them appropriately.

Asthma attacks

Many people who take part in sport suffer from asthma. They control this with a range of drugs, taken usually through an inhaler. However, adverse conditions, exercise and simply forgetting to take the prescribed dosage can all lead to an attack.

During an attack the sufferer may have difficulty breathing, shortness of breath and wheeze. In the worst cases he or she should be put in the recovery position and medical help called.

Shock

Serious injuries or accidents of any sort may cause shock. Someone in shock may look pale, have a rapid pulse and perhaps be on the verge of collapse.

D for Danger
- Assess the danger. Are you as the coach in danger? Is your participant in danger? Send for medical help. Clear the area around the casualty. Stop the activity if you have to.

R for Response
- Identify whether the casualty is conscious or unconscious. Shake him or her gently by the shoulders, and ask if they can hear you.
- If the casualty is conscious, find out if he or she is in pain, where the pain is and treat as appropriate.
- If the person is unconscious put them in the recovery position.

The recovery position

A for Airway
- When a person is unconscious their tongue can easily slip backwards and block their airway. Loosen any tight clothing. Raise and tilt the head back to open the airway fully. Remove obstructions such as a gum shield or vomit. Scrape away vomit with a tissue.

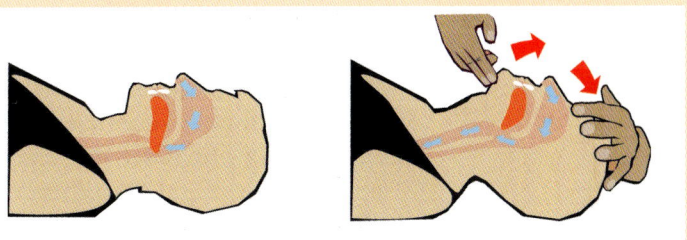

It is important to ensure the airway of an unconscious person is clear

B for Breathing
- Is the casualty breathing? Look to see if their chest is rising and falling. Listen for breathing sounds. Feel for breath on your cheek. If he or she is not breathing place them on their back, start mouth to mouth ventilation (MMV). Give two full breaths, then check for circulation.

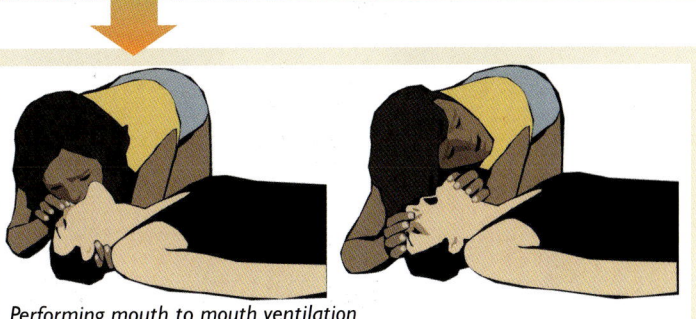

Performing mouth to mouth ventilation

C for Circulation
- Find the carotid pulse in the neck.
- If a pulse is present keep the casualty on their back and continue MMV, checking pulse and breathing regularly.
- If a pulse is absent start cardiopulmonary resuscitation (CPR). Check pulse and breathing regularly.

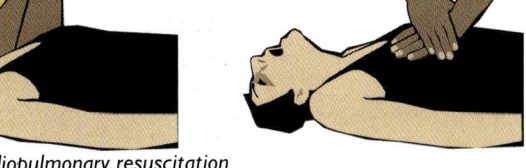

Performing cardiopulmonary resuscitation

An individual in shock should be laid down with their head low, kept warm and their breathing and pulse checked.

Hypothermia

In extreme cold an individual's body temperature can fall well below their core of 37°C. If it falls below 35°C they will be in danger of suffering from **hypothermia**. The individual will begin to shiver, look pale and slightly blue, have shallow breathing and a weak pulse. They may even collapse.

If someone shows signs of hypothermia they should be insulated with extra warm clothing and their head covered. If conscious they should be given warm drinks. Medical help should be called.

Hyperthermia

In extreme heat and sunshine – and especially when exercising in these conditions – the body temperature can rise above 37°C, sometimes as high as 39°C. In extreme heat the body can not remove heat generated by muscular activity quickly enough.

Sweating occurs naturally to remove the body's heat. During extreme heat sweating becomes excessive and the body loses too much salt and water. This can give rise to **heat exhaustion**. As a result the person becomes **dehydrated**, and in extreme temperatures **heat stroke** occurs. In this case the body loses the ability to sweat and the temperature rises rapidly.

Above: People who take part in winter sports should dress appropriately to avoid hypothermia

Right: Sportspeople must take care to keep cool when performing in hot conditions

A person suffering from heat exhaustion should be given a weak solution of salt and water. Dehydration should be treated with water to restore body fluids. When someone is suffering from heat stroke their body should be covered with cold wet sheets.

ACTIVITY

Diagnosing injury

The following case studies outline a range of sporting incidents, which have been reported in an accident logbook.

Analyse each case study. The table (right) shows you how you should organise your analysis.

- diagnose the injury
- identify the treatment and course of action
- state how and why the injury occurred
- state whether it is an acute or chronic/overuse injury.

Case study 1
Carl was jumping to perform a lay-up shot in basketball. He landed awkwardly and jarred his ankle. He fell to the floor and clutched his right ankle and moaned. When asked if he could stand, he tried to but could not put any weight on his right leg and fell back to the floor.

Case study 2
Suleima was playing hockey on an astro-turf pitch. She received the ball from a team mate and was left in a one-on-one situation with the goalkeeper. When trying to round the goalkeeper she tripped and landed heavily on her left shoulder.

Suleima let out a piercing scream and clutched at her shoulder. The goalkeeper said that she heard a snap. Suleima said the pain was between her shoulder and the base of her neck. On closer inspection the area she referred to looked deformed. Suleima felt sick and thought she might vomit.

Case Study 3
Charlotte is a long-distance runner and spends nearly seven hours a week road running. In the last few weeks she has been complaining of soreness and pain at the front of her shins. She has continued to train because she is preparing for a half marathon.

	CARL	SULEIMA	CHARLOTTE
What could the injury be?			
Treatment?			
How did it happen?			
Is it an acute or chronic/overuse injury?			

Revising factors affecting performance

This section is designed to help you improve your knowledge and understanding of the factors affecting performance in sport.

In order to answer the questions you may well need to look back through the chapter to help you. Completing these questions successfully will help you prepare for your examination.

Diet and nutrition

1 Name three factors in the diet that might affect an athlete's performance.
2 Give two reasons why the body needs food.
3 What nutrients are considered to be the energy providers?
4 Carbohydrates are broken down into glucose and stored as glycogen in which parts of the body?
5 There are two main types of fat that the body needs. Name both of them and give three examples of food sources in which each is found.
6 What mineral would be useful for a tennis player to help prevent cramp whilst playing a match? Which foods contain this mineral?
7 It is a hot day and Stanley has to run the 1500 m for sports day. What should he do before and after the race to prevent dehydration?
8 List three factors that affect the amount of energy required by a person.
9 Complete the following sentence:

   If you take in more kilojoules than you burn, your weight will ....
10 Give two reasons why it is important not to eat only an hour before taking part in sport and exercise.

Physiological factors

1 What effect does puberty have on the performance of boys?
2 List three physiological changes that occur as you grow older.

Drug use and abuse

1. Drugs are used to maintain and improve health. Name three beneficial effects that drugs can have on the body.
2. State two ways in which alcohol can affect the performance of an athlete.
3. Smoking can become addictive. Name the chemical that forms that addiction. Describe the impact of smoking on the human body.
4. Give three drug categories that the International Olympic Committee has identified as performance enhancing.
5. Give one example of an anabolic steroid and identify the way in which it works to enhance performance. List three possible side-effects of the use of this drug on the body.
6. Why do some athletes consider blood doping to improve the quality of their performance?

Safe practice in sport

1. Name three pieces of protective equipment used in the game of hockey.
2. Fahida's PE teacher has told her that she must remove all her jewellery before she can participate in the netball match. Give two reasons why this is important.
3. After raising the heart rate an athlete should stretch their muscles before participating in competition. List four guidelines for safe stretching.

Sports injuries

1. One of the categories of sports injury is acute (injury that occurs as a result of sudden stress). Name and describe the other category.
2. Name three signs or symptoms of a strained ankle.
3. RICE is considered to be the best initial treatment for a range of injuries. What does RICE stand for?
4. How is a blister caused? What is the treatment?

5 In a football tackle a player is tackled and hurts his ankle. On examination the limb looks deformed and twisted but the surface of the skin has not been broken. Define this injury and name two other symptoms that he might have.

6 The DRABC routine is used when a person has been found unconscious. What does DRABC stand for?

7 Describe the symptoms of hypothermia and hyperthermia.

CHAPTER 4: Acquisition of skill in sport

Learning new skills is a complex process. People are not born with skills – they acquire or learn them as a result of teaching, coaching and instruction or by trial and error.

In this chapter you will investigate the phases of learning that performers go through, discuss the way in which skills are practised and analyse the way performers process information and make decisions.

Riding a bicycle is a skill that most of you learnt a long time ago and now take for granted

CONTENTS

Skill in sport	144
Classifying skill	147
Stages of learning	151
Learning and skills practice	155
Learning and performance	162
Revising acquisition of skill in sport	165

Human performance in sport

Skill in sport

We perform a range of different movements throughout the course of each day that allow us to complete a variety of tasks. Those tasks may be as simple as sitting down, standing up or walking, or may be more complex, such as changing a car tyre. Our ability to perform these actions or movements relies on **skill**.

If you take part in sport or exercise you will be required to perform a number of sport-related skills: running, kicking, catching, throwing, dribbling and hitting are just a few skills that are required in order to participate in game-type sports.

In 1963, Knapp gave a definition for the term skill which can be related to the skills that are required to compete in sport:

> ***'The learned ability to bring about pre-determined results with maximum certainty, often with the minimum outlay of time energy or both.'***

In any skilled sports performance there are a number of key features to watch out for. Often the word skill is associated with elite level performers. You might hear commentators talk about 'a skilful player' or 'a skilful performance'.

In sport, skills are the complex, critical and intricate movements that are performed during practice, training and competition. A footballer needs to be able to run, dribble, pass, receive and shoot. Alongside these skills a player will need good vision, speed, strength and stamina.

ACTIVITY

Skill in sport

Pick an elite performer from your sport.

List the skills this person needs to take part in his or her sport. You might want to list the whole range of skills and include skill names – for example, in basketball shooting you may refer to the lay up, in cricket you may refer to spin bowling in terms of off break and leg break.

Skill and technique

You will often hear the terms **skill** and **technique** used together but there is a difference between the two.

- **Skill refers to a standard of performance** – how well you can perform a skill is a reflection of your ability level. For example, many people can jump up and down on a trampoline, and some can even do a seat drop – but few can do an open back somersault.
- **Techniques are basic movement patterns in sport** – for example, dribbling in football, a smash in tennis or a handstand in gymnastics. In sports performance a number of techniques can be

Jonathon Edwards had the ability, knowledge and confidence to achieve his goals of gold in the 2000 Olympics and 2001 World Championships

combined to create a skilled performance – receiving, dribbling, turning on the ball and making a pass could be classed as skilful. A handstand in gymnastics that is performed one-handed and involves a round-off is skilful.

Skilful performance

Skill refers to your ability to choose and perform the right techniques at the right time, successfully, regularly and with a minimum of effort.

Skill is not just physical ability but also involves mental qualities. A player needs to be able to perform the movement in competition where there is pressure and emphasis on the outcome. For example, in practice a footballer might be able to put nine out of ten penalty kicks in the back of the net, but can he do it in a cup game when his team are 2–1 down and there is just 90 seconds on the clock?

Examples of skilful performance:

- Timing a football tackle to take the ball cleanly.
- Timing a dive at the end of a short sprint to catch a ball when fielding.
- In cricket playing the most appropriate stroke to a certain type of delivery.
- Knowing when to come forward, and 'rush' the net in tennis.
- Receiving the baton cleanly at speed in the changeover of a relay race.

A skilful performance is one where the highest standard possible has been achieved

ACTIVITY

Skilful performance in sport

Think about some of the most well-known and talented performers in your sport. Can you identify examples of when they have produced a skilful performance? What specifically about that performance made it skilful? Can you describe it in words?

Components of skill

People take part in sport and exercise at all different levels: some play for their local club side in perhaps the fourth or fifth team, some people take part in national and international competition. One significant factor that distinguishes the level at which people compete is fitness, another is their skill.

In Chapter 2 we spent time defining and understanding the term fitness and started to consider the components of skill.

components of fitness, p.62

Skill in sport **145**

THE COMPONENTS OF SKILL

Agility
The ability to rapidly and accurately change the direction of your entire body. An agile athlete is 'nimble' or quick. To be a good martial artist, football goalkeeper, a slips fielder in cricket, a skier or a squash player you would need to be agile.

Co-ordination
The term 'hand–eye co-ordination' refers to a player's timing and ability in sports where there is emphasis on striking, throwing and catching. Badminton players, baseball players, rugby players and golfers need good hand–eye co-ordination. Co-ordination also refers to the ability to use your senses and body parts to perform motor skills fluently and accurately.

Balance
Balance is the ability to maintain equilibrium (your balance) while standing and moving. In order to balance performers need to able to distribute their weight evenly.

Power
Power is the ability to transfer your energy into force. The ability to produce maximum power occurs over a short period of time only. Athletes in jumping and throwing events and weightlifters need to be able to produce powerful or explosive movements.

Reaction time
If you have a short reaction time you will react more quickly to a stimulus. For example, a motor racing driver needs quick reaction times, not just to get off the grid but also to drive the car during the race – breaking, accelerating, changing gear, overtaking and reacting to others on the circuit.

Speed of movement
Skilful performers need to be able to perform a movement quickly. For example, a cricket batsman may have less than a second to play a delivery that is travelling at over 80 miles an hour, and long jumpers need to reach a have good sprinting speed before take off.

Acquisition of skill in sport

Classifying skill

Skill in sport can be classified in three ways:

◆ **Open and closed skills.**

◆ **Discrete, serial, continuous skills.**

◆ **Self-paced and externally paced skills.**

Open and closed skills

In order to understand the different types of skills it is important to consider the sporting **environment** in which they are performed. The environment refers to a number of factors including the venue, the opposition, the type of competition, the stage of the game, the weather and the surface.

Closed skills

Closed skills are used in a stable, predictable environment where the performer knows exactly what to do and when to do it. The athlete is in control. In activities such as the vault in gymnastics, diving or archery the movement pattern or skill to be performed does not change with the venue, weather or opposition.

The skill to be performed is in essence a number of movement patterns or techniques that have been added together and learnt as a whole until the skill has become second nature. A vault in gymnastics, a dive from a high board with somersaults and half twists, a long or triple jump and throwing events in athletics are all closed skills. With closed skills the performer must exactly reproduce the movement they have learnt.

Skills that do not change from one performance to the next, or from one environment to the next, are referred to as closed skills

Open skills

In **open skills**, the performer must be in touch with cues or signals from their environment and must be able to respond to the demands of the situation at that time. For example, a cricket batsman has to choose the most appropriate stroke to play as a direct response to the delivery.

Catching a ball and throwing it to a team mate is an example of an open skill

Games like volleyball, football, lacrosse, basketball and rugby require the use of a number of open skills. In these games the playing environment is constantly changing, and the skill to be performed will vary according to a number of factors:

◆ the opposition – for instance, whether they operate a man-to-man or zonal defence

◆ whether the team is attacking or defending and whether they have possession or not

◆ whether the team with the ball are about to shoot or are just breaking out of defence.

For example, when defending an attacking short corner a hockey goalkeeper may be uncertain about which opponent will shoot, when, from where and where he or she will aim the shot at. The goalkeeper will have to be aware of the movements of the attacking players in the circle and be ready to respond to a shot that may be taken at any speed, height or direction.

In an open skill the form of the action is constantly being varied according to what is happening to the performer.

Open and closed skill continuum

We can place skills on a line (a **skill continuum**) that goes from fully open at one end to fully closed at the other. Many skills fall somewhere between the two extremes.

A skills continuum

- Golf drive off the tee
- Bowling in cricket

- Driving a racing car

CLOSED ———————————————————— **OPEN**

- Gymnastic floor routine
- Archery or target shooting

- Sliding tackle in football
- Playing a stroke in cricket

ACTIVITY

Open and closed skill in sport

Make a list of sports skills from across a range of sports.

Draw a skills continuum and place the skills you have listed onto it according to whether you think they are open or closed.

Compare your work with that of your classmates. Some may have chosen the same examples – have they placed theirs in the same place as yours on the continuum?

Discrete, serial and continuous skills

◆ **Discrete skills** have a definite start and end point. Examples include a somersault in gymnastics, driving a golf ball, throwing a javelin, taking a free throw in basketball and bowling a tenpin ball.

◆ **Serial skills** string discrete movements together. Examples are a netballer receiving a ball, turning and throwing at goal in the same movement, a complete floor routine in gymnastics, a complex high dive involving twists and rotations. These skills may require many seconds to complete, and often appear continuous, although they might have discrete beginnings and ends.

◆ **Continuous skills** have no fixed start and end points. Repetitive-type activities such as walking, running, rowing and swimming involve repetition of the same movement pattern over and over again. In the context of a race there will be a start and finish point to the repetition (usually the end of the race). For example, in swimming the movement pattern of swimming (continuous) is broken up by tumble turns at the end of each lap. Tumble turns are examples of serial skills.

The figure below places examples of different sports, activities or skills on a continuum to show whether they are discrete, serial or continuous.

Swimming is an example of a continuous skill. However, the movement pattern is broken up by tumble turns (a serial skill) at the end of each lap

Discrete – continuous continuum

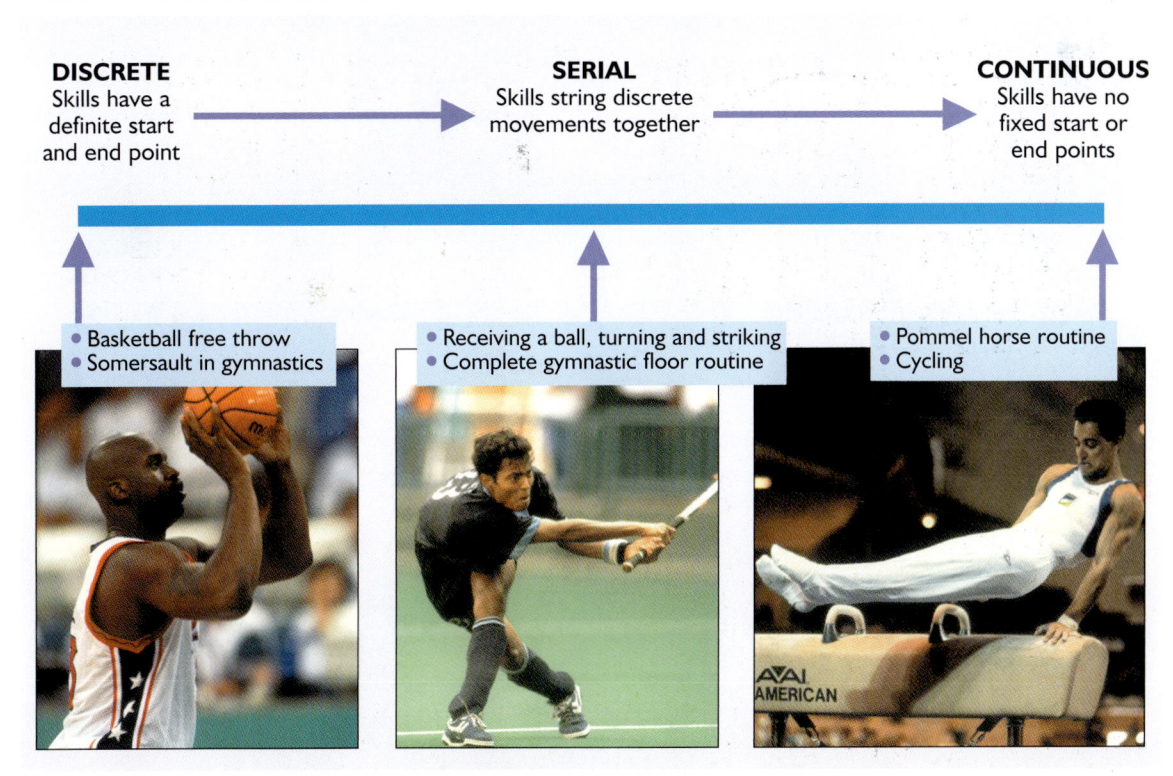

DISCRETE
Skills have a definite start and end point

→

SERIAL
Skills string discrete movements together

→

CONTINUOUS
Skills have no fixed start or end points

- Basketball free throw
- Somersault in gymnastics

- Receiving a ball, turning and striking
- Complete gymnastic floor routine

- Pommel horse routine
- Cycling

Classifying skill **149**

Self-paced and externally paced skills

Pacing refers to the degree of timing and control a performer has over the skill being carried out.

Self-paced skills are skills where the performer starts the action – for example, when striking a golf ball, serving at badminton, throwing a javelin and bowling a rounders ball.

There are situations in sport where the timing of movements and skill is dictated by the action of another. These are referred to as **externally paced skills** – a cricket batsman responds to the pace, pitch and angle of delivery of the ball; a tennis player's service return is dictated by the server and the quality of that serve. In some situations performers must react to the environment rather than to the action of their opponent – for example, a sailor is reliant on the strength of the wind, a sprint athlete is confined to their blocks until the pistol is fired.

The figure below uses another continuum, placing examples of skills and sporting movements at either end of the continuum. Remember, as with all skills, not all activities or movements will fall into an 'either/or' category and will be placed mid-way on the continuum.

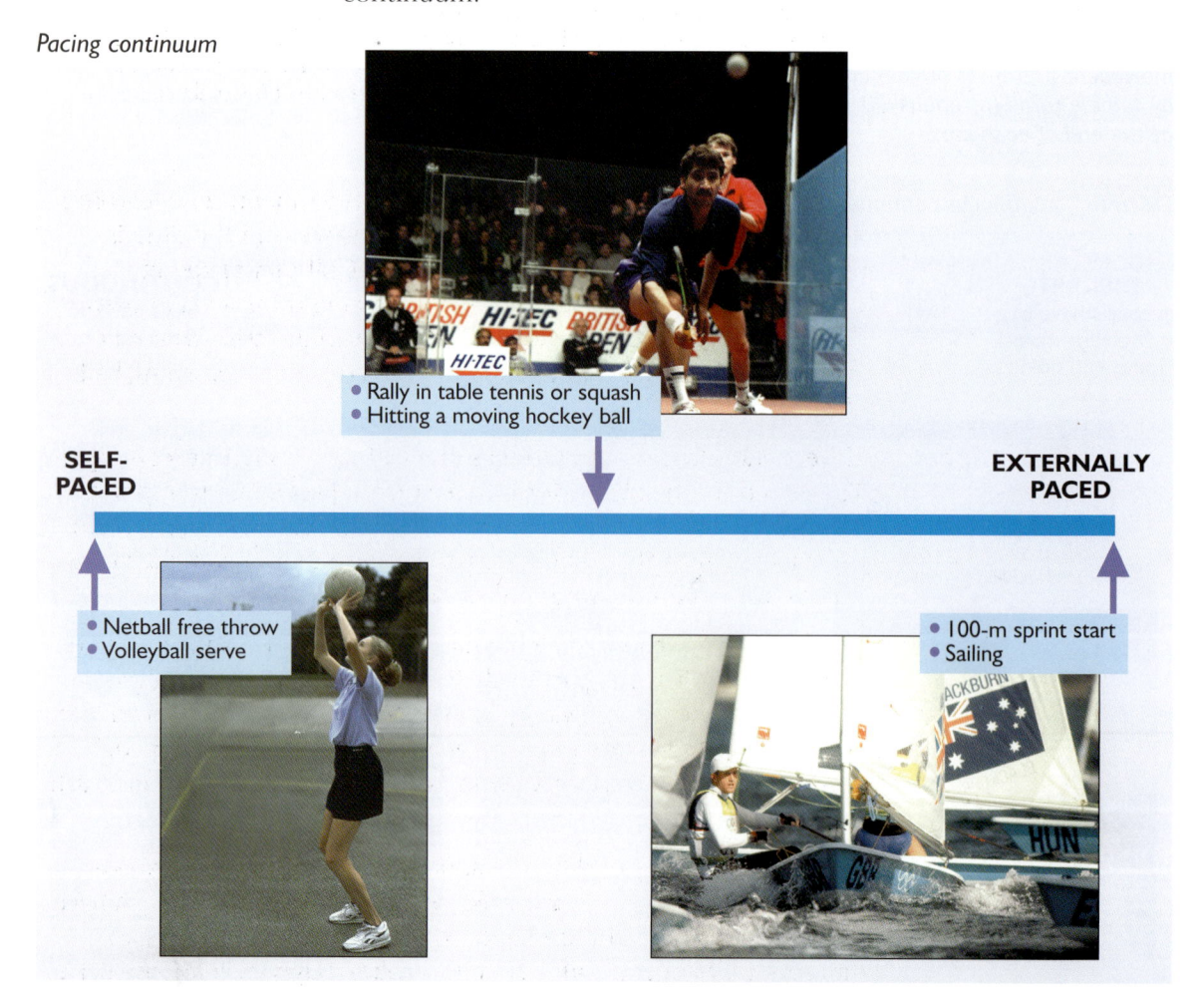

Pacing continuum

- Rally in table tennis or squash
- Hitting a moving hockey ball

SELF-PACED

- Netball free throw
- Volleyball serve

EXTERNALLY PACED

- 100-m sprint start
- Sailing

Acquisition of skill in sport

Stages of learning

Learning a new skill such as riding a bicycle can be broken up into three stages. Each stage represents a new level of understanding, awareness and ability. You can see an overview of this in the figure.

3 Autonomous stage
The last stage refers to a movement which is performed virtually automatically. At this stage little conscious attention is paid to the mechanics of the movement.

2 Associative stage
This stage allows the learner to practise the skill, correct errors and try again and again until the movement becomes more fluent. As time goes on the amount of errors being made is reduced.

1 Cognitive stage
In this stage the participant understands what needs to be done. They may have a mental picture or image of what the movement should look like. In terms of their own performance, however, the skill may feel alien, unnatural and uncomfortable and many errors will be made.

In order to become skilful, a performer has to spend time learning and practising – in terms of acquiring a skill most of the time is spent practising rather than being taught. Golfers will spend countless hours on the practice range, driving thousands of balls; during the course of a week's training a swimmer will swim mile after mile; tennis players will spend hours on court returning ball after ball.

Players and athletes need to master a variety of different techniques. They need to be able perform those techniques consistently and efficiently. In order to achieve this level of consistency performers need to be given the opportunity to practise their techniques in a variety of different competitive situations.

Selecting an appropriate technique to meet the demands of a given situation is an integral part of skilful performance. For example, in cricket a batsman's knowledge of which shot to play in response to a certain type of delivery improves with practice and experience. In tennis, timing is critical in knowing when to come forward and rush the net.

Practice in a variety of different situations allows you to master a range of techniques. For example, the tennis player will return balls on both backhand and forehand, with top spin or back spin, to different parts of the court. No two strokes played will be identical.

Stage one – the cognitive stage

In the first stage of learning participants are beginners. They are trying to understand what has to be done, how and when. The mechanics of the movement will seem difficult, awkward and unreal. Beginners will devote a considerable amount of conscious attention and thought to performing the movement.

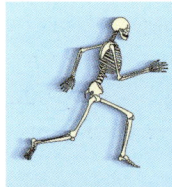

> **The cognitive stage**
> Can you understand or remember what it feels like to be a beginner in your sport? If you have forgotten what it is like to learn a new skill then try catching (and especially throwing) with your non-dominant hand. Throw a tennis ball overhand to a partner.
> Comment now on how you felt. What sensations did you have? Did it feel strange or alien? How accurate was the throw?

The movements in this early stage of learning are often awkward, jerky, fragmented and unsuccessful. Beginners will make many mistakes. Making mistakes is, however, all part of the learning process. Beginners will not be able to correct their own actions and will rely heavily on their coaches.

Working with beginners

Beginners need a clear mental picture of the movements they need to make and will need to be shown what to do. If the movement is complex or long it will have to be broken down into component parts or **sub-routines** that should be taught separately and then put together. For example, in cricket bowling the action involves run up, delivery stride, coil and release and follow-through.

In order to promote learning, coaches should:

- explain the aim of the technique or movement
- give a physical demonstration and allow the learner to develop a mental picture of the movement in action
- break the skill down if necessary and teach the steps in a logical order before performing the whole action
- give clear demonstrations, simple instructions, in short periods of practice time, emphasising the techniques not the outcome
- avoid overloading the performer with too much information
- include rest and recovery periods
- give praise for the correct action.

As you can see the coach plays a critical role in the learning process. You will consider the skills required by a coach to improve performance in more detail later.

Beginners in the cognitive stage of learning need a clear mental picture of what they are trying to achieve. The coach can help them in this process

NEXT *observation and analysis of performance, p.185*

Stage two – the associative phase

During this stage the performer has learnt the technique and now concentrates on practising the skill. The emphasis in learning shifts from *what* to do to *how* to do it. Performance of the skill improves considerably. Fewer errors are made and the performer is able to understand and correct some of these mistakes. For example, a golfer may be able to drive a ball more consistently well but may still make errors in some drives, such as those played with slice or hook.

This stage can last weeks, months, or even years – and some performers never progress beyond this stage.

During this stage performers are better able to deal with more complex information and they start to rely on different types of **feedback**.

Some performers do not progress beyond the associative stage during their playing career

Internal feedback

Internal feedback is obtained through the sense organs. For example, in catching a ball the fielder sees the height, flight, trajectory and pace of the ball. In interpreting this information the participants are able to move themselves into a catching position. The performer is also able to gain feedback from their proprioceptors (sense organs located in the muscles and joints) about various states of muscle tension and joint angles.

BACK *proprioceptors, p.43*

There are also sensory receptors in the inner ear that provide important information about balance. These give the performer a sense of awareness of their body in relation to other body parts, and of their body in flight or during movement. For example, gymnasts or divers are able to work out where their body is in relation to the floor or water, whether they are upside down or not and when to come out of a somersault.

In this stage of learning the performer is still reliant on the coach. The diver or gymnast may wait for the instruction 'now' to come out of a tuck or dive until they are comfortable with the timing and can rely on their own instincts. This is **external feedback**.

External feedback

External feedback comes from outside the body through sound and vision. Participants will receive verbal feedback in the form of instruction, correction or direction and input from the coach. Some coaches use video recordings to allow the participant to see what others can see and they cannot while they are performing the movement.

Stage three – the autonomous phase

At this stage skills are used without any conscious control or thought dedicated to the mechanics of the movement ('how do I do this?'). Thought is dedicated to the outcome of the movement and to the incorporation of strategies and technique in the game. Some performers never reach this stage or level of consistency in their performance.

Participants can give their attention to decision-making processes. For example, a snooker player is not simply thinking about the next red and setting up for any colour but will be thinking three or four shots ahead; a tennis player will not be thinking about merely getting the ball over the net but also specifically about where to place it; a badminton player will be giving thought to placement, positioning and out-manoeuvring their opponent. The skills and techniques of the game are performed largely automatically.

Performers at this level can detect and correct their own errors and will use their own analytical powers to do this rather than relying on the coach.

Elite-level or world-class performers do not think about the mechanics of the skill but about how to outplay the opposition

ACTIVITY

Understanding the stages of learning

Copy the table below. In the left-hand column write what stage of learning the performer is in. Complete the right-hand column using examples of your choice.

STAGE OF LEARNING	DESCRIPTION
	Li is practising his tennis serve and his coach has placed markers on the corners of the service box to encourage accuracy.
	Sammie is in the tenth week of a trampolining course and has been working on somersaults with the help of the support harness and her coach.
	Mrs Smith is just about to start teaching hockey to her Year 7 girls' groups. Most of them have not played before.
Associative	
Cognitive	

Acquisition of skill in sport

Learning and skills practice

Players and athletes will learn best by a combination of **guidance** (teaching, coaching and instruction) and **practice**. A training or instructional session is planned, directed and delivered by the coach. It is the coach's responsibility to ensure that learning and the acquisition of skills take place.

The coach has to decide how best to give the participant the information that he or she requires in order to learn and improve. They must identify the most appropriate demonstration techniques, delivery styles and guidance to use. The way the guidance is given will depend on:

- the personality, motivation and ability of the performer
- the nature of the skill being taught or developed
- the situation in which learning and the development of skills is taking place.
- The facilities and equipment available and the weather might also factor in the decision about how to deliver a session.

The rate of learning is affected by:

- the **guidance** or instruction given to the performer
- the type of **practice** used
- the **feedback** received.

Guidance

There are three basic forms of guidance or methods a coach may use to relay information:

- **visual**
- **verbal**
- **manual**.

These are sometimes referred to as 'show–tell–do'.

In learning a new skill it is important to have a visual image of how the skill should be performed

Visual guidance

This is used at all stages of teaching and learning but is particularly valuable in the early stages of learning.

Physical demonstration relies on imitative learning – the learner must mimic the action accurately.

The skill must relate to the performer's age and ability level. Expecting beginners to be able to mimic a forehand drive with topspin in tennis or a reverse stick sweep in hockey might be expecting too much but a more able learner is more likely to understand complex demonstrations than a beginner.

A coach will use verbal guidance and instruction to tell the performer what to do

Verbal guidance

This is the most common and widely used form of guidance in sport today. The coach will describe in words the action and state how to perform the activity. The coach is trying to create an image in the performer's mind of what it is and how it needs to be done.

This guidance has limitations if used on its own.

During a coaching session the coach must consider a number of questions:

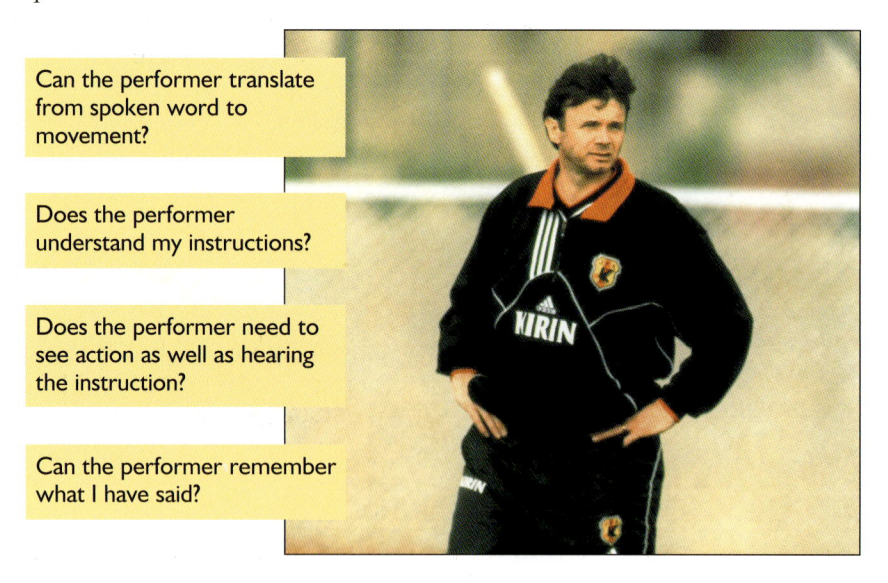

Can the performer translate from spoken word to movement?

Does the performer understand my instructions?

Does the performer need to see action as well as hearing the instruction?

Can the performer remember what I have said?

Without verbal guidance a drill or practice will be difficult to explain and set up. In explaining a drill or skills practice coaches will often assemble the group and will ask a smaller section of that group to work with them. They will give these players instructions and will use them to show the rest of the group how the drill is supposed to work.

With the advanced performer verbal guidance is more effective in giving information such as tactics or positional play.

Manual/mechanical guidance

The aim of physical guidance is to reduce error and fear (such support is usually given to young performers or those with special needs) and can be given in either of two forms:

- **Physical support for the performer by another person.** In this situation the performer is guided through the movement.

- **Physical manipulation of the performer through the skill.** The coach directs the participant manually and physically through the technique. This is commonly known as a 'forced' response. Holding the arms and racquet hand of a young tennis player and forcing him or her through a forehand drive is an example of a forced response.

Such guidance allows the learner to discover the timing and spatial aspects of the movement, but does not help with a knowledge of the forces acting on their body or the movement cues.

In some activities physical support is essential whilst learning new skills

Practice

Learning a skill often involves putting together a number of different movement patterns. For example, a tennis serve is made up of the ball toss, contact of the racket head with the ball and the follow through. These stages are often referred to as **sub-routines**.

ACTIVITY

Sub-routines in sport

Think about a skill in your sport. Imagine yourself or someone else performing the skill. Can it be broken down into distinct parts or sub-routines? Write these parts down.

Training and practice sessions should be structured so that the transfer of information and skills or can take place. There are a number of ways in which skills can be broken down and taught and practiced.

Whole or part practice?

In teaching a skill thought should be given as to whether skill should be taught as a whole or broken down and taught in its distinct or sub-routines. Deciding on which method to use may depend on your answer to the following question:

> **Is the skill or movement easy to break down into sub-routines without changing it beyond all recognition?**

For example, the triple jump with its run up, hop, skip, jump and landing phase has distinct parts, as does the tennis serve with its ball toss, contact of racquet head with the ball and follow through.

The triple jump can be easily broken down and taught using the part method

Regardless of the method of practice you use you should ensure that all participants have fixed in their mind a mental picture or 'moving image' of what the whole skill or movement pattern looks like. You will need to make sure that demonstrations are clear.

Whole practice

Whole practice involves practising the technique as a whole unit. For example, it would be very difficult to break down a somersault in trampolining – which is therefore best learned and practised as a whole. Either the coach or the overhead harness would support the movement until the performer became competent and no longer needed assistance.

Part practice

In part practice the coach breaks the skill down into its component parts and each part is practised separately. This can be done in either of two ways:

- **Part continuous** Each component or sub-routine is introduced in a continuous, logical and progressive sequence so that they gradually all build up to form the whole technique. For example, in trying to do the swivel hips in trampolining the performer would start with and master:

  - a seat drop
  - then a seat drop with a half twist to feet
  - then a seat drop, half twist to feet to seat drop
  - then a seat drop, half twist to seat drop – swivel hips.

- **Part progressive** Each component or sub-routine is practised alone before being performed together. In swimming front crawl, the arm action, leg action and breathing action can all be practised separately and then pieced together and learnt as a whole after all the sub-routines have been mastered.

Massed and distributed practice

The coach or teacher must decide whether practice is better all at once (massed) or whether breaks are required (distributed).

If the performers are highly skilled then a **massed practice** may be the most appropriate form of organisation. This means performers will work continuously without any breaks until the skill is mastered.

The alternative is a **distributed** (or **spaced**) session. In this the practice session is split into several shorter periods with 'rest' intervals in between. The 'rest' intervals could involve performing tasks that are unrelated to the main practice activity but they should not involve activities that could interfere with the learning and acquisition of a new skill. Rest intervals might be between sessions, that is, from one day or one week to the next.

Massed or distributed practice – which to use?

When choosing the form of a practice session a coach should take into account the following factors of the participants:

- age
- ability level
- fitness levels
- motivation
- the type of skill or movement to be taught.

Distributed practice is generally best – massed practice can lead to poor performance and hinder the learning process because the performer may become tired or demotivated. Beginners are more likely to be affected by a lack of attention or concentration and may not be fit enough (mentally or physically) to sustain long periods of practice.

Massed practice may help a performer learn discrete skills that are short in duration but distributed practice is best for learning continuous skills because the player rapidly becomes tired.

MASSED PRACTICE	DISTRIBUTED PRACTICE
Better when the individual is: • *experienced* • *older* • *fitter* • *more motivated*	**Better when the individual is:** • *beginner* • *less experienced* • *has had limited preparation* • *less motivated*
Better when the task is: • *simple* • *discrete (has a distinct start and end point)* • *dangerous*	**Better when the task is:** • *complex or long and requires precision* • *continuous – that is, the same movement pattern is repeated continuously*

Mental rehearsal

One of the advantages of distributed practice is that the rest intervals can be used for **mental rehearsal**. This is the process whereby the performer, without moving, runs through the performance in his or her mind to establish a mental image of the skill to be performed or game to be played.

This can be done in several ways:

- by watching a demonstration or film
- by reading or listening to instructions
- by **mental imagery** if the skill is established.

Mental rehearsal can help to eradicate unnecessary and energy consuming movements. For the novice, mental rehearsal may improve confidence and control arousal levels.

▶ **arousal and performance, p.171**

Think about the penalty kick taker who is told to imagine the ball hitting the back of the net, or look at the gymnast or freestyle skier before their routine – their eyes are shut as they mentally run through the movement pattern or routine before actually doing it. How many times have you imagined yourself performing a skill? It is a useful strategy for experienced performers and many use it in preparation for competition.

Feedback

In order to develop and improve their skill levels performers need relevant, correct and positive feedback. This feedback comes from a number of sources. You have already spent some time looking at feedback in the section on the stages of learning.

◀ **stages of learning, p.151**

Feedback involves the collection and interpretation of information about performance from a number of sources. It might come from the performer's internal sensory receptors in terms of how the movement felt. This is called **internal** or **intrinsic** feedback. A golfer will feel the movement sensation as they swing through and make contact with the ball, a pole-vaulter or high jumper will feel the sensation of their body in flight through the air and will be able to tell (without seeing the bar) whether they have cleared it or not.

Performers can also see the outcome – whether the ball that was passed reached its destination, whether the shot was on target or not. In athletics, times, places and measured distances will give statistical information about the result of a performer's efforts.

A cricketer will often know when they have made good contact with the ball

Their efforts may also be recorded on video for the purposes of analysis. All of this is referred to as **external** or **extrinsic feedback**.

Extrinsic information is useful during the early stages of learning when the performer is uncertain about how the technique or movement pattern is reproduced. It is also useful in the advanced stages when performers want to refine or adapt their technique. Jonathon Edwards (the world triple jump record holder) spent a whole season taking his jump phase apart and putting it back together to gain extra distance. He won gold in the Sydney 2000 Olympics as a result of the time he spent refining his technique.

Both internal and external feedback can provide information about knowledge of results and knowledge of performance:

◆ **Knowledge of results** gives information about the outcome of action –whether the first serve was in, whether the basketball went through the hoop, whether the penalty kick was scored.

◆ **Knowledge of performance** gives information about the feel, pattern and performance of the movement. For example, the flight and movement of the body through the air in freestyle skiing, the entry into the water from a dive, the sensation and feel of the ball as it is struck off the bat.

ACTIVITY

Understanding and using feedback

Think about your sport.
Identify the different methods of feedback available to the performer. An example has been completed for you.

SKILL	INTERNAL FEEDBACK	EXTERNAL FEEDBACK
Cricket bowling	How it felt. Was the movement rhythmical and fluent or did it feel fragmented and jerky?	• Was it a no-ball or a wide? • Did it get the batsman out? • What type of delivery was it? • Was it playable? • Did the batsman hit it, for how many? • Statistics from the over

Learning and performance

In Chapter 1 we considered the structure and function of the body systems and their role in human movement. The brain and nervous system have a crucial role to play in the production of human movement, skills and technique in sport. The brain and nervous system are responsible for the control and co-ordination of movement.

◀ BACK **the nervous system, p.41**

Learning and performing skills does not rely solely on practical ability: it also relies on the ability of your brain and mind to process and store the information it is receiving.

Information processing

During sport and exercise you are constantly receiving information from the environment in which you are performing. ('The environment' refers to a number of factors, including your team mates, the opposition, the officials, the venue, whether you are playing at home or away, the weather, the type of competition, the score and the stage of the game.)

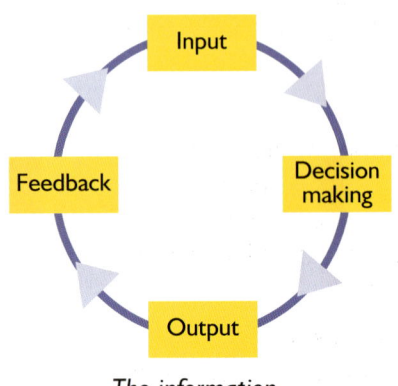

The way this information is processed and the way it will affect the outcome of the skill or performance can be viewed using an **information-processing model**. The model has distinct stages, as shown on the left.

This model is a cyclical or ongoing process of learning and skill reproduction. If the chain of learning events were to end at the feedback stage how would the performer continue to learn and improve their performance?

The information - processing model

Input

Input is the incoming information. A significant amount of the information you receive is visual (through your eyes) and refers to factors such as what is happening, where your opposition are and how much time is left on the clock. You will, however, also be aware of sounds around you – from your team-mates, the opposition, the crowd or far away irrelevant noises. You will also receive information though your senses of touch, taste and smell.

Your brain will also receive a large amount of internal information from your proprioceptors.

◀ BACK **proprioceptors, p.43**

During sport you will receive information from your muscles, joints and tendons. This information is most useful to athletes such as gymnasts, high board divers and freestyle skiers, who need to be able to orient themselves in space. For example, divers need to know where they are in relation to the water so that they can make a clean entry with little splash. Marks in diving are also awarded on the quality of the movement. Divers are not able to see what they look like so must be able to feel the quality of the movement.

Decision making

At any one time there is a significant amount of information coming through your senses, which can create information overload.

Some of the incoming information is irrelevant. For example, in returning a tennis serve the information that the player needs to focus on relates to the ball:

- the point of contact with the racquet
- the speed of the ball off the racquet
- the trajectory or flight of the ball across the net
- the point or anticipated point at which the ball lands in the service box.

Information not relevant to the return of the serve includes what the crowd is doing, the noise, the flashbulb photography, the weather, the score and the stage of the competition. If a player is distracted by irrelevant information it could affect their service return.

The brain has to use a filter mechanism to sort out the relevant information from the irrelevant information. There are two different filter mechanisms that can be used.

Selective attention

Some athletes are able to cut out all the distractions and focus completely on the task in hand. For example some players when taking a penalty kick will not hear the noise of the crowd, others will. Performers who can achieve this completely focused state are said to be in the 'zone'.

Being able to 'selectively attend' is achieved as a result of memory and perception. For skilled performers perception allows for some anticipation – anticipating the sound of the gun in order to get a 'flyer', a goalie anticipating where the penalty kick will be placed, returning a tennis ball travelling at over 100 miles per hour.

There are two types of memory to be considered:

- **Short-term memory**. Information can be stored here for a short time only. If it is not used or acted upon it is lost. Important information coming into this memory bank will be transferred to the long-term store. Competing items of information can interfere with the information stored in short-term memory and affect the outcome. This store operates in the learning and performance of all activities and is referred to as the 'working memory'. Most sporting movements are produced from information in the short-term memory.

- **Long-term memory**. The long-term memory has a huge capacity to store all kinds of information. You could liken it to the hard

High board divers must rely on information from their proprioceptors to tell them their position in relation to the water

Some players are able to selectively attend to only the most relevant information

drive of a computer. In sport long-term memory will store not only the rules of the game but also how to play them, what skills or techniques to use and when and how the player performed on previous occasions.

Movements stored in long-term memory are 'filed' under **verbal labels**, which, when thought about or recalled, can produce a **mental image** of the correct movements. For example, if you heard the term penalty kick it would immediately conjure up a mental or moving image.

Limited channel capacity

The information as it arrives at the brain hits what might be regarded as a bottleneck, much like traffic queuing when a road narrows.

Only part of this information can go forward and be processed – the other part cannot be acted upon. For example, a tennis player will select an appropriate shot or stroke with which to return a serve but if the ball clips the net and lands short in the service box the player will have to react quickly to the new 'flight' information. Similarly a batsman in cricket who has preselected a shot to play to a quick bowler will be caught out, stumped or bowled if he fails to 'read' the slower delivery.

Output

The decision made is based upon the information received or attended to. At this point the brain will respond to the information and give a number of muscles or muscle groups the order to contract. It is this series of co-ordinated contractions that creates the movement response – which may be a catch in the slips, dipping across the finish line or kicking a conversion.

The output is also referred to as a motor skill, motor output or movement response.

Feedback

As a result of the action or skill output the brain receives further information or feedback.

feedback, p.153

The way in which feedback is used in the information processing model or cycle is known as the **feedback loop**. This loop is a critical part of the learning process. If the feedback given is used constructively then skills will be modified or adapted where needed and learnt so that they can be reproduced in competition.

Revising acquisition of skill in sport

This section is designed to help you improve your knowledge and understanding of the acquisition of skill.

In order to answer the questions you may well need to look back through the chapter to help you. Completing these questions successfully will help you prepare for your examination.

Skill in sport

1. 'A skill is a learned ability.' Is this statement true or false? Explain your answer.

2. Name three skills other than vision, speed, strength and stamina that a footballer needs to become a premier league player.

3. Copy the table below. Match the sportsperson with the component they need most to perform.

   co-ordination   reaction time   balance
   speed of movement   power   agility

SPORTSPERSON	COMPONENT OF SKILL
Ice hockey goalkeeper	
Gymnast	
Archer	
Shot-putter	
Sprinter	
Cricket batsman	

4. Copy and complete the following sentence using phrase a, b or c.

   A skill can be affected by :..

   a the environment in which it is performed.

   b the colour of the performer's shoes.

   c the make of the equipment being used by the performer.

Classifying skill

1. What is meant by the term 'a closed skill'? Give an example of a sport or skill which is closed in your explanation.

2. Give a sporting example of:

   a A self-paced skill.

   b An externally paced skill.

3 Copy the table and match a type of skill with the correct definition.

discrete   serial   continuous

TYPE OF SKILL	DEFINITION
	They string discrete moves together
	Skills have no fixed start or end point
	Skills have a definite start and end point

Stages of learning

1 Copy and complete the sentences below.
   a The first stage of learning a skill is known as the .... stage.
   b When a skill has been perfected it is known as the .... stage of learning.
   c The .... stage of learning allows the sportsperson to practise and refine the skill.
2 Give examples of what a coach may need to include in a training session to help a beginner in the cognitive phase of learning learn a new skill.
3 What is meant by internal feedback? When is it useful in the process of learning a new skill?

Learning and skills practice

1 What are the three basic techniques a coach may use when teaching a new skill?
2 Copy and complete the sentence:

   Once an athlete has learnt a new skill he or she needs to .... the skill in order to perfect it.
3 Complete the sentence using the correct phrase.

   The best way to learn a tennis serve is to ....:
   a learn the whole skill at once.
   b break it down into sub-routines.
   c learn a number of different skills at any one time.
4 Before a race an athlete might go through how she is going to run the race in her mind. Can you name the term given for this process?
5 Draw a simple diagram representing an information-processing model.

CHAPTER

5 Psychology and sports performance

Successful performances in sport are often not simply just due to superior physical ability or performance. Athletes at any level must overcome pressure to be able to perform. Is it possible that an athlete's basic personality would have something to do with this? The venue, the competition, the stage of the game or competition, the opposition, the crowd, the weather, even the surface may have an impact on performance.

In this chapter you will analyse the roles of different personality types in sport, investigate the effects of stress and arousal on performance, consider how the environment affects performance and look at aggression and motivation in sport.

CONTENTS

Personality	168
Arousal and performance	171
Aggression	176
Motivation	179
Goal setting	181
Revising psychology and sports performance	184

167

Personality

The study of personality and its role in performance in sport is relatively new. In 1985, Bunker said that:

'it will be the athlete's ability to control his or her own body and mind in action and in all areas of life that will determine the level of ultimate athletic performance.'

Your personality is the set of characteristics that makes you the person you are. Even if you have an identical twin you are still unique because no two people have exactly the same set of personality characteristics.

The characteristics you own are often referred to as **traits**. Are you lively and outgoing? Confident? Shy? Nervous? Friendly? A constant talker? Mostly happy? Do you ever get angry? Are you aggressive? Your traits can influence your behaviour, the way in which you respond in certain situations, even the sport or activity you take part in.

Personality types

In analysing personality there are distinct types: **introvert** and **extrovert**.

These types can be placed on a **personality continuum**.

A personality continuum

INTROVERTS ———————————————————————— **EXTROVERTS**

Introverts tend to be thoughtful, quiet and careful. They may appear to be lacking in confidence and shy in social situations. Introverts often like to keep themselves to themselves. They may be reluctant to express their own views and may not enjoy new situations.

At the opposite end of the scale are the extroverts. They are typically very confident and socially outgoing. They are often at the centre of attention or the 'life and soul' of the party. They may be quite talkative and dominate a conversation.

ACTIVITY

Introverts and extroverts

Draw a personality continuum with introvert at one end and extrovert at the other and mark where you think your personality lies.

Ask your classmates, team mates and members of your family to mark where they think you lie on the continuum. Is their placement different from yours? Are you surprised by these results?

It is difficult to label someone as either an introvert or extrovert until you have observed them closely in a variety of different situations.

Introverts and extroverts in sport

Researchers have found a number of links between sport and personality types.

The table below compares introverts and extroverts and their participation in sport. But note that these findings are only **general** findings and will not apply in all cases.

INTROVERTS	EXTROVERTS
Prefer individual sports	Prefer team sports
Dislike contact sports	Enjoy contact sports
Perform intricate skills well	Enjoy sports with lots of action
Enjoy sports with more restricted movements	Get impatient with intricate skills
Have lower tolerance for pain	Have a high pain threshold
Get nervous before a competition	Can get bored quickly in training
Have a low level of excitement	Prefer a high level of excitement
Perform better at low levels of arousal	Perform better at high levels of arousal

Research suggests that extroverts tend to prefer to compete in team sports whereas introverts prefer to work in isolation

ACTIVITY

Introverts and extroverts in sport

Make two lists – five famous sports personalities, athletes or performers you think are introverts and five you think are extroverts. From what you know about these athletes, what you have read and the way in which they compete, make a list of their traits. Look at the definitions of introverts and extroverts and look at the table above to help you.

Try to obtain photographs of these performers in action and start to compile a 'picture board' of introverts and extroverts.

Personality

Personality traits and sports performance

Much research has been done into personality traits and performance in sport.

Ogilvie (1976) found that a number of personality traits were closely linked to athletic performance. These traits are:

- tough mindedness
- conscientiousness
- self-discipline
- self-assurance
- trust
- extroversion.

Do you have any of these traits?

Another study found that extroverts are more likely to take up sports and excel in them – they are 'thrill seekers'. It could be concluded from this that extroverts would be more likely to take part in extreme sports like bungee jumping than introverts.

Cooper (1969) suggested that athletes tended to exhibit the traits of extroversion and self-confidence. He also found that they are highly competitive and have a tolerance for pain.

Do you think that athletes and sportspeople are so very different from non-athletes?

Among all of the research that has been done, however, nobody has as yet written down a psychological recipe for success. There is no one set of personality traits or characteristics that will guarantee success in sport.

Research suggests that extroverts are thrill seekers. Extroverts are therefore more likely to do a bungee jump than introverts

Arousal and performance

Can you remember your first day at school? Have you ever had sports trials? Were these in front of selectors or coaches? Have you ever been in the final of a cup match, race or competition? On all of these occasions, how did you feel? Can you put your feelings into words?

Most of you might have been nervous, felt anxious or even felt sick. You were in fact in a state of **arousal**.

Arousal can be defined as a state of excitement or alertness. You are in a physical state of readiness, and the more aroused you are the more '**psyched up**' you are and ready to perform. This state can be represented on a continuum:

A performance continuum

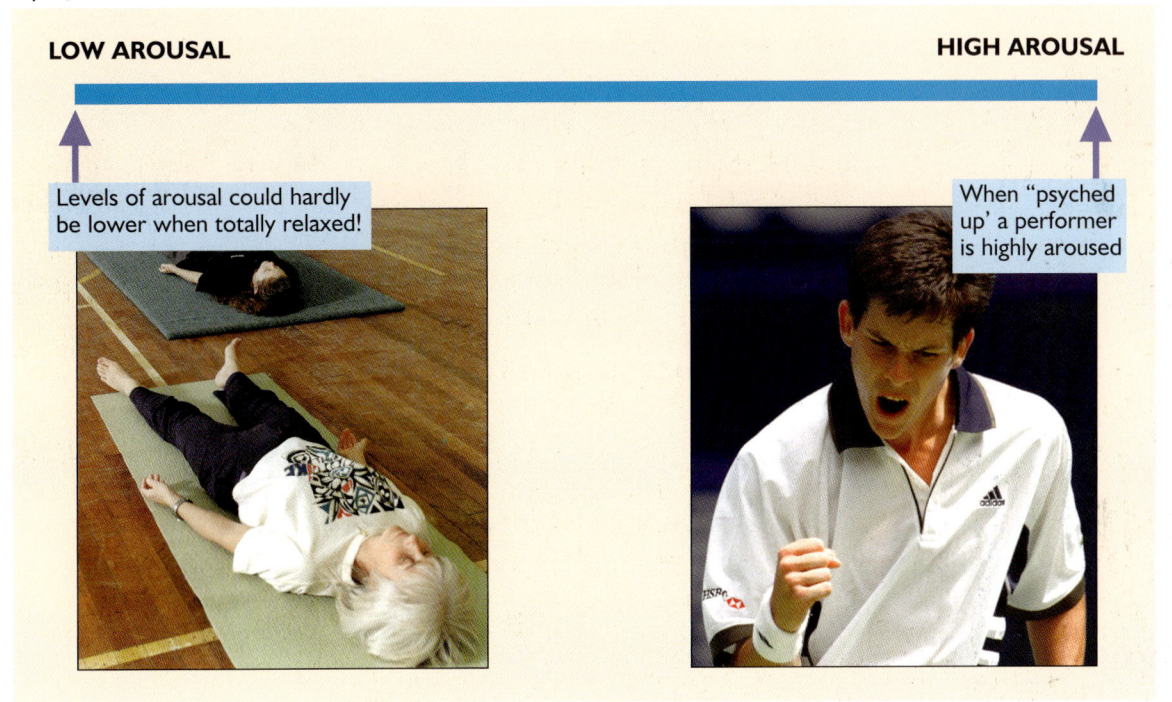

LOW AROUSAL — **HIGH AROUSAL**

Levels of arousal could hardly be lower when totally relaxed!

When "psyched up' a performer is highly aroused

Your state of arousal, anxiety or nerves can affect you physically. Your body may show the physical signs of arousal and anxiety:

◆ your heart rate and breathing rate increase

◆ the palms of your hands may become sweaty and clammy

◆ your mouth may feel dry

◆ you may have butterflies in your stomach

◆ you may be nervous, edgy and sometimes even shaky

◆ you may even feel sick.

All of these symptoms occur usually on the day of competition and in the build up to it. How do you suppose you might feel the day before, or the week before? Would you experience any physical symptoms in the preceding days?

Arousal and sports performance

Have you ever seen the New Zealand Rugby team perform the 'Hakka' right in front of the faces of the opposition before the start of the game? Why do you suppose they perform this dance? Is it to scare the opposition or is it to make sure they are fully aroused, physically ready and 'psyched up' to play?

The hakka is a ritual that the New Zealand rugby union team perform before every international. They use it to ensure that all players are psyched up before the game

Arousal in sport is very important. Your level of arousal can affect the quality of your performance. Duffy (1962) stated that the quality of an athlete's performance often depends upon how aroused the athlete is. The graph below shows how arousal levels can affect your performance.

On the graph you can see that in the centre of the inverted (upside down) 'U' there is a plateau (flat portion of the line). This plateau represents the player's optimum or best levels of arousal.

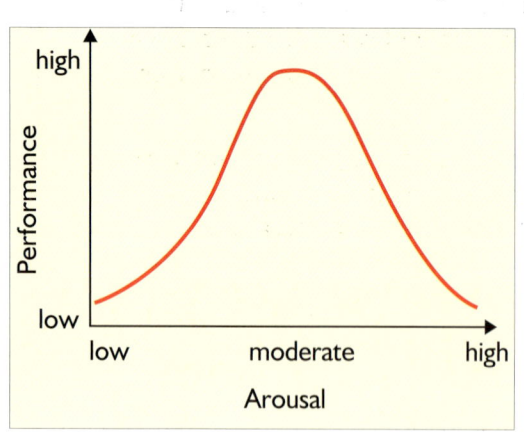

From the graph you can also see that insufficient (not enough) levels of arousal will mean that the player does not perform to the best of their ability. At this point he or she may be bored, distracted, tired or simply not interested in the game or competition. They may not be sufficiently 'psyched up'.

Too much arousal will also have a negative impact on performance. A performer may start to worry or become anxious – because they are serving for the match, because they are moving into the last 10 minutes of the game and they are losing, because they have to take and convert a penalty to win, because it is the last jump of the competition or because they have just made a huge mistake. There are dozens, possibly hundreds, more sporting situations that may cause a performer to become anxious or '**psyched-out**'.

When arousal levels start to go beyond the optimum performance will be affected. Think about the footballers who have missed crucial penalty kicks, golfers who have missed 3-foot puts, tennis players who have double faulted on match point and gymnasts who fall.

Different sportspeople have different levels of arousal. Some performers may have high levels of arousal already and not need as much 'psyching up'.

This link between arousal levels and performance is called the **Inverted 'U' Theory**.

ACTIVITY

The anxiety–performance relationship

Think about actual sporting situations in which a performer has made a mistake or performed poorly.

Name the performer and describe the situation in which they were performing. Can you explain why their performance was affected? Do you think it had anything to do with pressure situations and rising anxiety or arousal levels? How do you think you might have felt in that situation?

Arousal levels in sport

Different sports need different levels of arousal. Think back to the example of the New Zealand rugby team performing the 'hakka'. Why don't swimmers, fencers or gymnasts perform this? A golfer requires lower levels of arousal than a weightlifter. High levels of arousal are best in sports where the body movements are large, explosive and rely on power.

In performing a fine controlled movement that requires attention to detail and considerable accuracy (like putting) a golfer needs to avoid loss of control. High levels of arousal or anxiety may cause a golfer problems in stance, grip and ability to judge line and length. These problems, although not necessarily noticeable to the human eye, are sufficient to affect the accuracy of the shot and the player's ability to comfortably putt the ball.

It is much easier to make mistakes in sports and performance where the emphasis is on accuracy, timing and precision. Optimum levels of arousal are essential in sports like rifle shooting and archery.

ACTIVITY

Optimal levels of arousal

List five sports or activities that you have participated in or watched.

Now look at the sports in relation to one another and think about the levels of arousal that performers in that sport need. Place them onto a graph like the one on page 172, using the inverted U theory.

Anxiety in sport

In sport if there is some emphasis on the outcome of the event – for example in trials and selection, in cup competition and in race finals – performers may suffer from nerves, anxiety or stress.

Anxiety can be defined as a personal feeling of apprehension and fear. Performers experience anxiety for a number of reasons:

◆ Failure may result in a lack of confidence or threaten the player's self-esteem.

◆ The threat of personal harm and injury during competition.

◆ Fear of the unknown, particularly in extreme situations where the performer has little or no control over the environment. For example, the southern oceans are meant to be some of the most extreme conditions that sailors may find themselves in. Extreme conditions have sunk boats and killed even experienced sailors.

◆ The fear of failing in front of others (team mates, coaches and significantly the media – who can make or break a player's career). Classic examples of this have been seen in penalty shoot-out situations in World Cup football competitions. Some players will not step up or volunteer to take a penalty for fear of missing and being held accountable for the team not progressing through the stages of the competition.

Feelings of anxiety may reduce over time as an athlete becomes familiar with aspects of the 'environment'. For example, a young tennis player walking onto centre court at Wimbledon for the first time may be overawed by the occasion, the venue and the history associated with the court. They may feel nervous and anxious and as a result will not be able to cope with the occasion and will lose the match. As a player returns to Centre Court time after time, they may feel like they are almost playing at 'home'.

Pete Sampras is one the few players who is not overawed by playing on Centre Court

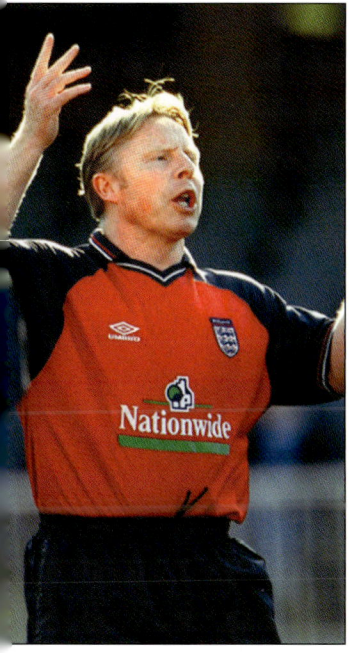

Reaching optimal levels of arousal

Reaching an optimal level of arousal does not happen automatically. It is often difficult for performers to achieve this by themselves.

The coach or manager has a key role to play in the 'psyching' process. It is his or her responsibility to identify whether the team needs psyching up or calming down. Coaches may talk through the game plan or identify key roles for each team member. These roles will give the player some focus and motivate them to play or perform well.

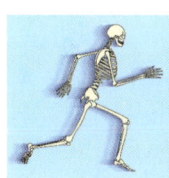

> **Team talks**
> Think about some of the team talks that you have been part of. Were they used to psych up or motivate the team? What was said to individual players? Did some players need more encouragement than others?

The crowd or audience can also be important in a performer's arousal. There are a number of triple jumpers and long jumpers who 'invite' the crowd to clap. If you listen you will hear the clapping get faster and faster. The athlete uses this fast and increasing beat in their run up and by the time they take off from the board the clapping will be at its fastest – and the jumper should have achieved maximum running speed.

The coach plays a key role in helping athletes reach their optimal levels of arousal

Long jumpers and triple jumpers have to increase their arousal levels before a jump – they may choose to use the crowd as a source of encouragement

In some instances a crowd can be quite hostile, particularly at an elite level or during international competition. Some players find it difficult to play against both another player and an 'away' crowd and still win.

Aggression

Sport at any level by its very nature is competitive. Players compete against opponents, the elements, the clock and themselves. In order to win or to be the best, performers sometimes resort to aggressive behaviour.

Aggression in sport has been accepted for a long time as simply 'part of the game', particularly in contact sports like football and rugby. No doubt you will have seen many acts of aggression, both verbal and physical. You may have even displayed aggression yourself on the field, or been the victim of aggressive behaviour.

Defining aggression

Aggression can be defined as:

> *'behaviour in which a deliberate intent to harm or injure others is evident.'*

This definition can be broken down further:

◆ Aggression must be intentional, so accidentally causing injury or harm is not included in the definition.

◆ Willing harm to someone is not aggression and neither is anger, unless it is expressed as intention to do harm.

◆ The inclusion of 'harm' in the definition suggests that aggression can be verbal if the words used are intended to embarrass or hurt.

◆ The definition refers to people, so smashing the ball into the wall or throwing your stick down would not be aggressive.

Aggressive styles of play often affect the outcome of games, decrease their quality, heighten crowd reaction and cause unnecessary injury.

Types of aggression

The amount of aggression seen in sport depends upon the type of sport being played. For example, you would not see fist fights between gymnasts like some of those that you see between ice hockey or rugby union players.

Little or no aggression

In order to compete and win in sports like ice dancing, gymnastics and diving the performer has to be in total control of their own mind and body. Any aggression must be channelled into controlling the quality of the movement. There is no advantage to be gained from acting aggressively.

Venting your frustration or anger like this is not technically aggression in sport

There is no advantage to be gained from aggressive behaviour in these sports

Indirect aggression

Players who use **indirect aggression** do not usually intend to harm anyone but act without due care for others and so injuries do occur. For example, in cricket a fast bowler may bowl bouncers or pitch straight at the batsman's body. This type of bowling is not meant to hurt the player but to unsettle him, to make him nervous and so pick up a quick wicket. The Ashes Series between England and Australia in 1932/33 saw this type of aggressive bowling for the first time. It is referred to as 'The Bodyline Series'.

Assertion

In sport injuries and accidents also occur as a result of assertive play – forceful, decisive play. For example, in football a player may go to tackle the ball but his timing may be out, or he may go in far too hard and injure the person he is tackling.

Direct (hostile) aggression

Boxing, judo and rugby are all contact sports. There is direct physical contact between the players. Boxers will hit hard and rugby players will tackle hard. Out of view of the referee, however, players may well barge, punch, nip and taunt the other players verbally. This is not acceptable. It is against the rules and if players are caught they will be penalised. These are all acts of **direct aggression**.

Performers have to play within the confines of the rules and should be able to control their levels of aggression. In some situations, however, it is difficult. Mike Tyson is well known for his aggressive behaviour, none more so than when he bit off a portion of Evander Holyfield's ear. Acts like this are referred to as **direct** or **hostile aggression** – they involve a deliberate intent to do somebody harm. Hostile aggression is illegal.

In many sports the boundary between hostile aggression, instrumental aggression and assertiveness is hard to distinguish.

Aggressive bowling, that is aiming your delivery directly at the batsman, is considered to be an act of indirect aggression

Aggression in sport

The amount of aggression evident in some sports can be represented on a continuum like the one below.

An aggression continuum

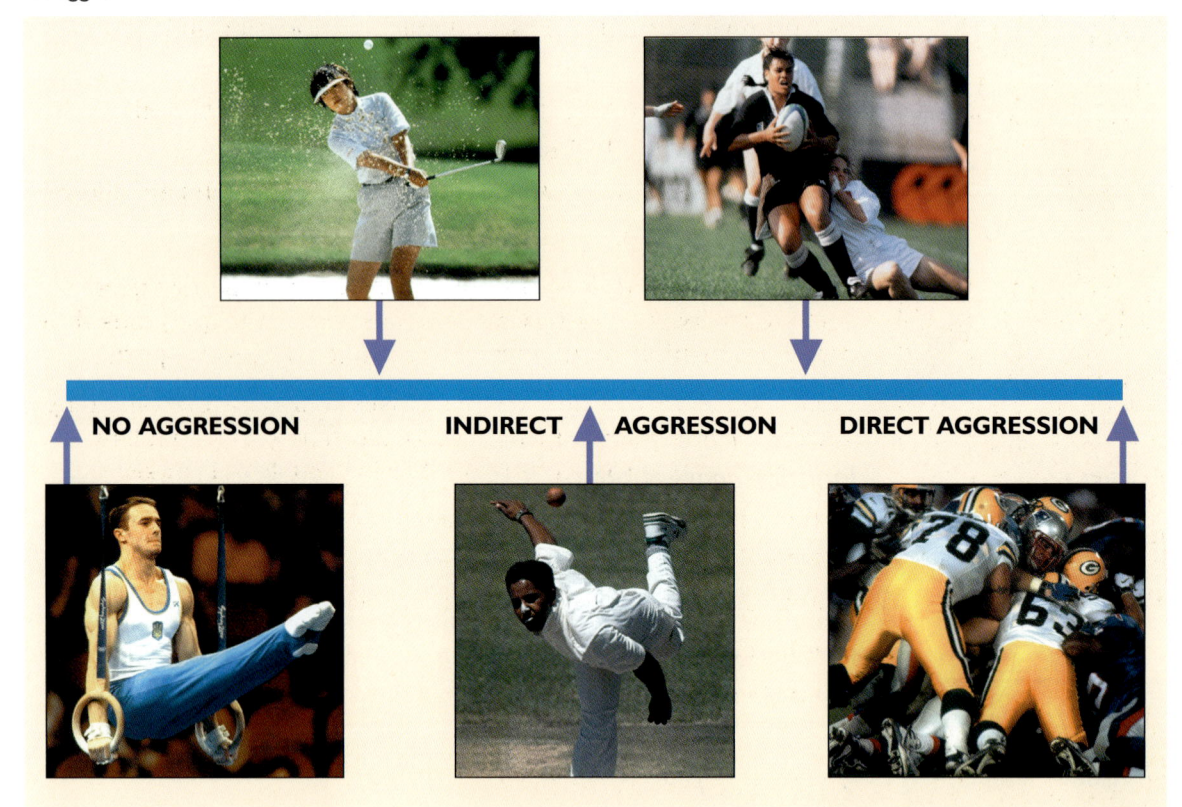

NO AGGRESSION   **INDIRECT AGGRESSION**   **DIRECT AGGRESSION**

ACTIVITY

Aggressive acts in sport

Look at the continuum above. Create a pictureboard of your own to show the various levels of aggression in sport.

You will have to look at newspapers, specialist magazines and even the Internet to source your pictureboard.

ACTIVITY

Many of the aggressive acts discussed here (and some of the ones that you have listed) are seen as simply part of the sport. In order to promote some discussion in your class, consider the following questions:

◆ Does competition cause aggression?
◆ Does participation in sport reduce aggression or prevent people being aggressive in non sport settings?
◆ Does watching a 'bad tempered' game cause spectators to be more violent to each other?

Athletes who can win Olympic medals have levels of motivation way beyond those of the average person

Motivation

Consider the following questions.

- Why do you participate in sport and exercise?
- What are your goals, dreams and ambitions in sport?
- How much time do you spend training, practising and competing?
- How much more effort are you prepared to put into your programme of training and competition?
- How hard would you work to achieve your goals and ambitions?
- What sacrifices are you prepared to make?

In order to take part in sport, exercise and activity people need some **incentive** or **motivation**. Your answers to the questions above reveal information about your motivation to succeed in sport.

Motivation is the driving force that makes somebody do something, whether that is getting up and out for a run or giving up full-time paid employment to focus upon achieving an Olympic medal.

To be the best in the world requires more than just motivation – it needs almost superhuman effort and sacrifice.

Motivation can be categorised into two types:

- **intrinsic** motivation
- **extrinsic** motivation.

Intrinsic motivation

Intrinsic motivation has also been referred to as **self-motivation.** The drive to participate, practise, train and compete comes from inside or within you. An individual who is intrinsically motivated takes part in the sport or activity for no other reason than simply to take part.

A player or athlete who feels in control over their movements and their level of skill is intrinsically motivated. Some performers have total control over their performance. The timing of their movements and actions is almost perfect. They seem to be unable to do anything wrong. They will have every confidence in their ability to defeat their opponent. Such performers are experiencing the 'ultimate intrinsic experience' – they are 'in the zone'. Getting into the zone requires:

- confidence and positive thinking or a positive mental attitude
- the ability to relax yet find your optimum arousal level
- the ability to selectively attend to only the most relevant information from the environment
- a state of physical readiness, that is training and preparation for the competition.

The zone is a mental state of being able to focus specifically on the task in hand and to achieve success and perfection.

◀ BACK **selective attention, p.163**

Extrinsic motivation

An outside source of motivation is **external** or **extrinsic.** Something else or somebody else gives you the motivation you need.

Motivation may be in the form of physical rewards such as badges, certificates, trophies, medals and cups. In schools young performers are encouraged to improve by taking part in award schemes.

For many professional athletes the main source of extrinsic motivation is money – not just the money earned or won from competing but the money that can be generated from sponsorship deals which may include clothing, equipment and advertising contracts.

ACTIVITY

Extrinsic motivation

Think of a number of different sports and make a list of the various different incentives (such as cups, money, badges, prizes, rankings, etc.) on offer that would motivate performers.

Now identify two incentives for the same competition, for example prize money and a cup or trophy. Discuss with your classmates which you think would be the biggest motivator.

Was Martina Navratilova's motivation to compete intrinsically or extrinsically driven?

Some athletes are motivated extrinsically by rewards that cannot be touched or placed in a trophy cabinet – a place in a representative side (county, region or national side, maybe the Olympic or Commonwealth team), or the publicity or recognition associated with winning. Some are seeking no more than praise from their coach, teacher or team mates.

The motivation that a player needs to compete will change over time. At an early stage in their career external rewards are a key source of motivation. However, performers who have earned enough money and won enough medals will continue to participate purely for the love of the game. There are now 'veterans' tours in both men's tennis and golf.

Players who have achieved everything in their sport often continue to play simply for the love and enjoyment of the game

Goal setting

Many athletes have dreams and goals – to play football at Wembley, to win at Wimbledon, to win an Olympic gold medal. These are **long-term** goals. Other dreams might be less ambitious, for example making the county team or first eleven, winning the junior tennis club knockout, getting a single figure handicap, running a marathon or learning to ski.

In order to achieve long-term goals you will need to be realistic in the challenges you set yourself. Most performers, as part of their training programme, will set (in conjunction with their coach) achievable **short-term** goals or objectives that will help them achieve their long-term goal. For example, before winning an Olympic medal an athlete or swimmer must achieve the qualifying times and distances set. Short-term goals can act as incentives and signposts as to whether you are on target. Achieving short-term goals can build the confidence to carry on and achieve long-term goals.

Setting goals is important for development and progress.

Goals and ambitions in sport

There are two types of sporting goals:

- **Outcome goals** are linked to the result of a competition or match – for example winning, or achieving second place.

- **Performance goals** are concerned with comparing the standard of performance with previous performances.

Individuals have more control over their performance goals than the outcome goals. For example, it is still possible to achieve a personal best without winning a race. Performance goals give a performer a better chance of success and success can in turn increase motivation and confidence.

Performance goals can be achieved without winning or even obtaining a medal. In the 2000 Olympics Paula Radcliffe broke her own personal best yet did not place in the medals

Setting 'SMARTER' goals

The National Coaching Foundation (now Sports Coach UK) has designed a way for coaches to work with their players or athletes to identify performance goals. These goals are usually written down so that both the performer and the coach can see exactly what needs to be done in order to move to the next goal or a higher level. The list is also a useful tool to refer back to, to see how the athlete has progressed.

In designing or setting goals you should consider the **SMARTER** principle:

Specific	Goals should be focused and as specific as possible. For example: • 'I want to increase my personal best for the high jump.' • 'I want to be more consistent in my first serve.' A goal that is too vague – for example 'I want to jump higher' – will not focus the performer's attention or give them any real target to aim at.
Measurable	A performer will need to be able to assess their progress. He or she may wish to assess progress against a set standard. For example: • 'I want to increase my personal best for the high jump by 3 centimetres.' • 'I want to get 60% of my first serves in.'
Accepted	Goals should be set jointly between the coach and the performer and accepted by both as realistic and achievable.
Realistic	Are you going to be able to achieve these goals? For example, improving personal best times for a mile from 6 minutes to 5½ will not happen overnight. However, it may happen if the time set for the distance is reduced in stages.
Time phased	Target dates should be set for goals to be achieved. Completion dates act as motivation to achieve the agreed objectives.
Exciting	Goals should be exciting, challenging and rewarding. If the goal is too easy or too difficult it will not hold the performer's interest. Performers who achieve their goals will experience feelings of self-satisfaction, achievement, competence, self-confidence and euphoria.
Recorded	Goals should be written down to allow the performer to evaluate their own progress, to gain relevant feedback and provide motivation.

The SMARTER system can be used for a specific session or a series of sessions over a period of time. The SMARTER system can be individual or group specific – in a team of players one or two may want to have personal goals or targets set. SMARTER systems can be designed for most athletes in most situations.

The table below is an example of the SMARTER system designed by a coach and a young tennis player and focuses on improving the player's serve over a three-session period.

Specific	*To improve the percentage of first serves going in.*
Measurable	*To get 60% of first serves in, as opposed to the 48% that are going in now.*
Accepted	*Yes, by both the player and coach.*
Realistic	*Yes. 75% may be too high but 60% in this time period is reasonable.*
Time phased	*Three weeks.*
Exciting	*Yes. The coach has said she will include a range of different drills and practices to focus the player's attention, improve her accuracy and help her achieve her goal.*
Recorded	*Statistics from practice and club/league matches over the next three weeks and beyond will be recorded in the coaching diary and player's training log.*

ACTIVITY

Setting your own goals

Participation in sport and exercise gives you the opportunity to achieve success. Performance can be measured by a stop watch, a measuring tape and statistics, so you can set yourself challenges to beat – your own best time, distance or height. You can also set challenges as a team. Each improvement is an achievement.

Can you identify what you want to achieve out of your next training session or series of sessions in order to help you achieve your long-term goal?

Use a table like the one below to help you identify a series of performance goals using the SMARTER system. You might want to discuss these with your teacher.

Specific	
Measurable	
Accepted	
Realistic	
Time phased	
Exciting	
Recorded	

Goal setting

Revising psychology and sports performance

This section is designed to help you improve your knowledge and understanding of psychology and sports performance.

In order to answer the questions you may well need to look back through the chapter to help you. Completing these questions successfully will help you prepare for your examination.

Personality

1. Describe the general characteristics of an introverted sportsperson. What sort of sports would an introvert take part in?
2. Patrick is known to enjoy contact sports, has a high pain threshold and gets bored quickly during training. Do these characteristics suggest that he is an introvert or extrovert?

Arousal and performance

1. Identify three physical symptoms of anxiety.
2. If someone were over-aroused what would be the impact on their performance?
3. If Tiger Woods were putting at the 18 hole in a major golf competition, would he want the crowd to cheer him or keep quiet until he had finished the put? Briefly explain your answer.
4. During a basketball game how could a coach help the players reach their optimal performance?
5. Would a triple jumper perform best at a low level or a higher level of arousal?

Aggression

1. At match point down a tennis player serves a double fault and loses the match. In his frustration he smashes his racket on the ground. Would you consider this aggressive behaviour? Why?
2. Define the term 'direct aggression'. Give one example of an instance of this in sport.

Motivations

1. Give another phrase to describe self-motivation.
2. What is meant by the expression 'being in the zone'?
3. What is meant by the term 'extrinsic motivation'? Give a sporting example of extrinsic motivation.
4. What is the difference between outcome goals and performance goals?

CHAPTER 6
Observing, analysing and improving performance

Sportsmen and women, at all levels, are always looking for ways to improve their performance. The analysis of performance is an ongoing and continuous process.

In this chapter you will examine ways of studying, analysing and improving sports performance.

A coach's role in the performance of his or her team is critical

CONTENTS

Improving sports performance	186
The process of analysis	188
Other ways to help your analysis	194

185

Improving sports performance

Think about the football manager who watches from the dug out during the game. He will assess his team's performance and the performance of individual players. He will shout advice and tactics from the side, whilst considering what to say to the team at half time in order to capitalise on their performance. Each game that the team plays will be different in terms of individual and team performance and the score. The outcome of his analysis will allow the coach to plan the next phase of training. It will enable him to work with players to strengthen their individual skills, and develop team strategies and tactics.

It is not just national and international coaches who analyse performances. In your sports lessons at school your teacher is constantly assessing your performance and advising you on how to improve your skills and technique. That advice might have been technical in terms of how to perform the skill, might have referred to the timing of the skill, or it might have been about your positioning – where to move into the most appropriate receiving position.

A coach will need to be able to assess each performer's fitness levels, skill, technique and tactics to help identify, assess and implement the most appropriate methods to improve overall performance.

In order to analyse a performer and their performance a coach needs a good understanding of the rules and regulations of the sport, and know how to implement them in a game type or competitive situation. He or she will also need to understand the technical requirements of the sport – the range of skills required in order to participate or compete.

Tiger Woods has spent countless hours refining and practising his game to near perfection. His success is not just as a result of his natural talent but as a result of the advice given to him by golf professionals during his career

In any sport the players and athletes are required to reproduce a range of skills and techniques consistently well.

The table below shows the range of skills a cricket batsman or woman needs to play certain shots well.

TECHNIQUE	SKILLS
Forward defensive	• Bat and pad together going forward on the front foot

Back foot shots	• Back foot defensive
	• Back foot cross bat attacking:
	   – Pull
	   – Hook
	   – Square cut

Drives	• Square drive • Cover drive • Off drive • On drive • Lofted shots
Front foot cross batted attacking shots	• Sweep • Reverse sweep • Paddle
Glances	• Leg glance • Offside glance

ACTIVITY

Identifying skills in sport

Think about your sport, or a specific position within that sport.

Now list all of the skills required to participate in that sport or position. Check your list with your coach.

In order to improve technique and optimise performance you will need to be able to analyse the strengths and weaknesses of the performer. You will also have to be able to give appropriate and positive feedback. To do this effectively you will need experience in playing that sport, and experience in coaching or teaching. You must learn how to structure and deliver skills practices and instructional sessions, how to assess technique, how to correct errors and how to give feedback. This experience is gained from 'knowing' the sport or event through participating, competing, watching and officiating.

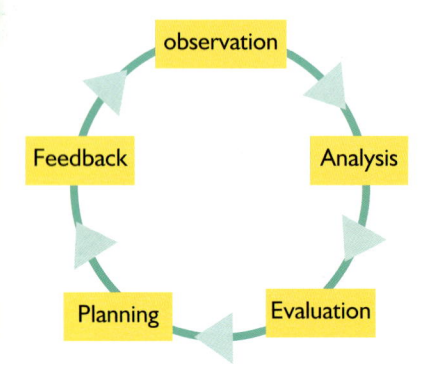

The process of analysis

Being able to analyse performance involves the coaching model or process shown on the left.

You may be asked as part of your course to consider the coaching process in more detail. You may be asked to undertake the role of a coach in order to improve the performance of others.

Observing the performer

There are a number of points a coach must consider when observing performers in action:

◆ Make sure you are safely out of the athlete's (and harm's) way, so he or she can perform freely.

◆ You may need to watch the performance from a number of angles to get an all-round view.

◆ Identify whether the performer is left or right handed or footed. This will determine how they will position themselves in order to execute a skill.

◆ Ask the athlete to repeat tasks to help you gain a better insight into their performance.

◆ Try to watch the performer on different occasions and in different situations. You may wish to watch a practice or training situation and then a competition. This will help you determine how well he or she can cope with the psychological demands of competition.

◆ Take into consideration the environment – venue in which the athlete or team is competing, the spectators (whether the crowd are supportive or hostile), the playing surface, the weather and other factors. As a coach you will be able to assess the impact of the environment and identify strategies or coping mechanisms for the performer.

ACTIVITY

Observing skill in sport

Observe a skill from your sport. During observation make a note of:

◆ How far away you will stand. Note down the optimal distance.

◆ Where you will stand in relation to the performer. You may even wish to draw the playing area and mark down the points from which you will get the best views. Write down where you should *not* stand to observe the performer.

◆ Which is the player's dominant hand or foot? This might influence where you stand to observe them.

◆ The different aspects of the environment – the venue, the weather, the crowd, the stage of the game or competition.

You should try observing a number of different performers from different sports performing different skills. Can you identify standard observation points?

Analysing performance

You will need to break the skill or movement down into its various **sub-routines** or sub-skills so that you can analyse the action thoroughly.

For example, the cricket bowling action is made up of the following sub-routines:

- run up
- delivery stride
- coil and release
- follow through.

In analysing movement and technique it is possible to isolate the sub-routines and focus future practice on them to improve performance. For example, in the tennis serve, if the ball toss is too low you should know that the player is rushing the serve. You should also realise that there will not be enough room for the player's racquet arm to extend and swing through above their head to make contact with the ball. So there will not be enough momentum and the serve will lack power (and possibly also direction).

During your analysis you should consider the performer in action. Observe:

- body position
- stance and centre of gravity when executing a skill
- arm action – are they using this effectively when initiating a movement?
- leg action – is it used correctly to help optimise performance?
- timing – have they read the cues in order to perform their movement successfully?

Once you have assessed these aspects you can build them up to help produce the perfect model – one that is technically correct.

Before observing and analysing the performer in action you need to make sure you really know the skill. Find a textbook, a coaching manual or video, or even a site on the Internet that gives the textbook definition or description of how to perform a skill. Write down the teaching or coaching points given. This will help you understand exactly what the perfect model is. It will help you identify errors in the performance of your players and will give you advice on how to correct errors and improve performance.

The tennis serve, like most sports skills, has a number of sub-routines

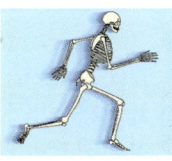

> **Understanding skills and tactics in sport**
> Check your library for any coaching books that might give you a better understanding of skills and tactics in sport.

Sometimes even the best sportspeople don't perform as well as they could

Use of other people's knowledge

A good way to gain an insight into a sport is to listen to other people's opinions. Insight can come from your teacher or coach, commentators, the panel of experts at half time, newspaper articles and interviews with players, athletes and coaches on television or in newspapers and magazines.

These people are often current or previous players and coaches who are up to date with the latest techniques and tactics.

It is easy for these professionals to view the game and provide expert advice and commentary. They have a wealth of playing, coaching and managing experience.

ACTIVITY

Commentary in sport

Name five football commentators. How many of them are ex-footballers?

How many analysts and commentators in other sports such as athletics, tennis and motor racing are also ex-performers?

The analysts and commentators are not directly involved with the game so can be **objective**. They often have a good vantage point, where they can see the 'whole' performance, and they will often have the benefit of replay, slow-motion and interactive television facilities. Sky Television's interactive sports channels now have the individual 'player cam', which allows viewers to focus on the performance of specific players.

Analysts and commentators have time to scrutinise aspects of play and key performances. They have statistical information at their fingertips to analyse individual and team performances. They can

Observing, analysing and improving performance

Sports like football, cricket and rugby are often subject to the post-match scrutiny of the experts and analysts

consider the various factors responsible for the outcome. They can give an accurate account of the game and are able to identify what tactical decisions they would make or have made under the circumstances.

In your role as an observer or analyst it is important to be a little detached from the situation so you can make informed, objective and rational decisions during and after performance.

Evaluation

Once you have observed and analysed the performer in action and considered their technique and skill you are ready to evaluate their skill, by identifying both good points and errors in the performance. Being able to identify errors is the first step in being able to correct technique. Your evaluation should be used to improve a performer's technique by:

◆ capitalising on what they do well to help enhance performance

◆ exposing their weaknesses and determining how they can improve these with isolated practises or drills

◆ discovering if your athlete's fitness level is good enough for them to sustain optimum skill throughout the game or routine. If an athlete tires during competition they will not be able to perform to the best of their ability.

Professional athletes have to concentrate purely on the event and how they are going to participate – what skills and tactics they will use and when. Spectators or other players will try to distract them (e.g. by chanting or shouting). Therefore an athlete needs to learn how to ignore distracting remarks and focus on the game and their own performance.

Planning

Once you have determined the athlete's level of performance you need to devise a training programme that includes both fitness and skill.

◀ BACK *fitness training, p.83*

If you are working with a team you need your players to work as a unit and know set plays. They need to train together in order to understand tactics and learn how to combat the approach of the opposition. You need to plan for all occasions.

For example, when playing a friendly game you may play with a weaker side to give other squad members playing experience. You may decide to try out new set play routines such as a free kick in football, a line out in rugby or a short corner in hockey. You may also change your playing formations in attack or defence according to how strong or weak your opposition are.

The emphasis on a cup match will be different as there is more at

Maurice Green, the 2000 Olympic Champion, is able to completely ignore the distractions of the environment around him

The process of analysis   **191**

stake. In this type of situation players often feel more nervous and may play differently under pressure. Some athletes have been known to make significant mistakes in high pressure situations, for example, Gareth Southgate and David Batty have both missed penalty kicks in penalty shoot outs in international competitions. As a coach you need to devise various strategies to help your players perform well under this added pressure. Such strategies may include relaxation techniques, visual imagery or psychological pep talks to get players and athletes fired up and ready to play with 'all guns blazing'.

The role of a coach is crucial in motivating his or her players in pressure situations

Feedback

In order to develop and improve their skill levels a performer needs relevant, correct and positive **feedback**. Some of the most important feedback, particularly in the early stages of learning, comes from the coach.

Feedback involves the collection and interpretation of information from a number of sources. It might come from the performer themselves, in terms of how the movement felt. This is called **internal** or **intrinsic feedback**. For instance, a golfer will feel the movement sensation as they swing through and make contact with the ball; a pole-vaulter or high jumper will feel the sensation of their body in flight.

In some sports the performers will be able to see the outcome – whether the ball that was passed reached its destination, whether the shot was on target. Times, places and measured distances will give athletes statistical information about their efforts. They could even watch video recordings of their performance for analysis. This is referred to as **external** or **extrinsic feedback**.

A high jumper is able to feel the sensation of their body in flight through the air. They will instinctively know whether they have cleared the bar

Extrinsic feedback is useful during the early stages of learning when there is uncertainty about how the technique or movement pattern is reproduced. It is also useful in the advanced stages when performers want to refine or adapt their technique.

◀ BACK **feedback, p.153**

The coach will play a critical role in giving feedback.

- ◆ Make sure your advice is clear.
- ◆ Give simple, specific instructions.
- ◆ Prioritise the skills that need to be developed.
- ◆ Give a maximum of three teaching points.
- ◆ Be positive when giving feedback, as a negative attitude could bring negative results by demotivating the performer.

To make the most of the feedback you give you should work with the performer to devise a schedule of when and how to work on technique.

ACTIVITY

Analysing and improving performance

Choose a sport and an athlete. They do not have to be famous or well known – it might be one of your classmates or somebody from your sports club.

Look at their performance. Choose an aspect of that performance (a single skill, technique or move) that they are trying to perfect.

Devise a plan to help that athlete take steps towards improving their play. Try to choose a skill that can be worked on before their next game.

The process of analysis

Other ways to help your analysis

Video recordings

By playing back a performance in slow motion – or even frame-by-frame – you and the performer can assess their strengths and weaknesses. Together you can then work on improving the various aspects.

Capturing a performance on video means you can analyse your technique move by move

Taking notes

When analysing an athlete make notes of points about their performance. This will be useful for the planning stages of the next coaching session, team talk and game plays. It also allows you to give constructive feedback.

Reading about the sport

Read coaching manuals on how the sport should be played, look at web sites dedicated to the coaching of specific sports. This will help you understand the perfect model of a performance and give you ideas as to how you can correct techniques and implement tactics.

You need to practise analysing others in coaching sessions, lessons and game situations to help improve your observational skills. You should practise analysing athletes in both individual and team scenarios. Try practising analysis in PE lessons or while watching sport on television.

CHAPTER 7 Current issues in sport

Sport plays a major part in society and in people's lives. As with all aspects of society there are a number of issues that tend to dominate the sporting headlines. These headlines are generated both on and off the field and relate to issues such as hooliganism, use of drugs, cheating and the role of women in sport.

In this chapter you will analyse the various factors that influence partitipation in sport, consider the role of women in sport, study the provisions for performers with disabilities and investigate the issues of hooliganism, cheating, gamesmanship and other antisocial behaviours.

CONTENTS

Participation in sport	196
Sport in society – current issues	203
Women in sport	210
Revising current issues in sport	215

Participation in sport

Why take part in sport?

People take part in sport for a number of different reasons:

- **Training for sport** Many people train, practise and exercise in order to compete in their sport.
- **To improve general health** for weight management or rehabilitation from injury or illness.
- **Mental well-being** Some people use exercise to work off feelings off stress and frustration. For some people, energetic activity is the way they relax.
- **Social and recreation** Some people will take part in sport to make new friends and meet and mix with people.
- **Excitement** Some people find being in danger or having their body out of their control (for example, in rock climbing, bungee-jumping or skiing) very exciting.
- **'Just because'** Some people participate in exercise simply because they want to.

Participation in sport offers excitement that can not often be found in everyday life

Participation rates in sport

Participation rates in a range of sports and activities have been estimated through the General Household Survey (GHS) conducted by the government's Office of National Statistics.

In 1996 81.4% of adults in Britain took part in at least one sport or physical activity during the twelve-month period leading up to the survey. In terms of more regular participation 63.6% of adults had participated in some form of sport or physical activity in the four weeks before the survey. The survey found that men were more likely to have participated in some form of physical activity than women (70.9% of men compared with 57.5% women). The most popular activity for both men and women was walking (for the purposes of the survey walking was defined as a walk or hike of two miles or more). Over two-thirds of adults had participated in the twelve-month period before the survey.

ACTIVITY

Participation rates in sport

Look back at the last four weeks and identify the number of times you took part in sport and physical activity – but not those sessions that were part of your timetable at school. Write down what you did, where you did it and how long you worked for.

Now ask your classmates, your teacher and parents what they did. What do these statistics tell you about participation in sport and activity?

Factors influencing participation in sport

Participation on a regular basis, or as much as you would really like to, depends on a number of factors.

- **How much leisure or free time do you have?** Remember that leisure time is the time you have to enjoy yourself when you are not committed to work, school, travelling, chores and sleeping.
- **What facilities are available in the local area?** How accessible are they? Are there facilities which cater for your interests?
- **How much does it cost to participate?** Can you afford it?
- **Are you able to participate and train?** That is, as a disabled performer, as a woman or as an ethnic minority individual can you participate fully?

An individual will take up one sport or activity rather than another for a variety of reasons.

Leisure time

Your life will revolve around the commitments you have:

- working or studying
- travelling to and from work and home
- completing chores, household or otherwise
- other essential activities such as sleeping.

The rest of the time is 'free time' in which you can pursue your own interests, activities, ambitions and goals.

ACTIVITY

Your leisure time

Analyse a typical day, one during the school week and one at the weekend.

Your analysis should identify how much time you spend sleeping, at school, travelling to and from school, doing homework or other chores. How much time is left? Is there a difference between the school day and the weekend?

Now analyse your leisure time. How much time on average do you spend watching television, playing on the computer, hanging out with friends, playing sport or doing exercise? Do you think you are wasting any of that time?

Compare your findings with those of your classmates.

Now start to think about any barriers that might stop you from doing what you want to do.

Parental influences

The sports your parents play or are interested in will often influence the sports you and your brothers or sisters participate in. You may play for same club as your parents, even on the same team.

Many families have gained international fame in sport. The Charlton brothers (Bobby and Jack) are an example, as are the Neville brothers

(Phillip and Gary). Their sister (Tracey Neville) has also had international experience, having represented England at Netball. And, of course, there are the Williams sisters, Venus and Serena.

Some parents will groom their children for a certain sport. Martina Hingis was introduced to tennis because her mother had been a professional tennis player, although not as successful as Martina. Martina was even named after the legendary Martina Navratilova.

Young performers often rely heavily on their parents during the developmental stages of their career, for a number of reasons. Some parents will volunteer their time and coach, others provide financial support and transport.

Martina Hingis was strongly encouraged to take up tennis by her mother

Education

Many young people have their first experience of participation in sport and activity at school. This experience can have long-lasting effects. For some the experience is a positive one and will foster an interest in sport that continues beyond the school years. For others, particularly girls, the experience can be traumatising and leave bitter memories. As a result many young women drop out of sport and activity completely when they leave school.

In 2000, the Youth Sports Trust in conjunction with Nike spent some time researching the attitudes, motivation and participation rates of girls aged 11–14. They found that rates were low. In an attempt to improve these rates they are developing innovative strategies for increasing girls' involvement.

New strategies have included involving girls in the planning and delivery of their lessons, introducing different games such as football and aerobics to the PE programme and relaxing policies on PE kits and showers. Positive imagery and more female role models have also been encouraged, along with teaching students in groups of like-ability or in single sex-groups and forming school club links.

By adopting these new plans, schools taking part in the research programme reported a dramatic increase in the number of girls willing to take part in physical activity and a far more positive attitude overall.

Schools and colleges have a key role to play in the continued participation of its pupils in sport and activity once they leave school

Financial situation

The amount of money that an individual or family has spare at the end of each wage period will affect the standard of living and the activities that are undertaken by members of the house. This spare money is referred to as **disposable income**. People with more disposable income have more money to spend in taking part in sport.

Taking part in sport and activity often requires some financial outlay in subscriptions and membership fees. Some sports may cost only a few pence to play but at the other end of the spectrum green fees at golf clubs can be enormously expensive. Costs of travelling, equipment and clothing can also mount up. Inevitably, when you are younger you rely on your parents' financial support to be able to compete. In some sports like sailing or golf, or in sports where there is much travelling and overseas competition, costs could run into thousands of pounds.

Where you live will determine the type of sports or activities that you take part in

Environment, facilities and access

The environment in which you live may also have a direct effect on the type of sport and activity that you take part in. If you live in the countryside you may have more opportunity to participate in outdoor activities such as climbing and abseiling than your city neighbours. If you live by the sea, a lake or river you may have had more chance to learn and master water sports like sailing or windsurfing. However, if you live in the country you might not have easy access to sports clubs and leisure centres. You may not have as great an opportunity to play for sports teams and clubs.

In order to participate in your chosen sports and activities you might have to go overseas for the better facilities and provision. For example, provision in the UK for skiing is not as good as in the rest of Europe, Canada and the United States, and you would be better to go to the Red Sea or Great Barrier Reef for scuba diving. Participation in these types of activity will be determined largely by the level of disposable income in the household.

It may be that the nearest facilities to you for your sport are inaccessible by public transport, or the times at which you train and compete do not tie in with the public transport timetable, and you need a car or at least a lift. This will increase your dependency on your family – and your parents in particular – to be able to participate.

Age

As people age their interests and priorities change, as may the choice of sport or activity they participate in. You have already spent time in this book considering the effects of ageing on sports performance.

age, p.112

Participation in sport

Most people as they get older tend to take less part in sport or sports that are not quite so demanding physically. Certain sports tend to be associated with the older person – for example, crown green bowling, walking and swimming. These sports, however, are also enjoyed by a significant number of younger people. Many older people do still engage in active and demanding sports – for instance, the London Marathon always has runners who are well over 60 years old.

Most sports clubs have veterans and senior sections; some sports – like tennis and golf – even have a senior tour. Players like Arnold Palmer, Gary Player, John McEnroe and Jimmy Connors are still capable of drawing in huge crowds and playing a game that would challenge many younger players.

Age is not necessarily a barrier to participation in sports like the marathon

Gender

Each year in the UK 33% of men participate in some form of activity whilst only 10% of women do. Women, however, make up over half the population. Why is there such a difference in the participation rates of men and women?

In 1999 Sport England established a steering group to look at women's participation in sport. The research found four key barriers to women's participation:

Choice
Some women feel they have little real choice of sports activities. Issues of childcare at times when activities are available increased this problem.

Comfort
Some women are worried about their personal safety when travelling to or from sports activities.

Convenience
Because women's leisure time is more fragmented many feel unable to commit themselves to a regular sporting activity.

Confidence
Many women lack the necessary confidence to participate. Some are unwilling to be seen in tight-fitting sportswear. Others do not want to be laughed at or ridiculed.

NEXT *women in sport, p.210*

Disability

One of the biggest factors influencing participation in sport for people with any disability is the provision and adaptations made for them. These adaptations refer to the buildings and their accessibility, the activities and services provided and – most significantly – the attitude of others towards their disability.

In 1993 the Sports Council published an action plan to help disabled people take part in sport. The plan had seven main objectives:

1. To raise the profile of disability in sport.
2. To ensure that plans for sport include people with disabilities.
3. To provide sporting opportunities for people with disabilities.
4. To improve access to sport.
5. To encourage people with disabilities in international sport.
6. To ensure the best use of resources and increase finance.
7. To make sure the sporting needs of people with disabilities are met.

Most sports and leisure centres are obliged by law to make facilities accessible by people with all manner of disabilities. Modern facilities now have wheelchair ramps, lifts, special changing rooms, specialist equipment.

The Disability Discrimination Act (1994) requires all service providers to make 'reasonable adjustments' to operations, if people with disabilities are having difficulties in accessing their services. These adjustments could include audio tapes, Braille, large print and sign language interpretation. Staff at sports and leisure centres should be trained to work with people with disability, and disabled people should be given the opportunity to take part in all sports where reasonably practicable. Reasonable physical changes to buildings must be in place by 2004.

Disabled people have as much right as able-bodied people to compete in sports at all levels

ACTIVITY

Analysing provision for people with a disability

Visit your local sports or leisure centre.

If you can, obtain a map or floor plan of the centre. Then walk around the centre and map the provision that has been made for disabled performers.

Look at access into and around the centre, including the car parking facilities. Inside, look at the toilet and changing facilities. Look at the width of the corridors – is there enough room for two wheelchairs to pass each other comfortably? Which way do the doors open? Could they be easily opened by somebody in a chair or on crutches? If the facility is on two floors how easy is it to move from one floor to another? If there is a lift how big is it? What is the provision for people with sight or hearing impairments?

Now think about the range of activities offered by the centre for those with disability. Some of the activities or equipment might have been adapted so that people can participate fully. Identify the different adaptations that have been made.

Modern sports and leisure centres are legally obliged to attempt to make full provision for people with disabilities

The profile of disability sport has risen since the Act was passed, its success reflected in the British medal haul in the Sydney 2000 Paralympic Games. Organisations involved with the organisation of disability sport in the UK will be discussed later.

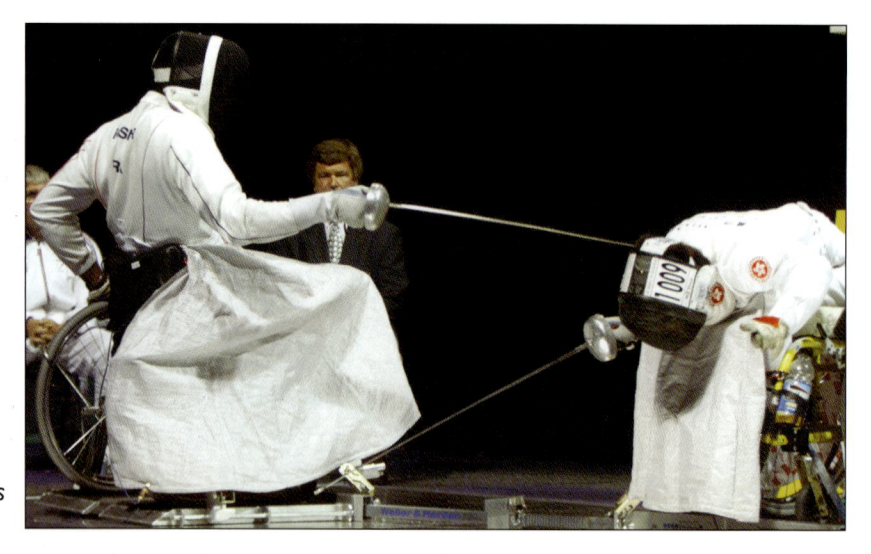

The Paralympic games include many of the same sports that the Olympics have – but some adaptations may be necessary

ACTIVITY

Paralympic sport

The Paralympic Games always takes place immediately after the Olympic Games, yet does not attract the same media attention.

List two sports that are included in the Paralympics and identify the adaptations that have been made to the game or sport in order that disabled performers can participate.

Current issues in sport

Sport in society – current issues

In elite-level sport the difference between winning or losing may be a thousandth of a second, less than a hair's breadth, the blink of an eye. However, the difference in terms of recognition, adulation and reward can be significant. What tactics will athletes resort to in order to win?

Some will use drugs to gain a physical advantage over their opponents. Ben Johnson, the Canadian sprinter, is one such example. Some will use **gamesmanship** or un-sportsmanlike conduct to put off their opponent. Martina Hingis, in the 1999 French Open Final, served underhand on Steffi Graff's match point to try to put her off. The American ice skater Tonia Harding had her closest rival, Nancy Kerrigan, 'knee-capped' before the American Winter Olympic qualifying championships. In the 1986 World Cup competition, Maradonna used his hand, rather than his head to put the ball into the back of the net and defeat England.

Such behaviour is often penalised by penalty points, cards, fines or expulsion from a tournament.

Deviant behaviour

Within sport, **deviant behaviour** goes beyond commonly accepted definitions of fair play and sportsmanship, and intentionally using illegal means to intimidate or injure an opponent.

Sport across the world and at all levels involves a number of different, perhaps not socially acceptable, behaviours – including gambling and violence. Sporting acts that would not be acceptable 'in the street' include boxing and motor racing: any boxer found fighting in the same manner outside the ring would become a criminal; a racing driver who drove on the road as he does on the track would be arrested, and even banned from driving, for speeding and careless driving.

When serious injuries or deaths occur in sports, criminal charges are often not filed, and civil law suits are generally unsuccessful. However, some footballers and rugby players have been found guilty of causing actual bodily harm on the pitch. For instance, Duncan Ferguson was prosecuted for a head-butting incident when he was playing Glasgow Rangers.

Even in non-contact sports, the use of hate as a source of motivation is evident. This feeling is often channelled into 'psyching up' the player.

◀ *arousal in sport, p.171*

In competitive, professional sports such as football hatred from the fans based on the terraces is directed at the opposing team's fans and players.

Hooliganism

Hooliganism in British sport today is most evident in football.

However, contrary to popular thinking, hooliganism is not a recent addition to British football – the timeline at the bottom of the page highlights the fact that hooliganism has long been a part of our national game.

Racism

Racism among football fans is a serious problem and is often blamed for outbreaks of violence, particularly at international matches.

Racist chanting and abuse from the terraces was arguably at its worst in the 1970s and 1980s, when football players from around the world began to join the English league. One of the most infamous examples was at John Barnes' debut for Liverpool in the 1986/87 season when the team played Everton and bananas, and even a live monkey, were thrown onto the pitch. Racist chanting at matches still occurs, but at nowhere near these levels. The recent decline may be due in part to campaigns designed to combat racism, such as 'Let's Kick Racism Out of Football'.

In the 1970s far-right groups rose to prominence as the problem of football hooliganism grew. The National Front was the most active group in the 1970s, giving regular coverage in its magazine *Bulldog* to football and encouraging hooligan groups to compete for the title of 'most racist ground in Britain'. Chelsea, Leeds United, Millwall, Newcastle United, Arsenal and West Ham United were all seen as having strong fascist elements in the 1970s and 1980s. After the Heysel stadium tragedy British National Party leaflets were found on the terraces.

As recently as 1995, far-right groups were involved in disturbances abroad, for example at the England v. Republic of Ireland 'friendly' match, when fights between rival fans caused the game to be abandoned after half an hour.

Disagreements among fans can rapidly escalate to large-scale violence

Hooliganism is still a problem in today's society. Acts of violence occurred at Euro 2000

1905	1909	1920	1924	1930	1949
Preston North End v. Blackburn. Several fans tried for hooliganism, including a 70-year-old woman.	6000 spectators involved in a riot at Hampden Park, Glasgow. The pitch was destroyed, 54 police constables were injured, and much damage was done to the town.	Birmingham City football fans used bottles as clubs and missiles.	After a match in Brighton the pitch was invaded, the referee chased by the crowd and a policeman knocked unconscious.	Rangers ground closed after unruly conduct of spectators during match against Northampton town. Clapton Orient v. Queens Park Rangers – police were called in to stop fighting between rival spectators behind the Rangers' goal.	Millwall v. Exeter City. The referee and linesmen were attacked by the crowd

Current issues in sport

Combating hooliganism

A number of methods have been tried to detect and stamp out hooliganism from the grounds and the terraces.

The Taylor Report

On 15 April 1989, 96 Liverpool fans were crushed to death on the terraces at the Hillsborough Stadium during the FA Cup semi-final between Liverpool and Nottingham Forest. In the wake of this tragedy the Taylor Report was published. The principal recommendations of the report were:

- Conversion of all football league grounds to all-seater stadia by the end of the millennium.
- The removal of spikes from perimeter fencing, which should be no more than 2.2 metres in height.
- Ticket-touting to be made a criminal offence.
- The introduction of new laws to deal with offences inside football stadia, including racial abuse.

Closed-circuit television (CCTV)

CCTV was introduced into football grounds around the middle of the 1980s and is now present in almost every league ground. The effectiveness of such camera surveillance has also been improved by the introduction of all-seater stadia across the country.

The photophone

The 'photophone' system allows the police to exchange photographs of football hooligans from CCTV and other sources via telephone and computer links, allowing vital information to be readily available to the police on match days.

The Hoolivan

The Hoolivan is a hi-tech item of machinery that enables police to maintain radio contact with all officers inside and outside the ground and is linked with the CCTV cameras in and around the stadium.

1954	1955–56	1985	1998	2000
Several hundred spectators came onto the field during a match between Everton Reserves and Bolton Wanderers Reserves. Fireworks were thrown and a linesman was kicked.	Liverpool and Everton fans involved in several train-wrecking exploits.	At Bradford, 56 people were killed by a fire in the ground. Serious disorder occurred at the grounds of Birmingham City, Chelsea and Luton Town. Liverpool fans were seriously implicated in the deaths of 39 Italian fans before the European Cup Final at the Heysel Stadium in Brussels.	At the World cup in France, England fans clashed with opposing fans in Marseilles.	English and German fans fought a pitched battle during the Euro 2000 championships.

Sport in society – current issues

Cheating

Cheating in sport can fall into a number of categories.

Drug use

When the rewards for winning dwarf the rewards for coming second, some athletes will use every means possible to win. Using drugs is possibly the most effective means of gaining the upper hand and is not as blatant as other tactics such as barging your opponent. It is also often the hardest to detect.

The different types and effects of drugs and their detection have already been discussed.

◀ BACK **drugs, p.117**

The sporting community considers the deliberate use of banned performance-enhancing substances to be cheating.

Why use drugs?
The second half of the twentieth century saw a dramatic change in sport from amateur status into big business, with millions of dollars of sponsorship and endorsements to be won by a few champions. This has placed pressure on athletes to become the best, and this has contributed to the growth in drug taking.

Elite athletes are extremely disciplined, motivated individuals, and often perfectionists. The accolades and rewards available to champions in sports such as basketball, football and athletics are enormous, and athletes usually have only a limited amount of time to reach the top. Athletes suffering injury can also be tempted to take substances that will aid the recovery process, enabling them to train harder.

Coaches can be another source of pressure. A successful athlete is often associated with a successful coach, and their wins can result in rewards for the coach in the forms of publicity, new athletes wanting to train under them, and endorsements.

Many athletes claim they resorted to drug use because they believed their competitors were using drugs and that they would never have any chance of success unless they also took drugs.

Expectations of family, friends, team mates and even spectators can create enormous pressure on an athlete to succeed. The 'win at all costs' attitude to sport that characterises international sport can be a heavy burden for athletes to carry, particularly when their efforts are being beamed back live to family and friends at home.

ACTIVITY

Taking drugs – is it worth the risk?

Look at newspapers, text books, the Internet and other resources to identify examples of the use of drugs in sport. Name some sportsmen and women who have been caught. Suggest reasons why they resorted to the use of drugs.

Now identify what happened as a result of them being caught. Discuss with classmates whether it was worth the risk. Think not just about the risks to their career but also to their health.

Match fixing

Some athletes, particularly those in a position of respect and authority may use their position and power to swing the result in one direction or another. Their main motivation is to win or gain money.

Most notable recent examples have been in the sport of cricket. Cricket is a team sport, the result of which may depend upon the achievements of individuals. The nature of the sport has created opportunities for betting on the performance of particular players and on the result itself. Hanse Cronje, once the South African cricket captain, was recently banned for life from playing cricket as a result of his involvement in a match fixing scandal. Mohammed Azharuddin, the Indian test captain, was handed a life ban by the Indian cricket authorities after he admitted to fixing three one-day international matches.

Hanse Cronje is just one of a long list of players who have been involved in match fixing allegations

Sportsmanship

Most sport relies on **sporting** or **sportsmanlike** behaviour. This behaviour means playing to the written and unwritten rules of the game and is often referred to as **etiquette**. For example, in football if a player has 'gone down' and the game has not been stopped then the ball is sometimes sent across the sidelines by the opposing team to allow the injured player to receive treatment. On the restart the ball is usually thrown back to the team who sent the ball off to allow play to continue.

- **Fair play** means playing to the rules of the game, abiding by the decisions of the officials and accepting the outcome of the contest without question.

- **Sportsmanlike behaviour** includes shaking hands with your opponent and giving them three cheers at the end of the game.

Gamesmanship

There are occasions in sport where players, coaching staff and managers have resorted to unsportsmanlike behaviour or conduct in order to win. This behaviour is also known as **gamesmanship**, which has been defined as:

◆ 'The art or practice of using tactical manoeuvres to further one's aims or better one's position.'

◆ 'The use in a sport or game of aggressive, often dubious tactics, such as psychological intimidation or disruption of concentration, to gain an advantage over one's opponent.'

Golf is a sport that is bound by history, tradition and rules and gentlemanly conduct. In recent years, however, golf has witnessed some classic examples of gamesmanship.

At the Solheim Cup (the women's equivalent of the Ryder Cup) held at Loch Lomond in 2000, the US team captain Pat Bradley invoked the rules of golf to force Annika Sorenstam to replay a shot that she had played out of turn and sunk for a birdie (one under par for the hole). Sorenstam was clearly upset and can be forgiven for suspecting that her opponents, Pat Hurst and Kelly Robbins, intentionally let her play out of turn. On replaying her shot she did not make her birdie.

In the Ryder Cup of 1999 at Brookline in the USA, America's triumph was overshadowed by a bitter row over the behaviour of the home team's players, officials and spectators in the closing stages of the competition. The USA were accused of 'disgusting' behaviour as the players and their wives ran onto the green just after the American

Below: The American team were accused of unsportsmanlike behaviour when they ran onto to the green celebrate a key putt. They did not wait for the European player to take his putt to equal the game

Right: John McEnroe is now famous for his 'you cannot be serious!' call to a tennis umpire. Was this an example of gamesmanship?

Justin Leonard holed a crucial putt in the decisive match. Opponent Jose Maria Olazabal had already been heckled while trying to play his second shot on the same hole and still had a chance to keep the match alive when the green was invaded. European vice-captain Sam Torrance reacted with fury, saying: 'The United States should be ashamed. It's about the most disgusting thing I've seen in my life. He still has a putt to tie the hole, we could still take the Ryder Cup home.'

However, golf is still a sport where the vast majority of players are honest – after all, in golf you are your own referee. An example of this occurred in 2001 when Ian Woosnam admitted to having one more club in his bag than he was allowed and took the penalty for it.

Other examples of gamesmanship have been witnessed in other sports. In tennis, players receiving serve will often take a short time out to tie their shoelaces, or receive physio treatment. These actions are sometimes seen as delaying tactics intended to put the server off. In football, the goalkeeper facing a penalty kick will often take more time in coming to his line than he needs. He may then try to put the striker off by moving on his line.

In 2001, golfer Ian Woosnam acted as his own referee when he found he had one more club in his bag than he should have

ACTIVITY

Unsporting behaviour

Write down the different unsporting behaviours that you have seen or heard about in sport. What was the unsporting behaviour intending to achieve? If it was punished state how.

Compare your examples with those found by others in your class. How many different examples have you found? Which unsporting behaviour was the cruellest?

Women in sport

British women have excelled in many sports. In team sports in 1993, the England Women's cricket team won the Cricket World Cup at Lords, beating New Zealand. In 1994, England women won the second Rugby Union World Cup, beating 22 countries.

Ellen MacArthur sailed single-handed around the world in the Vendee Globe race on her boat Kingfisher. She crossed the finish line in second place and in doing so she became the youngest and fastest woman ever to do so.

Throughout history women have taken part in sports, though not on the same scale as men. In most societies women's sport has taken second place to that of the men.

A hundred years ago women were regarded as fragile and delicate. It was thought that vigorous physical activity might harm their internal organs and possibly affect their ability to have children. Looking glowing, tousled or sweaty was considered unattractive and unladylike. These attitudes persisted for some time, but the barriers have gradually been broken down.

The first woman to swim the English Channel was Gertrude Ederle in 1926. She broke the then (male) record by two hours, proving that women were every bit as capable as men in some sports and activities.

Ellen MacArthur proved that women can compete with men on an equal footing

The individual foil event was first held in the Olympics in 1924. Ellen Osier of Denmark won

Women did not compete in athletics events such as the high jump and 800m until 1928

The Olympic Games

The modern Olympic Games were based on male competition. Baron De Coubertin, founder of the modern Games, stated that the role of women should be restricted to the admiring spectator.

The Olympic statement *'no discrimination is allowed against any country or person on the grounds of race, religion or politics'* did not include women in its list of categories identified under discrimination.

Women today still do not compete in the same number of sports as men. In Sydney, in 2000, women's events made up 44% of all events, and only 38% of the total athletes were women.

Cathy Freeman received the torch from a succession of Australian Olympic women athletes to light the Olympic flame in Sydney

The first woman to light the Olympic flame was the Mexican Enriqueta Basilio in 1968. In Sydney 2000, the Olympic torch was carried into Stadium Australia by a succession of Australia's most successful Olympic female athletes. The procession was designed to both acknowledge and celebrate the role of women in Olympic sport.

1896	1900	1912	1924	1928	1980	1984	1988	1992
First modern Olympics. No women allowed to take part	Golf and tennis	Some women's swimming events added	First winter Olympics. Number of women's events restricted	Some women's athletics events	Women's hockey	Women's marathon	Women's 10,000 metres	Women's judo

Participation rates in sport

A number of reasons for the low participation levels in women's sport have been identified by Sport England as a result of their research programme. If you cannot remember these follow the back button.

◀ BACK **gender, p.200**

Society and stereotypes

For generations, women have been expected to conform to a certain role. Girls were encouraged to play with dolls and learn how to cook, while boys were encouraged to play ball games, climb trees and explore. Women traditionally have been constrained by their role in society as the mother, carer and the homemaker. These roles are **gender stereotypes.**

Male and female stereotypes continue into adult life, although some of these are gradually being broken down. Some women think that playing sport will make them unattractive to men. Married women are expected to take responsibility for the home and the children. This leaves them little free time to pursue their own goals and interests. For some mothers sport is a low priority in family life.

Fanny Blankers-Koen was the mother of two children when she won four gold track medals in the 1948 Olympics in London. She was the first woman to prove it was possible to juggle the commitments of being a mother with being a professional, full-time athlete. More and more mothers are now competing successfully at all levels of sport.

To be a top sportswoman, you have to train for long hours and be psychologically tough. Physical training often involves the development of muscles, muscle definition and in some cases masculine characteristics. These characteristics are viewed by some sections of society as unacceptable for women.

Myths

There have been many myths about what sports are suitable for girls and women and what are not. In the 1928 Olympic 800 metre race a number of women collapsed, casting some doubt over whether women could compete over distances. Before 1980, women were not allowed to compete in the Olympic marathon event. The authorities felt that women did not have the physique for endurance sports and that 26 miles was too far for them to run. Top female endurance athletes have since proved that women are more than capable at competing over long distances. Sports scientists think that women may in fact be better suited to longer endurance-type events than men.

The fastest growing sports currently in the UK are women's rugby and women's football. In 1990, there were only 80 girls' football teams, but by 1998 there were over 1000. The number of female players also increased dramatically – from 21,5000 in 1996 to 34,000 in 1998.

The coverage by the media (the press and television) of women's sport is gradually increasing.

Removing barriers

The principles of **equal opportunity** are now being applied to women's sport. Women are being identified as target groups by a number of organisations whose aims are to widen participation by women in a range of sports and activities. Such organisations have included the Sports Councils. The 'What's Your Sport?' campaign was deliberately set up to try and encourage more women to take part in sport.

Many sports centres are now making specific provision for women. Some programme in sessions for 'mums and toddlers' and others have provided crèche facilities to look after children whilst mothers take part in sport or activity. This is referred to as '**positive discrimination**'.

A number of successful women endurance athletes, including Paula Radcliffe, have dispelled the myths society have long held about women in sport

Women's boxing was only recently made legal in England, although it is now a growing sport. The sport is really challenging the stereotype of womanhood

ACTIVITY

Provision for women

Visit your local sports or leisure centre.

Have a look at the programme or schedule of activities currently available. Are there any activities geared specifically for women? What provision or additional facilities does the centre offer so that women can take part in sport?

Much of the increase in women's participation in football is due to the FA's decision to launch the female Talent Development Plan. The main aim of the plan is to make women's football the top female sport in the new millennium. This will be achieved by putting in place a system for the identification and development of talented young players from the age of 10 through to the England senior side.

Both the Women's Sport Foundation (WSF) and the Home Country Sports Councils (HCSC) are working towards increasing the participation of women in sport.

WSF p.263

Women in the media

Venus Williams, Martina Hingis, Laura Davis and Denise Lewis are all sportswomen whom you would have heard of. This is largely due to the coverage their sports receive on TV and in the press. Women's tennis, golf and athletics are possibly three of the biggest sports in terms of media coverage, salaries, prize money and endorsements received.

How many of you know the name of the England Women's hockey captain? The England women's cricket captain? The current English squash champion? Can you name any British women swimmers, identify their stroke or what their most recent achievements have been? Do you suppose this has anything to do with the media coverage afforded each of these sports?

This representation contrasts strongly with the coverage given to men. More attention is often paid (particularly in tennis) to the physique, dress and looks of the player than to her performance.

Male sport tends to dominate both TV and the press. However, there have been some changes in recent years. Channel 4 now has a policy of showing a number of minority sports, including women's cricket, football and rugby.

There are also now a significant number of female sports presenters and commentators. Sue Barker is possibly the most well known since she has presented BBC1's very popular *A Question of Sport*. Sharron Davis is usually to be found pool side interviewing swimmers at all of the big competitions. Claire Balding has broken into the traditionally male-dominated domain of horse race commentary.

Venus Williams is not the only player whose style of dress has been the subject of much debate

The Women's Sport Foundation carried out a survey of the amount of coverage given to women's sport in the Monday editions of four newspapers over a three-month period. The table below shows the coverage given to women's sport as a percentage of the total column centimetres allocated to sport in these newspapers.

	TOTAL COLUMN CM	WOMEN'S COLUMN CM	% OF TOTAL
The Times			
April	11,098	531.5	5.0
May	9,775	373	4.0
Jun	12,075	788	7.0
Daily Telegraph			
April	10,903	326	3.0
May	10,885	221	2.0
June	11,447	919	8.0
The Guardian			
April	9,094	117	2.0
May	10,152	305	3.0
June	10,965	553	5.0
Daily Express			
April	4,632	187	4.0
May	4,328	128	3.0
June	5,240	28	5.0

Women's sport typically accounts for between 4 and 5% of total sports coverage in the Monday sports sections of the newspapers. Those months with higher representation tended to be as a result of major events featuring women and men competing at the same venue, such as athletics meetings.

Most of the coverage tends to be given towards professional women's sports, such as tennis, golf and athletics. Maximum coverage of sports like tennis coincides with the grand slam events of the Australian, French, Wimbledon and US Open championships.

ACTIVITY

Women's sport in the press

Collect two different types of papers. One should be a tabloid, such as the *Sun*, *Star* or *Daily Express*, and the other should be a 'broadsheet', like the *Times*, *Guardian* or *Independent*.

Look at the sports section of a Monday morning newspaper. Count how many pages of sport there are in that section. Now list the women's sports that received some coverage in that section. Identify the names of the women that were mentioned in the article. Had you heard of them before? Were any photographs included? Of whom? Was it an action shot?

How much coverage was given to women's sports compared with men's sport?

Revising current issues in sport

This section is designed to help you improve your knowledge and understanding of the current issues in sport.

In order to answer the questions you may well need to look back through the chapter to help you. Completing these questions successfully will help you prepare for your examination.

Participation in sport

1. Give four reasons why people might want to participate in sport.
2. With reference to a specific geographical area (for example, the coast, water or mountains) state how the location might influence the sport or activities that you take part in.
3. Sport England in 1999 identified four barriers to women's participation in sport. Name two.
4. State three adjustments that centres would need to make to their provision to conform with the Disability Discrimination Act.
5. The Youth Sport Trust has discovered that adolescent girls drop out from playing sport. What ways have they thought of to help encourage more girls to participate in sport?

Sport in society – current issues

1. Explain the term deviant behaviour. Give examples of sporting conduct to help explain your answer.
2. Hooliganism is an unacceptable feature of British football. Give two reasons why it occurs. Identify three ways in which the authorities are trying to stamp it out.
3. There are a number of different ways in which sportsmen and women try to cheat in order to win. Identify two methods of cheating and use actual examples from sport to explain your answer.
4. Give one example of sportsmanlike behaviour.
5. Give one example of gamesmanship in football.

Women in sport

1 What was the attitude towards women's participation in sport 100 years ago?

2 What positive health influence does sport and exercise have on women?

3 In what year were women first allowed to run the marathon in the Olympics?

4 What term is now being applied to women's sport in a bid to try to increase opportunities for participation?

5 What do the initials WSF represent?

6 Women's sport on average occupies between 4 and 7% of the space in the sports section in the major papers. During Wimbledon this increases significantly. Give three reasons why.

CHAPTER 8 Finance and funding in sport

Today sport is worth billions of pounds to the UK economy. Without finance and funding we would not be able to build or run sports facilities, operate leisure centres or be sports spectators. If you are involved in sport it is important to know where the money comes from – and where it goes!

In this chapter you will consider the various ways sportsmen and women obtain funding to take part in sport.

Sports managers obtain funding for their athletes or teams in many different ways, including sponsorship and product endorsement. Many football clubs sell shares in the team, which can be big business.

CONTENTS

Money in professional sport	218
Amateur and professional sport	224
Government spending in sport	226
Sports clubs and the sports governing bodies	229
Sport and the media	232
Sponsorship	237
The National Lottery	239
Answers to activities	242
Revising finance and funding in sport	243

217

Money in professional sport

In order to understand the concept of money in sport we will look at some of the ways that professional sport is funded.

We will look at the world of finance within football so that you can learn some of the key terms in finance. Once you know these terms you can use them to talk about the finance and funding of any sport. The money that a club earns in a year is known as its **income**. The amount a club earns and spends over a year is called its **annual turnover**.

ACTIVITY

The world's richest football clubs

You can do this exercise on your own or in small groups as a competition.

Compile a list of the world's top 20 football clubs in terms of their annual turnover in the year 2000. Copy the table and put the clubs in order of their turnover, with the highest in the number 1 position.

You will get one point if you place a club within three places (either way) of its actual position and a point if you can guess each club's turnover to the nearest £5 million.

Three clubs have been entered to get you started.

CLUB NAME	TURNOVER (£ MILLION)
1.	
2.	
3. Real Madrid	76.1
4.	
5.	
6.	
7.	
8.	
9.	
10.	
11. Liverpool	45.3
12.	
13.	
14.	
15.	
16.	
17. Rangers	36.5
18.	
19.	
20.	

Inter Milan
Barcelona
Juventus
Leeds Utd
Real Madrid
Manchester Utd
Liverpool
AC Milan
Rangers
Tottenham
Bayern Munich
Lazio
AS Roma
Newcastle Utd
Chelsea
Parma
Arsenal
Celtic
Borussia Dortmund
Aston Villa

Finance and funding in sport

The Nou Camp Home to Barcelona, one of the biggest earning football clubs in the world

In contrast to the money earned in football, the sports giant Reebok has sales of almost $3,000 million – giving it a turnover way above that of the top 20 football clubs in the world put together!

Sources of finance

Where does all that money come from?

Originally almost all the money coming into sport was due to fans and customers paying to watch a match. This is still of course very important but now the top clubs have a variety of ways of bringing in income. Some of the main sources of finance (other than gate receipts) are:

- merchandising
- advertising
- product endorsement
- conferences, banquets and catering
- TV rights
- sponsorship.

Merchandising now generates millions of pounds each year. Some of the bigger clubs have their own merchandise megastores

Merchandising

Merchandising is selling goods with the club's colours, name and logo on them. Often these are far more expensive than they would be if they were not covered in the club's images. Merchandise can range from replica football kits to sports bags, towels and baseball caps.

ACTIVITY

Merchandising in football

Make a list of all the things that you can think of that clubs sell with their club name, logo and colours on.

Have you got any ideas of new and different items a club could include as part of its merchandising?

Look at a club web site or visit a club store. List the prices that the club charges for a range of merchandise. Compare your answers with those of a classmate who has looked at a different club.

Money in professional sport

Clubs sometimes try to get extra money through merchandising by changing their kits so that the old ones become out of date. Many people think this is very unfair to the fans, and especially to children who have spent a great deal of money buying their club's strip. Now the Football Task Force has recommended that football kits should have a minimum lifespan of two seasons. Do you agree?

Advertising

At one time it was not thought right that sport should sell itself to companies that had nothing to do with sport. Now you will see adverts all around the pitch, from drinks and fast food to banking and insurance. Most types of industry now advertise in sport in one way or another.

Many clubs now have revolving advertising hoardings that can show the adverts of several companies in the one space during a game. If the advert is likely to be seen on television the club will be able to charge more because the adverts will reach millions of people. Adverts can also be found on places such as club web sites and in match day programmes.

If this match is shown on television millions of people will see the adverts

ACTIVITY

Advertising in sport

How far would you go with advertising?

Draw up a table with two columns, headed 'acceptable advertising' and 'unacceptable advertising'. In each column give examples of your views. Think for example about tobacco companies – should they be allowed to be involved in advertising in all sports, some sports or none? Should adverts be allowed everywhere or can advertising become too much? Would you like, for example, to see the England strip covered in adverts like a Formula 1 racing driver if this brought more money into football?

Find photographs or images from the newspapers to show what you mean by acceptable and unacceptable advertising in sport.

Product endorsement

Top players and clubs do not pay for their sports clothing and equipment – they are paid to wear and use goods by the manufacturers. Seeing a top player or team wearing or using something is thought to encourage others to buy the same goods. This is called product endorsement.

Conferences, banqueting and catering

Not so long ago the main image of food at a sports event was a simple hot dog with a drink. Now the top stadiums have a range of bars, cafes, restaurants and refreshment outlets. This is not only for match days. At other times the grounds are used for business conferences and meetings and people go to eat in club restaurants or visit the stadium museum.

Almost all the top clubs now have **executive boxes** where people can watch the game in luxury with services such as televisions, food and drink as part of the entertainment. Sometimes these facilities are not used by individuals or fans but by businesses who, for example, would hire an executive box on a match day and then use it to entertain their own guests. This is called **corporate hospitality.**

Seeing top players wearing a particular brand encourages fans to buy the products

ACTIVITY

Corporate hospitality at the big events

Imagine you are an executive of a major company who is going to entertain six guests from a Japanese company. You are hoping they will agree to sign a big deal with you so you have decided to take them out to a sports fixture on Saturday.

Browse through the web sites of major sports stadiums to see how much it would cost to hire executive boxes. You may think about looking up facilities for:

- Rugby Union – Twickenham, Millennium Stadium
- Horse Racing – Aintree, Epsom, Newmarket, Cheltenham
- Football – any Premier League ground
- Cricket – any of the major county grounds
- Tennis – Wimbledon.

Identify what each sport or facility can offer you as part of your corporate hospitality day.

TV rights

The television companies all want to show the main sporting events on their channel. They are prepared to pay enormous sums of money to do it and to make sure their rivals do not have coverage! The TV Company has bought the **TV rights** to broadcast the match, series of matches or whole season of fixtures.

▶ **sport and the media, p.232**

Sponsorship

Many sports clubs and individual players are sponsored by commercial companies. In return for associating themselves with the sponsoring company, they receive sometimes very large sums of money. This benefits both the sponsor and the performers.

▶ NEXT **sponsorship, p.237**

Gate receipts

This means simply the money that clubs earn from fans paying to get in to see the game. Now that major grounds are all-seater, entry prices tend to be quite high. More people now have season tickets.

ACTIVITY

The cost of watching live sport

Using the web site addresses and other sources of information you found in the previous activity find out how much it costs for a ticket to see:

- one County Cricket match
- one Premier League football match
- one major horse racing event
- one Home Nations rugby international at Twickenham
- one major basketball game.

How do the prices compare? What about the price of a ticket to an Olympic sport, say the athletics, or to view the Ryder Cup?

Total turnover

The income of top football clubs has soared in recent years. One of the main reasons for this is the large amounts of money generated from TV deals.

The pie charts show how this turnover is compiled for three professional football clubs.

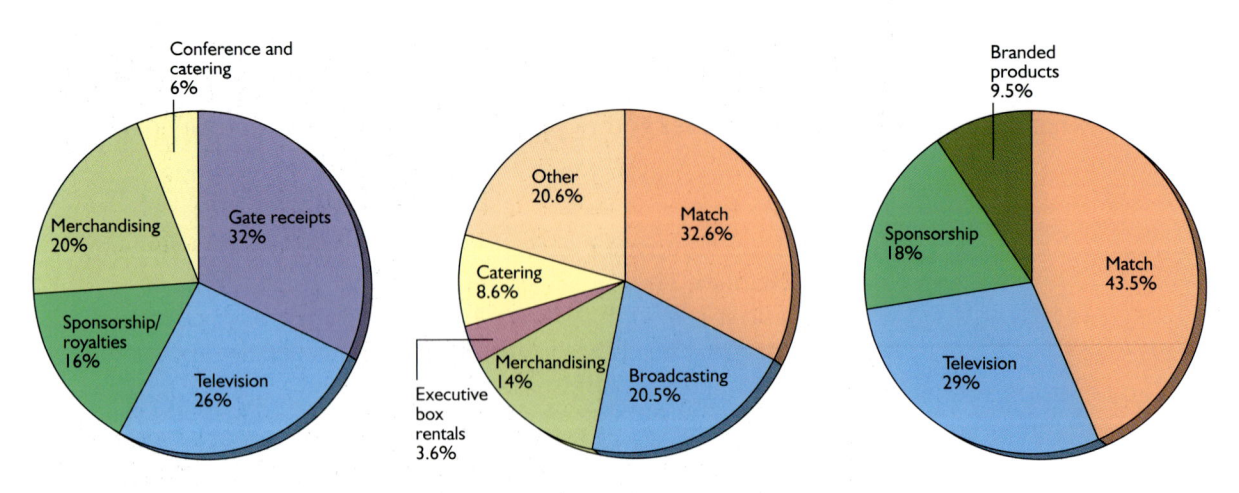

Club 1:
- Conference and catering 6%
- Gate receipts 32%
- Television 26%
- Sponsorship/royalties 16%
- Merchandising 20%

Club 2:
- Other 20.6%
- Match 32.6%
- Broadcasting 20.5%
- Merchandising 14%
- Catering 8.6%
- Executive box rentals 3.6%

Club 3:
- Branded products 9.5%
- Match 43.5%
- Television 29%
- Sponsorship 18%

How important are each of these sources of finance, not just to a professional football club but to any club or sport?

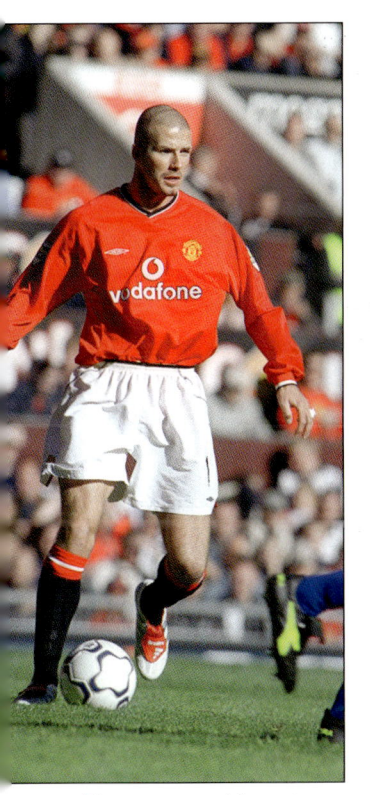

Where does the money come from?

Football clubs use their income to operate on a day-to-day and week-to-week basis. The money that is spent on running a club is known as its **expenditure**.

The largest item of expenditure is usually staff costs. Mostly this means salaries for players and other staff. In recent years players' wages have soared so much that they now earn in a week what some players not so long ago could not earn in a year!

The table shows the money the three clubs listed opposite paid on staff (including players) in the year 2000.

CLUB	STAFF FEES (£)
Manchester United	44,791,000
Aston Villa	21,551,000
Newcastle United	28,869,000

Aston Villa is a typical Premier League football club. It employs the following staff:

Players, managers and coaches	80
Commercial and merchandising staff	71
Office management	41
Grounds and maintenance staff	26
Community projects	5
Part-time staff (on match days, etc.)	970
Total	1,193

Source: Annual report Aston Villa 2000

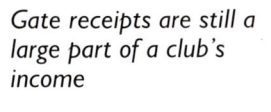

The wages paid to top professional players have increased dramatically in recent years

Gate receipts are still a large part of a club's income

Money in professional sport

Amateur and professional sport

Only a tiny minority of sportspeople earn the vast sums of money that we associate with top footballers, tennis players, golfers and racing drivers. For the rest the story is very different.

Defining amateurs and professionals

When we think of the differences between amateur and professionals today we tend to think that professionals are fitter and more skilful and that amateurs are not so good. But these were not the original definitions.

The history of amateurism and professionalism

The words **amateur** and **professional** have changed their meaning somewhat in sporting terms over the last hundred years.

At one time amateur simply meant that you were not paid and professional meant that you **were** paid. In the early days of organised sport amateurs were often better players because they had time to develop their skills.

However, to be paid to play sport did not mean you were rich. In fact, the wages were just a little better than were earned by the average worker. It was frowned upon to be paid at all for playing a sport – to be paid meant that you were not wealthy enough to support yourself. Professional sportspeople were often from poorer backgrounds while amateurs had probably gone to public school and were considered gentlemen. This led to the distinction between 'gentlemen' and professional 'players'.

The incredible CB Fry

CB Fry was one of the greatest all-round athletes of all time. Born in 1872, he attended Repton public school, where he excelled at cricket, athletics and football. He represented Oxford university at cricket, football and athletics in his first year, running 100 yards in 10.2 seconds. While still a student he played football for England, and broke the world long jump record, jumping over 23 yards 6 inches.

He was one of the best cricket batsmen of his day, and captained Sussex and England. He also played football for Southampton in the FA Cup final and Rugby for Blackheath and the Barbarians. He only didn't enter the 1896 Olympics because he didn't know they were on!

Later he went on to be a sports journalist, a diplomat in the League of Nations – and was even offered the throne of Albania. No wonder his autobiography was called *A Life Worth Living!*

However, CB Fry was not rich. He had to struggle to survive in the 'gentleman' class by working as a teacher, a journalist and even once as a nude model! If he had become a professional sportsman his status would have nose dived, and he would have lost many of the privileges that came only with being an amateur. For example, amateurs had to sit at separate tables during cricket lunch and tea breaks, had less comfortable dressing rooms and were given less appetising food. Moreover, he would not have been able to count as friends many of his amateur team-mates, who would have shunned him.

Players and gentlemen often played in the same international sides but there were strict differences between them. For example, gentlemen were unpaid and referred to as 'Mister', while professionals were referred to simply by their name (e.g. a 'gentleman' would be referred to as 'Mr Smith' while a player would simply be 'Smith'). At one stage it was unthinkable that a mere professional could ever captain England at cricket. There were also strict rules about gentlemen and players mixing with each other on occasions like international tours.

Arguments over professionalism and amateurism have raged since the late 1800s and helped to cause the splits between the Football Association and the Football League and between Rugby Union and Rugby League in the nineteenth century.

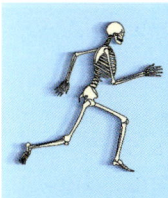

Professional and amateurs – then and now
When the Football Association was founded all footballers had to be amateur. After a while many clubs began secretly paying players or finding them jobs in order to persuade them to play for them. This became known as *shamateurism*. Eventually footballers were allowed to be paid but under strict conditions. In 1884 the *Manchester Guardian* stated:
- 'The admission into amateur ranks of professional players is possibly the beginning of the end …!!'

How does this statement compare with the status of football today?

The attitudes and definitions of amateur and professional status continued to influence sport in the late twentieth century. Only in the 1960s was the minimum wage abolished for footballers and professional tennis players allowed to play at Wimbledon. More recently athletics, Rugby Union and the Olympics have become more relaxed about sportsmen and women being paid.

Semi-professionals

Many top sportspeople compete for the honour of winning, representing their country and being as good as they can be. They do not get paid enough through their sport to both earn a living and pay their expenses so they have to take other work as well. They are **semi-professional**.

Outside of the elite there are many semi-professionals in sports such as football, cricket, and rugby. In some sports even top performers are semi-professional and could not earn enough to live well if they just relied on the money they receive from sport. Until recently the only way that some athletes could prepare for the Olympics was through sponsorship. Now they can obtain lottery funding in order to be able to train without the distractions of working.

Lottery funding, p.239

Government spending on sport

Local government spending on sport

People must pay **council tax** in their local area, which depends on things like the value of the house they are living in and which local authority they come under. However, council tax does not make up all the income that local authorities receive. Businessess must also pay for the services they use and local authorities obtain a large part of their income from central government.

Local authorities provide a wide range of services from street cleaning to housing. They also provide a wide range of sports facilities where the general public can take part in sport.

- swimming pools
- leisure centres
- playing fields
- astro-turf pitches
- parks
- youth clubs
- community centres
- tennis courts
- bowling greens.

The section of a local authority that deals with sport is usually called the **Leisure and Recreation Department**. Some Departments also provide other facilities such as sports grounds, local stadiums and pitch and putt courses. Some are far better at providing sports facilities and services than others.

Local authorities provide a wide range of facilities to cater for the interests of people within the community

ACTIVITY

Local authority provision

Make a list of the sport and leisure facilities in your area.

Be careful to select only those facilities that belong to the local authority and do not pick, for example, tennis courts that belong to a private club.

These facilities also have to properly managed. Money is needed for staff wages, maintenance and repairs, replacing broken equipment, heating and lighting and cleaning. These are the running costs or **operating costs** of the facility.

Although councils charge for admission to many of their facilities, the income they receive does not usually cover the running costs. For this reason councils put money in to make up the difference. This is called a **subsidy**.

Value for money

There are very powerful arguments for local authorities spending money on sports facilities. For instance:

◆ 'Sports facilities help to keep people healthy and active for longer.'

◆ 'They help to keep kids off the streets and to reduce crime.'

◆ 'Sport is a valuable part of children's education and growing up '

◆ 'Adults need sporting opportunities as well. It's never too late to learn.'

◆ 'Sports facilities are good places to meet other people and to develop a community.'

◆ 'Sports facilities help to prevent the "couch potato" child.'

◆ 'If we do not invest in sport at the grass-roots level we cannot expect to be any good at sport at the international level.'

◆ 'Sport is fun and having sports facilities improves the quality of our lifestyle.'

◆ 'With modern traffic and road congestion, sports playing fields and parks are the only chance of green space in some areas.'

Some local councils feel that their facilities are best run by their own staff. Others prefer to pay a private company. In this case the subsidy will take the form of a fee paid to the company. This is sometimes called a **contract fee** or a **management fee**.

Sometimes councils have to look at whether the subsidy they are paying is worth the money. The following activity will help you to understand this.

ACTIVITY

How valuable is that sports facility to you?

You can do this activity on your own or in small groups.

Use the list of local council sports facilities you compiled in the last activity.

Beside each facility, write down the benefits that you feel each is providing for people in your area. To help you consider the range of benefits provided to the local community, look at the list of user groups below:

◆ children
◆ youth
◆ older people
◆ active sports people

◆ people playing for fun
◆ sports clubs
◆ people playing in competitions
◆ schools.

Now list which facilities you feel are providing the most value to your community.

Being able to think about value for money and who benefits from the services is an essential part of the work of a council's Leisure and Recreation Department.

Sports and leisure are among the few things councils provide which you have a choice in. You cannot choose who cleans your streets, for example, but you can choose not to use a certain swimming pool if you do not like it there.

Provided you have transport you can use sports and leisure facilities from any area you like – you do not have to use the facilities provided by your own council.

National government spending on sport

National government does not have money of its own to provide us with the services we want. It needs to raise money to fund these services through **taxation**.

There are many government departments that each deal separately with areas of our national life. The government department that is most involved with sport is The Department of Culture, Media and Sport. We will consider the structure of sport in the UK in more detail in the next chapter.

structure of sport in the UK. p.255

The Department of Culture, Media and Sport provides money to:

◆ UK Sport

◆ Sport England

UK Sport and Sport England have a number of goals:

◆ to help our top athletes to perform at the highest level

◆ to improve sporting standards

◆ to improve the numbers of people playing sport

◆ to promote sport generally.

The sports councils of Scotland, Wales and Northern Ireland are funded through their national regional assemblies.

Home Country Sports Councils, p.255

Sports Councils are examples of what are called **non-governmental public organisations** because they are paid for through taxes – they are in the public sector. But they are not government departments.

UK Sport obtains around £12 million from the Department of Culture, Media and Sport. Over half of this goes in grants to sports governing bodies.

This money goes to fund the work of the sports councils that we will consider in the next chapter.

Central government, local government and non-governmental public organisations make up the **public sector** because they belong to and are paid for by the general public.

Sports clubs and the sports governing bodies

Sports clubs

Sports clubs are part of the voluntary sector because much of the work in running them is done voluntarily by members for the benefit of the club. Voluntary sector sports clubs can range from your local Sunday Football team to your local tennis or bowls club.

▶ NEXT **voluntary sector organisations and clubs, p.253**

Sports clubs obtain their money from their members in two main ways:

♦ **Membership fees** are paid each year as members rejoin the club. Normally all members must pay their annual fees. However, sometimes clubs have honorary members, people who, possibly in return for their services to the club, do not have to pay to be members. Sometimes you have to pay an extra fee when you join for the first time. This is called a **joining fee**.

♦ **Subscriptions** (usually called 'subs') are often paid weekly. They are very often paid when clubs who play team sports train during the week before playing at the weekend.

Some larger clubs have facilities such as bars and refreshment areas that can earn them valuable extra income. Sometimes clubs apply and receive grants from organisations such as their local council or from the National Lottery.

Huge numbers of people take part in sport at their local clubs

ACTIVITY

Funding a voluntary sports club

The Alderslink Tennis Club was founded in 1930 and has eight outdoor tennis courts and a small clubhouse, which contains a bar and a small changing room. The bar is staffed by club volunteers and opens three nights a week and after club matches and tournaments. Unfortunately, the courts and the clubhouse are in a bad state of repair.

Imagine that you are a member of this sports club.

Make a list of all the fund-raising activities that you can think of that would help to raise funds for new showers in the clubhouse and to repair the tennis courts.

The organisation of a voluntary sports club

Who organises, manages and runs a voluntary sports club? The members do.

Normally a **committee** of club members will meet from time to time to manage the affairs of the club. Usually the most important people on the committee are the **chairperson**, the **secretary** and the **treasurer**.

▶ NEXT **club structure, p.253**

Once a year all club members meet at the **Annual General Meeting** (AGM) to elect a committee for the following year. All members are entitled to vote or to stand for election to the committee. An important part of the meeting is the **treasurer's report**. The treasurer will talk about the club's income and expenditure. Any money left over after expenditure has been paid in a club is usually known as a **surplus.**

People who play at the grass-roots level often have to pay to do so

A local league cricketer explains the typical costs to a member of a sports club:

'We pay a membership fee of £30 a year at the start of the season, usually in April, and we each pay £3 in subs after our Wednesday night practice session in the nets at the sports centre. This helps to pay for the use of the sports centre. Luckily we can keep the cost down for the members because we have a local sponsor. At the AGM I wanted to increase the subs for this year so we could afford more pads and equipment, but I was outvoted. At last year's AGM the treasurer told us that we had a surplus of £150, which will go towards new equipment next season.'

ACTIVITY

Where does the members' money go?

Imagine that you are the treasurer of Alderslink Tennis Club and you will be speaking to the annual general meeting in front of all the members.

Write a report to present to the club members to tell them where the money has come from and how it has been spent over the last year.

Sports governing bodies

One expenditure a club treasurer usually has to pay is the club's membership to the sports **governing body.** This is usually called an **affiliation fee**. Once the club has affiliated they will have the right to play in leagues, tournaments and cup matches. Some governing bodies, such as the Football Association or Lawn Tennis Association, are household names.

For some governing bodies, the money from the member clubs is an important source of income. Governing bodies also obtain money through areas such as:

- sponsorship
- TV rights
- profits from tournaments.

There are as many variations in the way sports are organised, the numbers of fans they have, and the number of people who play them as there are in the way sports are played. For this reason the way that a sports governing body will obtain its income will depend largely on the organisation of the sport itself. For example:

Tennis The LTA gets most of its income (about 73%) from the Wimbledon Championships.

Rugby Union The Rugby Football Union gets a large share of its money (about 37%) from representative matches.

Athletics UK Athletics gets a large share of its money through its media deal with the BBC and sponsors.

Governing bodies that cannot rely on major events or mass TV coverage for their income must rely on support from their members, their affiliated clubs and organisations such as the sports councils.

How do sports governing bodies spend their money?

As an example the annual report from the Lawn Tennis Association (1999) identifies the way in which their finances were spent:

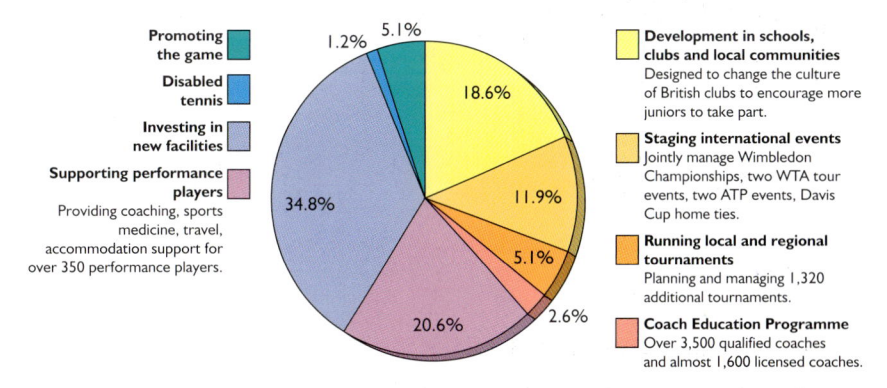

Promoting the game — 5.1%
Disabled tennis — 1.2%
Investing in new facilities — 34.8%
Supporting performance players — 20.6%
Providing coaching, sports medicine, travel, accommodation support for over 350 performance players.

Development in schools, clubs and local communities — 18.6%
Designed to change the culture of British clubs to encourage more juniors to take part.

Staging international events — 11.9%
Jointly manage Wimbledon Championships, two WTA tour events, two ATP events, Davis Cup home ties.

Running local and regional tournaments — 5.1%
Planning and managing 1,320 additional tournaments.

Coach Education Programme — 2.6%
Over 3,500 qualified coaches and almost 1,600 licensed coaches.

Money from the Wimbledon Championships supports the work of the LTA

Sports clubs and the sports governing bodies

Sport and the media

A large part of the income of sports comes from the media.

Sport on television

Sport is now a big part of television and television a big part of sport. At one time television companies showed sport but did not pay a great deal of money to do so.

At that time there were only a few channels. Now, with satellite and cable TV, the competition to show sporting events is intense. Companies try to out-bid each other to win the rights to screen events. This means that sports can charge the television companies far more in order to allow them to broadcast.

ACTIVITY

Sport on television

Below is a list of major sporting events. Copy the list and match up the events with the TV channels that broadcast them. Some TV channels broadcast more than one of these events and some events are shown on different channels.

EVENT	TV CHANNEL
Wimbledon Tennis Championships	
Test Cricket Matches (home)	
County Cricket Matches	
The Grand National	
Formula 1 Grand Prix racing	
Live Premier League football matches	
Highlights of Premier League football	
The FA Cup final	
The Football Champions League	
Rugby Union Six Nations	
Rugby Super League	
Golf's Ryder Cup	

Channels that everybody can watch (BBC, Channel 4, ITV and Channel 5) are the **terrestrial TV channels**. Companies like Sky have **subscription channels** (you have to pay or subscribe to join them). These channels also operate **pay per view**, which means that you can only view a sporting event if you pay an extra fee. Many top boxing fights are now pay per view.

The benefits of a sport being shown on a terrestrial channel include:

- The sport is accessible to all people who have a television set.
- Television is a medium for advertising, promotion and product endorsement.
- Television also promotes the athletes, performers and players. Many, such as Venus Williams, Tiger Woods and Ryan Gigs, have become household names, instantly recognisable.

TV pays sport a lot of money for the right to broadcast sporting events. This money is very useful for the sport. You might think that a sport should take all the money it can get from TV but it is not that simple. If sport is shown only on channels where you need to pay to watch, many fans will not be able to see may lose interest. Being on the terrestrial channels means more people get to watch that sport. This means more fans.

At one time Rugby League was shown on BBC on winter Saturday afternoons. Now it is on a subscription channel and not everybody who likes Rugby League can watch it.

ACTIVITY

Subscription channels

Conduct a small survey amongst your classmates, friends and team-mates.

How many of them have access at home to Sky or cable television? What percentage is this of the group? Now ask them which of the following reasons most influenced their family's decision to subscribe.

- Films
- News coverage
- Entertainment and music
- Sporting events

What conclusions can you draw from your findings?

Restrictions on sports broadcasting

The Department of Culture, Media and Sport has stipulated that some sporting events must be shown on terrestrial TV. This means that the sports are not allowed to sell their major events exclusively to satellite companies or cable TV companies. The government believes that these sporting occasions belong to the whole nation and that everybody should be allowed to see them.

This can be a difficult choice to make. While it is good that sports events are available to everybody it is not so good for the sport because they will not be able to charge as high a fee or the broadcasting rights. Restricted sporting events are placed in one of two lists:

- **List A** sporting events must be available to everybody on terrestrial TV.
- **List B** sporting events may sell the event to subscription channels but must allow edited highlights on terrestrial channels.

The sports on these lists have been given the name the 'crown jewels' because they are such a valuable and important part of our national life.

ACTIVITY

TV Rights

You can conduct this activity on your own or in small groups as a competition.

Below are a number of sporting events. You may have watched many of them yourself over the last year.

The Wimbledon Tennis Finals	The Scottish FA Cup Final (in Scotland)
Wimbledon Tennis (not final matches)	The Rugby League Challenge Cup Final
Great Britain Davis Cup Tennis matches	The Rugby World Cup Final
The Rugby Union six Nations	Other matches in the Rugby World Cup
The FA Cup Final	Cricket Test Matches played in England
England Football internationals	The Commonwealth Games
Premier League Football matches	The World Athletics championships
The Grand National	The Cricket World Cup Final semis & matches involving home teams
The Derby	
The Boat Race	The Golf Ryder Cup
FIFA World Cup Finals tournament	The Open Golf Championship
The European Football Championships Finals tournament	The Olympic Games
Champions League Football	

Identifying the crown jewels

◆ Which events are in list A?
◆ Which are in list B?
◆ Which are not part of the crown jewels?

LIST A	LIST B
(live coverage must be made available to all viewers on terrestrial TV)	(broadcasting may be allowed by a non-terrestrial channel provided edited highlights are available on terrestrial TV)

Here are some clues:

◆ Ten of the events listed have full live coverage protected and are on List A.
◆ Nine are in List B.
◆ Five events have no government restrictions on them and so can simply go to the highest bidder

You gain one point for every sporting event you put in the correct column.

Source: Department of Culture Media and Sport

TV rights

Often a number of channels will enter into **negotiation** with the sport over how much will be charged for TV rights.

For example:

- In 1988 the television rights across the world for the Seoul Olympic Games were $403 million.
- The rights for the Sydney Games in 2000 were over $1318 million, and the rights for the Athens Games are already over $1400 million – and they're not until 2004!

The rights to show a sport across the world are called **global TV rights**.

The International Olympic Committee likes to see the Olympics broadcast to as many people in the world as possible. For this reason it aims to sell its TV rights to television companies that broadcast to as wide an audience as possible.

ACTIVITY

Television rights

Can you estimate what the TV rights will be for the Athens Olympics in 2004?

Draw the figures for Olympic TV rights from 1984, 1996 and your estimated 2004 figure as a line graph. If the line continues to grow at the same rate what will the television rights cost for the Olympics in 2012?

Other sports media

Television is not the only media outlet for sport. There has never been more variety of sports coverage:

- a wide range of radio channels, including specialist channels such as Talk Sport and BBC 5 Live
- sports magazines
- newspapers devoting wholesections or colour supplements to sport
- the Internet
- fanzines (small magazines written by the fans themselves).

One of the recent trends is for newspapers to become more and more interested in the private lives of stars and less on their sporting performance.

Some of the media tend to focus on players' private lives as much as their sporting ability

Positive and negative aspects of the media

Many people are concerned about the relationship between sport and the media. Some of the common arguments are:

Television gives sport exposure. This means more fans become interested and players become household names and celebrities	**But...**	Sports that go on subscription TV get less exposure because not everybody can see them. This could mean fewer young fans in the future and fewer star-making opportunities for the players
Television companies have paid a great deal of money into sport	**But...**	Television companies are becoming increasingly powerful because they pay so much to buy the TV rights. This means that they can change the way sports are played to suit viewing figures.
Newspapers now have far more sports coverage, with colour supplements and many pages of sport	**But...**	Often tabloids are not interested in sport but gossip and speculation about the private lives of stars. This is known as **sensationalism**.
With the new TV channels, magazines, radio and Internet there have never been more ways to find out about a sport you are interested in	**But...**	This makes sport very attractive to advertisers and sponsors. Some people worry that too much commercialism is spoiling sport.

ACTIVITY

Pros and cons of sport in the media

Draw up a table with two columns: advantages (pros) and disadvantages (cons).

Now consider your own arguments for and against sport in the media and complete the table. Ask the views of classmates, team-mates and your parents to help you draw up your arguments.

You may want to discuss your views with classmates in a debate, with one group looking at the advantages and one the disadvantages.

Sponsorship

Sponsors pay vast sums of money to be associated with sport. Why?

◆ Sponsoring a sport is great advertising. The sponsoring company's name can appear on sports kits, at sports grounds – and if a company sponsors a competition the name is heard repeatedly every time a match is played, such as the Barclaycard Premiership.

◆ Sport is seen as something good and bringing out the best in people. It can unite people as perhaps nothing else can and can lead to greater understanding across nations. In short it has a great image and companies who invest in sport become associated with this image.

◆ Sponsors also get to sell their products through the club. For example, a drinks company who sponsors a football club will not only have its name across the front of the shirt but will sell its drinks at the ground and may use the club's name in advertising elsewhere. This could also give greater publicity to the club. When two organisations are supporting reach other like this they are often referred to as **partners**.

ACTIVITY

Who sponsors sport?

Look up the web sites of sports governing bodies and sports clubs and make a list of how many sponsors you can find in each one. On some web sites you may need to click on 'partners' to find them.

Copy the table below. If you recognise which category a company is in, place it in one of the following boxes. One has been filled in to get you started.

CATEGORY	SPONSORING COMPANY	NAME OF EVENT
Sports goods	Nationwide Bank	(Nationwide League)
Financial Services (banks/insurance)		
Alcoholic Drinks		
Catering and leisure		
Automotive		
Electrical/IT		
Media		
Telecommunications		
Food and drink		
Other		

The actual figures in terms of the number of sponsorship deals in sport are:

	NUMBER OF DEALS
Sports goods	177
Financial services (banks, insurance companies)	167
Alcoholic drinks	105
Catering	70
Automotive	93
Electrical/IT	80
Media	74
Telecommunications	33
Food and drink	35
Manufacturing and construction	38
Retail	28
Household/consumer products	30

Source: Sport England web site

How did the results of your survey compare with the actual figures?

The traditional form of sponsorship could be described as a simple two-way deal with the sponsor putting money into the club in return for exposure through the company name being portrayed around the ground and on the club shirt. Now sponsorship deals can be far more complex, involving both sports club and sponsor servicing each other's interests.

Manchester United and Vodaphone

In 2000 Manchester United made very important sponsorship deals with Vodaphone and Coral. The club report stated:

'Over the past twelve months we have realigned our sponsorship programme and appointed a new principal sponsor Vodaphone. The new arrangement is ground breaking within the sports sponsorship world in so far as it combines a traditional sponsorship element with a transactional aspect, with Manchester United benefiting from both.

'ManUMobile has been launched as the first service of its kind to provide all the latest Club news as it happens. Text messages provide live match day updates, kick off times and other ground breaking stories as they happen. The WAP site provides full news, match information and player biographies.

'The agreement with Coral's betting offshoot Eurobet also combines sponsorship with transactional activity with Eurobet becoming our on site and on line betting partner. Visitors to www.manutd.com can view the Eurobet microsite or link to the Eurobet site to review odds and place bets across a variety of sports.'

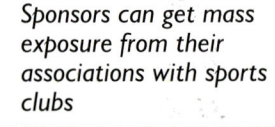

Sponsors can get mass exposure from their associations with sports clubs

The National Lottery

The National Lottery started in November 1994. Originally money was to be distributed to five good causes:

◆ sport

◆ the arts

◆ heritage

◆ the millennium

◆ charities.

There is now a sixth good cause, the New Opportunities Fund, which superseded the millennium fund.

Lottery sport funding

By the end of 2000 the total amount donated by the Lottery to the good causes was around £10 billion, of which £1.5 billion had gone towards sport.

For every pound spent on a lottery ticket 28p goes to the good causes. More importantly, about 4p (actually 3.8p) goes towards sport.

It is the responsibility of the home country sports councils to allocate the money to the various lottery bids once they have received funding. The table below shows the amount that had been awarded by each sports council by 2001.

	NUMBER OF PROJECTS RECEIVING LOTTERY AWARDS	TOTAL AMOUNT GIVEN OUT IN MILLIONS OF POUNDS
Sport England	7033	1,224.20
Sport Scotland	2633	101.17
Sports Council for Northern Ireland	472	35.50
Sports Council for Wales	471	62.46
UK Sport	53	25.59

Lottery money is making a big difference to the funding of facilities such as leisure centres, swimming pools and the sports facilities in schools and colleges.

Often lottery money only goes part of the way for paying for something and will be given only on the condition that the rest of the money can be found from somewhere else. This is an example of **partnership funding** because two or more organisations come together as partners to fund something.

Two-strand approach

The Lottery money given to sport can be divided into two strands:

SPORTS LOTTERY FUNDING
- Supporting our top athletes and world class programmes
- Supporting sport in the community

Without Lottery funding fewer British athletes would have won medals in the 2000 Olympics

Supporting our top athletes

There was a strong feeling in the late 1990s that as a nation we really should be doing far better at sport.

This desire to win on the international stage prompted calls for financial schemes to support our athletes. It was felt that winning and achieving international success might:

- encourage more people to play
- make people throughout the country feel good
- generate more money that can be put back into sport to continue to fund improvements and drive standards of performance even higher.

Lottery funding is now used to try to help our national teams to do better on the international stage through the World Class Programme. Below are some of the ways that this done.

- **By giving athletes money to support themselves**. In order to reach the top sports people need to train for hours and hours, day after day. They also need to rest. You can imagine how difficult this is if you also have to work to support yourself.

- Lottery money is used to **support governing bodies** so that coaching, training, planning and facilities can all come together to give our athletes more chances.

- Lottery money is used to help **fund the United Kingdom Sports Institutes** where athletes can receive all the help and support they need, from sports medicine to specialist facilities.

- **Developing international facilities and encouraging major sports events to come to the UK**. For example, around £41 million of Lottery money was used to help the Millennium Stadium in Cardiff, which hosted the 1999 Rugby World Cup. This was around a third of the total cost.

There are also other uses for sports Lottery money, such as trying to encourage top sporting events to come to the UK, and funding our top coaches so that they can be better at what they do.

Supporting sport in the community

A wide range of organisations benefit from Lottery funding – from schools to sports clubs. Money has been allocated to a range of different projects, such as:

- Development of new sports facilities or renovating and upgrading existing ones.

- Small projects aimed to help organisations such as schools or voluntary groups. One particular focus has been poorer areas where facilities might not be so good or where disadvantaged groups do not have the chance to play.

- Awards to help all sections of society become involved in sport. An example is the Active Sports projects for young people.

In the early days of the Lottery most of the money went on big projects. In 1995/96 the average amount given to a sports Lottery bid was £250,000. By the year 2001 the average amount had gone down to £40,000, which shows that more and more grants are now being given to smaller projects.

ACTIVITY

Your Sports Lottery bid

You can do this activity on your own or in small groups.

Imagine that your school is putting in for a grant to the Sports Council for Lottery money to develop new sports facilities or to improve your existing sports facilities.

- List what improvements you would like to see at your school.

- Produce a sketch plan of the facilities you would like to see built or improved. This can be a simple drawing of what your facility will look like when the improvements are finished.

- Besides PE lessons state how else your new sports facility could be used – for instance, after-school sports clubs or other groups or clubs from the local community using the facilities in the evening. Remember, the more people who are going to use the facility, the more likely your chances of success in getting the money.

You may wish to look at neighbouring facilities to see what provisions they have for sport. Your report should consider the new sports that will be catered for by the facility so think about the specific facilities and equipment you will need.

Present your findings in a report format.

Answers to activities

Page 218

	£ IN MILLIONS
1. Manchester United	110.9
2. Bayern Munich	83.5
3. Real Madrid	76.1
4. Chelsea	59.1
5. Juventus	58.5
6. Barcelona	55.7
7. AC Milan	54.1
8. Lazio	50.0
9. Inter Milan	49.1
10. Arsenal	48.6
11. Liverpool	45.3
12. Newcastle United	44.7
13. Parma	44.4
14. Borussia Dortmund	43.9
15. Tottenham	42.6
16. AS Roma	39.4
17. Leeds United	37.0
18. Rangers	36.5
19. Aston Villa	34.9
20. Celtic	33.8

Note: figures are for the period 1999–2000.

Page 232

LIST A	LIST B	NOT LISTED
The Wimbledon Tennis Finals	Cricket Test Matches played in England	Great Britain Davis Cup Tennis matches
FIFA World Cup Finals Tournament	Wimbledon Tennis (not final matches)	England Football Internationals
The European Football Championships Finals Tournament	Other matches in the Rugby World Cup	Premier League Football matches
The FA Cup Final	The Rugby Union six Nations	The Boat Race
The Scottish FA Cup Final (in Scotland)	The Commonwealth Games	Champions League Football
The Grand National	The World Athletics Championships	
The Derby	The Cricket World Cup Final semis & matches involving home teams	
The Olympic Games	The Golf Ryder Cup	
The Rugby World Cup Final	The Open Golf Championship	
The Rugby League Challenge Cup Final		

The figure for the Athens Games is estimated at $1482 million!

Revising finance and funding of sport

This section is designed to help you improve your knowledge and understanding of finance and funding of sport.

In order to answer the questions you may well need to look back through the chapter to help you. Completing these questions successfully will help you prepare for your examination.

Money in professional sport

1. What does the term 'source of finance' mean?
2. Name four sources of finance other than gate receipts that provide football clubs with their income.
3. What is meant by the term 'product endorsement'?
4. Complete the sentence. The money that is spent on running the club is known as the ....

Amateur and professional sport

1. What is the difference between an amateur and a professional sportsperson? Use examples from different sports and different levels of performance to help you explain your answer.

Government spending in sport

1. What is the name of the local authority department that deals with sport?
2. Give four reasons why local authorities should spend money on sport and leisure facilities.
3. What is the role of UK Sport and Sport England in terms of the receipt of government funds?

Sports clubs and the sports governing bodies

1. Most sports clubs belong to the voluntary sector. How do they obtain their money?
2. If a member of a voluntary sport club is made treasurer, what is their role?

Sport and the media

1. A huge amount of sport is shown on television. Give three advantages to showing a sporting event on terrestrial television rather than on subscription channels.
2. Name three media (other than television) that cover sporting events.

Sponsorship

1 List three reasons why sport is used as a medium for sponsorship.

2 A cricket team are trying to gain sponsorship for the coming season. Identify two benefits that the club could give to a company to secure a sponsorship deal with them.

The National Lottery

1 How much money from every pound spent on the Lottery is invested in sport?

2 How much money has been invested in sport since the launch of the Lottery?

3 Name the two strands of sport that the National Lottery provides for.

4 Give two reasons why British sport needs to succeed on the international stage.

CHAPTER 9 Organisation of sport

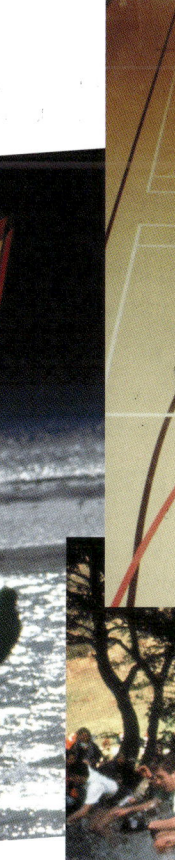

Many of you will participate in a number of activities during your leisure time. These activities are considered to be recreational as they are done at will, with no specific time scale. They do not have a regimented rule structure and can be seen as a form of play undertaken for enjoyment. An activity is usually regarded as a sport when it becomes more structured and organised with an element of competition.

In this chapter you will analyse the ways that people participate in sport other than as active players, investigate the organisation of sport at local, national and international levels and evaluate the roles of the bodies that are responsible for the organisationation of sport.

Hundreds of thousands of people take part in organised sport and recreation

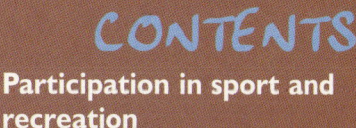

CONTENTS

Participation in sport and recreation	246
Organisation of sport at a local level	250
Organisation of sport at a national level	255
Organisation of sport at a international level	264
Revising organisation of sport	267

Participation in sport and recreation

Many people of all ages participate in sport at different levels. They may swim for a club, play hockey for their county, umpire cricket for their region or coach football at a national or international level. Some people do not play, officiate or manage but are involved in the organisation of sport.

Student

Many of you play sport or take part in recreational activities in your own time away from school. Most of you will take part in sport and recreation at school.

Your school provides you with the opportunity to take part in a range of sports and activities, and you will be taught the skills and techniques required to compete in that activity. You will also be given an understanding of the rules and laws governing that sport.

As part of the National Curriculum schools are required to offer a variety of sports. The sports and activities that schools can offer will often depend on teachers' abilities, specialisms and the school's' facilities and equipment.

You have the opportunity to study PE in more depth through your GCSE PE course. Some of you may want to work in sports and recreation when you leave school, perhaps as a coach, a teacher, an instructor, a physiotherapist or in management. You may have to do further study at college or university to achieve these goals.

ACTIVITY

Occupations in the sports industry

Identify the range of jobs or occupations that there are in the sport and recreation industry. You might like to do one of the jobs you have listed when you finish school.

Now identify the qualifications that you will need to pursue that role.

The government has also tried to promote sport in schools by offering an opportunity to gain The Sports Mark Award. To achieve this award a school must offer two hours a week for PE, organise extra-curricular sport, organise teams to play against other schools, enable teachers to attend further coaching courses and encourage students to participate in the governing bodies' award schemes.

Many of the national sports organisations are optimistic that if pupils and students are given the opportunity to participate in sport and have had a positive, enjoyable experience they will continue participating beyond their school years.

Whilst at school you will be given the opportunity to participate in a number of different sports. You may even want to continue participating in them when you leave school

Coach or teacher

In order to reach a certain level of skill a player needs instruction, advice, guidance, direction and motivation. The **coach's** job is to improve the performance of their athletes by:

◆ identifying technical and tactical faults

◆ correcting errors

◆ developing skill in their players

◆ analysing performance and monitor progress

◆ improving fitness

◆ encouraging mental preparation.

It is the coach's responsibility to nurture their performers and bring out their abilities.

The **teacher's** role is to introduce students to different sports, within the National Curriculum by:

◆ introducing students to the basic techniques

◆ developing skill in all students

◆ trying to develop competence across a range of sports

◆ developing a positive attitude about a healthy lifestyle

◆ developing an interest in at least one sport and so help students move from the school to the club or recreational sport system.

The roles of a coach and a teacher are very different. A coach usually has specialist and in-depth knowledge of one sport or one discipline within a sport. A coach will work with specialist performers from grass roots through to elite and world-class athletes; a teacher works across a range of sports and activities within the school environment. Coaches have responsibility for planning programmes of training for athletes over defined periods of time, say a season or an Olympic cycle, as opposed to a scheme of lessons. They will also know how to work within the world of competitive sport.

The role of the teacher is to introduce pupils to a range of sports at a grass-roots level.

Participation in sport and recreation

Official

All sports are governed by rules and regulations, which are designed to ensure that competition and play is both fair and safe.

The role of an official is to ensure fair play by ensuring that athletes compete within the rules. An official has to know and understand the rules of the sport and govern the competition in a controlled manner. Officials should be neutral, showing no bias towards one team or player.

If a player is seen to be breaking the rules then it is an official's job to give them some sort of punishment. For example, a player who intentionally fouls another player may receive a warning, a spell in the 'sin bin', a card or be sent off.

Some professional sports now have a 'third umpire' – the video referee – who has a crucial role to play if the action is too quick, the view of the official on the field is blocked or simply if he or she is in any doubt. For example, in cricket the third umpire (who has access to television replay) will often be asked to determine whether a player has been run out. In rugby league and union the video referee may be called to determine whether the ball has been grounded and the try should be awarded.

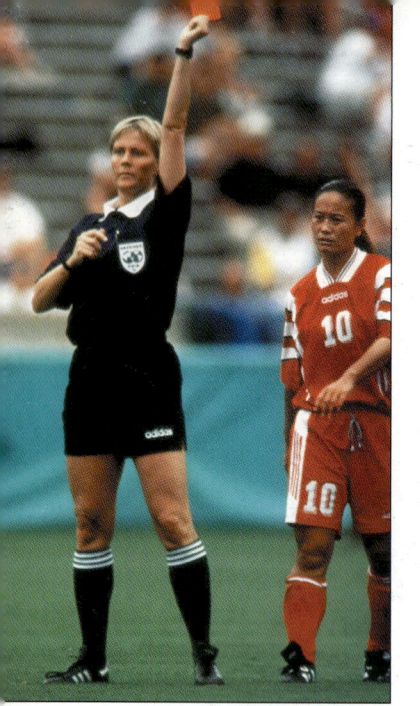

The role of the officials in sport is to promote fair play and penalise any player who breaks the rules and regulations

ACTIVITY

Officiating in sport

Choose a sport – it might be your favourite sport. What is the name given to the officials? How many are there? What is the role of each official?

Fitness instructor or trainer

People are now paying more attention to their individual levels of fitness, which has resulted in a sharp rise in individual and group or class training. There are now a vast number of jobs available within the industry as fitness instructors.

A fitness instructor or trainer has the task of getting a person physically fit. This may be for general fitness or to help players and athletes cope with the demands of their sport. Some people even have a personal trainer to help keep them motivated.

The fitness instructor plays a vital role in helping all people improve their levels of health and fitness

Spectator sport is a massive business. Millions of people every week will watch sport both live and on television

Spectator

Sport is exciting because nobody, not even the players, knows what will happen until the event is finished. Sport can be very dramatic and attracts large numbers of viewers or spectators. Millions of people all over the world watch sport at all levels – from proud parents, family members and friends who watch performances at the local club or school to ardent fans who hold season tickets and follow their team wherever they go, even overseas.

A large crowd can add to the excitement of the game or tournament and sometimes can influence the outcome of a game or match. Imagine the pressure Goran Ivanisovich felt on centre court at Wimbledon in 2001 playing against Tim Henman. A crowd of thousands of supporters can be difficult to play in front of and win. Listen at an International Rugby game when England are playing – the noise of 'Sweet Chariot' being sung will often drown out all other noise.

Fans help bring in revenue. At a voluntary sport club spectators may buy refreshments or attend fund-raising events to help the finances of the club. At professional level fans buy tickets, programmes and merchandise such as replica kits. All of these sales (in addition to sponsorship and TV rights) generate an income for the club.

Sport can attract a global TV audience. Events like the Olympics, The Superbowl, the FA Cup Final can be watched anywhere in the world. Watching from the comfort of your own home is often cheaper and more convenient than attending the match in person. There are now, especially on cable and Sky television-dedicated sports channels. Some of these are interactive and allow the home viewer access to various statistics, replays and individual 'player cams'.

Organisation of sport at a local level

In order to cater for the wide range of interests, ages and needs that people may have within a local community sport must be organised on a wide scale.

In your local area there may be many different facilities. There are outdoor areas, which will include local parks and sport pitches, and possibly lakes, reservoirs or rivers that are used for water sports such as sailing or water skiing and outdoor pursuit facilities. Indoor facilities are usually purpose built in areas where there is a demand. These may include swimming pools, leisure centres and fitness gyms. A large majority of these facilities are provided and maintained by the local council.

Local authority provision

It is the responsibility of the **local authority** or council to provide facilities for the people living in their area. These can include educational facilities (such as schools or libraries) and recreational facilities such as leisure centres. Some schools have sports and leisure centres on their site which 'double up', acting as education providers and catering for community sport and recreation interests. They are referred to as **dual-use facilities**. The school has exclusive use of the facility during the school day and school term and the community has access at all other times, including evenings and weekends. **Sports colleges** provide increased opportunities for participation and performance, and have some of the best facilities available.

Local authority sports centres can cater for a wide range of interests

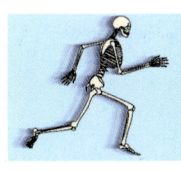

Sporting facilities in schools
Is your school a Sports College or dual-use facility? What facilities does it have? How does it differ from other schools in the area?

Council planners have to ensure that the public can get to facilities easily by both private and public transport. Access to the building must be acceptable for both able-bodied and disabled visitors.

Some dual-use facilities have a pool, track, an all-weather turf and grass fields. They may have a health suite, aerobic studios and sports halls. Sport and leisure centres do not just cater for the recreational sportsperson but also organise games, leagues and events for those who like to compete against others.

ACTIVITY

Recreational facilities in your local area

Name as many indoor centres, outdoor areas and clubs available in your area as you can. State whether they are dual-use facilities or not. Give examples of some of the activities and services they provide. List them as either sport or recreation.

Funding

Local authority facilities are organised, managed and funded largely by national or local government. They have a duty to provide a range of services for the local community and are not profit oriented, although they do have be cost effective.

Access to a large number of facilities is free and no direct payment is needed – examples are libraries, playgrounds, urban parks, beaches, picnic areas and country parks. Payment for use of these facilities is indirect, that is they are paid for through rates and taxes (specifically the council tax), which are charged to each household.

For the use of other facilities such as swimming pools, sports centres, playing fields, golf courses, marinas and art centres there is direct charge, although this is often highly subsidised. You may find that the costs of participation in a similar activity at a private or commercial centre will be higher as there is often no subsidy. Private facilities may, however, employ a range of concessions for 'under-privileged' groups during off-peak times.

◀ BACK *local government spending on sport, p.226*

The private sector

Private sector facilities (also referred to as **commercial organisations**) are profit oriented and their aim is to achieve a significant return on their investment through the provision of leisure and recreation products and services.

The private sector has developed a range of facilities and activities to cater for a wide range of interests. These include:

- active leisure and health clubs
- sports clubs (both indoors and outdoors)
- holiday villages
- golf and country clubs.

ACTIVITY

Private sector provision

From the list you compiled earlier choose one facility in your area that is privately run.

Compare that facility with a similar one that is run by the local authority. Make a list of the similarities and differences. Compare prices, facilities and the quality of service.

Funding

Private clubs can offer a wide range of activities and may even be attached to a hotel or holiday park, offering membership to the public as well as allowing guests to enjoy the facilities. Private clubs are organised on a business basis to make a profit. Larger companies will have more outlays (such as paying staff and for the upkeep of the venue) so they find many ways of making money – such as selling merchandise (sport shirts, mugs, key rings, etc. with the company logo printed on them).

An example of the private sector health clubs is the David Lloyd Centres, the premier racquet, health and fitness chain. There are 54 clubs all over the country that focus primarily on tennis, usually providing both indoor and outdoor courts. They also have fitness gyms, squash courts, swimming pools with spas, beauty salons, bars and restaurants. In some clubs there is access to sports injury clinics, personal trainers, lifestyle counselling and nutritional advice. The clubs cater for individuals and families and there are usually facilities for children including a crèche. There is a joining fee and an annual membership. Members are given a free lifestyle magazine that includes discounts on a number of services. Such centres are more than just a means of keeping fit – they provide a social centre for people.

ACTIVITY

Analysing the fitness industry

Find out if there is a private gym complex in your area. Is it a national organisation? What facilities does it provide?

How does the gym compare with other private companies or the local authority in terms of prices, the ranges of activities, classes, equipment and instruction?

Who in your opinion provides the best service?

Voluntary sector organisations and clubs

Voluntary sector organisations exist to provide a service that may not otherwise be provided by the public or private sectors.

It is estimated that there are 150,000 voluntary sports clubs affiliated to the national governing bodies. Local voluntary sporting clubs make up a large part of the framework of organised sport in the UK.

Sports clubs are organised to perform a variety of functions.

- To provide facilities for people wishing to participate in sport.
- To organise competition within their club and against other clubs. Often a club may have a number of different teams in county, regional and national leagues or competitions.
- To encourage younger people to participate in the sport by providing junior teams and coaching.
- To promote the sport to involve more people.

There are clubs for almost every sport – from cycling to scuba diving. Some have their own facilities and others simply hire public or council-run facilities. For example, a hockey club may have its own clubhouse and grass pitches but could also hire artificial hockey pitches for extra practice.

The organisation of sport in the voluntary sector relies on the work of unpaid volunteers. Sport England (1997), in their survey of the voluntary sector, noted that volunteers are the 'backbone' of British sport, making a massive 'in kind' contribution as coaches, managers and officials. In 1995 it was estimated that the total annual value of the UK sports volunteer market was over £1.5 billion and that there were about 1.5 million volunteers in UK sport.

Club structure

The way in which a club is organised will depend upon its size, its facilities, its membership, how many teams it runs and the range of fixtures or competitions it is involved with. Martial arts clubs, for example, tend to be led by one or two people who set up classes in leisure centres or community halls and affiliate to their governing body. Bowls and tennis clubs and many team sports often have a more democratic structure.

This traditional organisational structure for voluntary sector sports clubs involves the election of officers to a club **committee**. Normally the club members elect the committee to administer the club for a year at an annual general meeting. Each position on the committee has a distinct role or job.

- The **Chairperson** or **President** is usually considered to hold the most senior position. They have overall control at club meetings and may represent the club at other meetings.
- The **Vice-chairperson** or **Vice-president** is deputy to the Chairperson and covers for them where necessary.

- The **Secretary** has to take minutes (notes) at the meetings and deal with any other written work (answering letters, etc.).
- The **Treasurer** deals with the financial aspects of the club, collecting members' subscriptions and match fees.
- The **Fixture Secretary** organises the team's home and away fixtures for the playing season.
- The **Social Secretary** usually organises social events and fund-raisers for the club.
- **Team captains** are responsible for the welfare of their players and organise the team for each week, sometimes in association with the coach.
- The **Coaches** train the teams and prepare them for games and important competitions.

In small clubs the committee members usually do their work on a voluntary basis. However, at larger or more professional clubs people are paid for their committee work.

A club normally affiliates to the national governing body through the local county or regional association, depending on the structure of the governing body. Once affiliated to the governing body the club is able to enter leagues and tournaments and send representatives to local meetings of the governing body association.

◀ BACK **The National Lottery, p.239**

Funding

One of the voluntary sector's most distinguishing characteristics is its constant struggle for financial security. Funds are usually generated through a variety of sources, in the first instance from its member's pockets via annual membership fees, subscriptions and participation costs or admission fees. Often players in amateur sports clubs have to play for the privilege of training and competing.

Voluntary associations and clubs also rely heavily on fund raising, through the traditional jumble and car boot sales, raffles, race nights, etc.

Sometimes voluntary clubs receive financial grants such as National Lottery funding to build new facilities.

◀ BACK **The National Lottery, p.239**

Organisation of sport at a national level

The figure shows an overview of the central government departments responsible for sport in the UK.

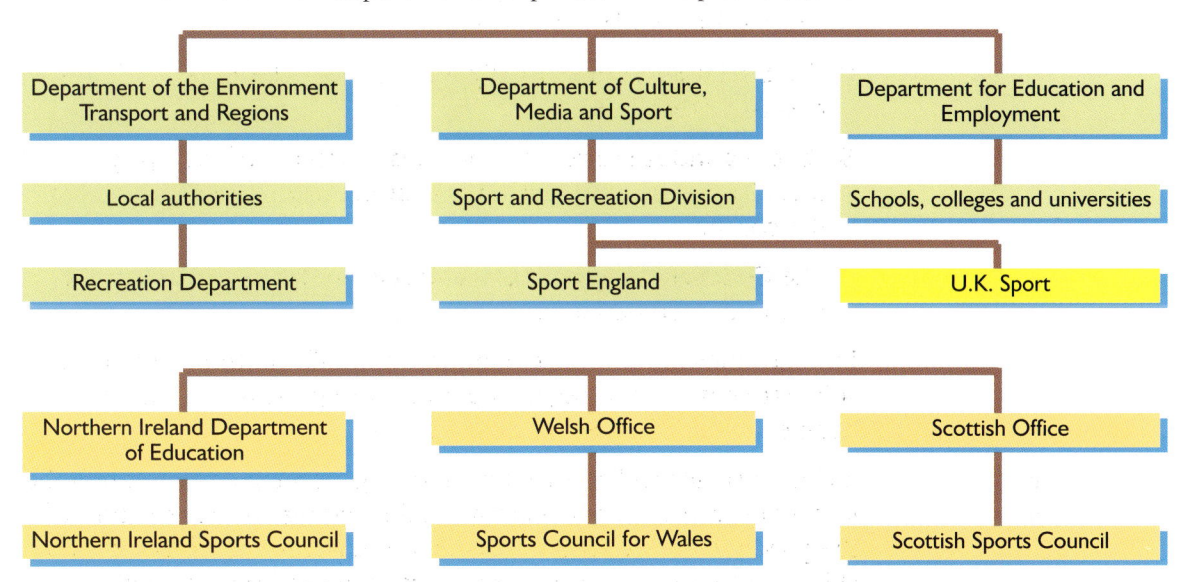

```
Department of the Environment        Department of Culture,           Department for Education and
Transport and Regions                Media and Sport                  Employment

Local authorities                    Sport and Recreation Division    Schools, colleges and universities

Recreation Department                Sport England                    U.K. Sport

Northern Ireland Department          Welsh Office                     Scottish Office
of Education

Northern Ireland Sports Council      Sports Council for Wales         Scottish Sports Council
```

Central government departments responsible for sport in the UK. Source: Sport England Information Fact Sheet 17

The **Department of Culture, Media and Sport** aims to promote wider participation in sport and support the development of sporting excellence.

In 1997, following the government policy paper *Sport – Raising the Game*, the GB Sports Council was abolished and in its place two new organisations were created. The English Sports Council (**Sport England**) was created to take overall responsibility for the development of sport in England. The Sports Councils in Wales, Scotland and Northern Ireland were already well established.

The UK-wide responsibilities were taken over by a new organisation called **UK Sport**.

Sport England

Sport England is funded by the Department of Culture, Media and Sport and is accountable to parliament through the Secretary of State for Culture, Media and Sport.

The main objective of Sport England is to work in partnership with the public, private and voluntary sectors in order to achieve:

'More places to play sport, More people playing sport, More medals.'

In order to achieve these aims Sport England has developed a number of initiatives as part of their **Active Programme**:

◆ Active Schools
◆ Active Communities

Organisation of sport at a national level 255

Holme Pierrepoint is one of the National Sport Centres. It specialises in water sports

- Active Sports
- World Class.

Most of these initiatives are delivered through partner organisations including local authorities, governing bodies and schools.

Sport England runs six national sports centres – Crystal Palace, Lilleshall, Bisham Abbey, Plas-y Brenin, Holme Pierrepoint and the Manchester Cycling Centre.

ACTIVITY

The National Sports Centres

Find as much information as you can about the National Sports Centres of the UK, including the sports, the performers and teams that train at these sites and their location.

UK Sport

UK Sport was established in January 1997, to focus on high performance sport at the UK level, with the aim of achieving sporting excellence on the world stage. UK Sport is divided into three directorates:

- Performance Services – through distributing lottery funds to UK level sports with world Class performance plans and through providing support through United Kingdom Sports Institutes.
- Ethics and Anti Doping Control.
- International Relations and Major Events – responsible for assisting bids to bring major sports tournaments to the UK.

In 1998/99 UK Sport received approximately £11.5 million from the government and around £20 million to distribute as Lottery grants.

Sport Scotland

Sport Scotland has a new strategy for the twenty-first century, called Sport 21.

- As part of its *Widening Participation* strategy £4.5 million has been pledged to offer every school in Scotland a sport co-ordinator. About 200,000 children have taken part in Team Sport Scotland Camps and activities. Over £200 million of new facility investment has been created by its Lottery fund.

- As part of the *Developing Potential* campaign 12,000 coaches and leaders have taken part in Team Sport Scotland activities and training courses. In 1998/99 Sport Scotland national training centres delivered over 50,000 student days of sports training.

- As part of the *Achieving Excellence* programme 50 coaches supported by the Performance Coach Development Programme and five Scottish Institute of Sport coaches were appointed.

- Two million pounds was used to support 500 athletes from 40 different sports and a further £1.6 million awarded toward a hockey training and competition centre.

Sports Council for Wales

The mission of the **Sports Council for Wales** is:

'Increasing Participation, Raising Standards, Improving Facilities, Providing Information and Advice.'

The Council supports the Welsh Institute of Sport and the Plas Menai National Water Sports Centre.

In 1999/2000 its income was over £9 million (of which around £6.7 million was grant in aid from government) plus around £11 million of Lottery money to distribute.

The Sports Council for Northern Ireland

The aim of the **Sports Council for Northern Ireland** is:

'Starting Well, Staying Involved, Striving for Excellence.'

The Council supports the Tollymore Mountain Centre and is involved with the development of the United Kingdom Sports Institute Northern Ireland.

It also contributed £2.5 million towards a 200 m hydraulic athletics track, an activity floor and an international-scale ice-hockey pad at the Belfast Odyssey. In 1999/2000 it received government grants totalling £2.27 million and Lottery money for distribution of around £7.5 million.

The national governing bodies of sport

Sports governing bodies like the Football Association, the Rugby Football Union or the Lawn Tennis Association are names that you might recognise. The main role of these bodies is to administer their sport within their home country and to represent their sport abroad by affiliating to their international sports federation.

Many sports governing bodies were established towards the end of the nineteenth century as a result of the need to harmonise rules, organise competition and co-ordinate the clubs or the local associations that had formed them.

Today there are over 400 independent governing bodies, some of which are organised on a home country basis while others are responsible for that sport within the UK as a whole. They have the responsibility to oversee the national development, administration and organisation of their sport.

Governing bodies range in size from large organisations such as the Football Association to smaller associations that rely on volunteers. All governing bodies, regardless of their size, share a number of common responsibilities:

- framing and amending rules
- implanting disciplinary procedures
- organising national competitions and events
- developing coaching award structures
- selecting and training national squads.

sports governing bodies, p.230

ACTIVITY

Governing bodies in sport

Can you name the national governing body of your favourite sport? For three other sports? Look at the roles and responsibilities of the governing bodies.

In the 1990s many governing bodies changed their structure in order to respond to the growing commercialism in sport and the need to produce athletes who can compete with the best.

Governing bodies employ development officers and coaches to help promote the sport, increase participation levels and improve performance. This helps keep sport alive and people interested enough to participate in some fashion.

A national governing body is usually connected to the international sports federation.

organisation of international sport, p.264

sports coach UK

In April 2001, the National Coaching Foundation (NCF) was renamed **sports coach UK** (**scUK**). The intention of the new name was to emphasise commitment to raising the profile of coaching, developing coaching as a profession and supporting individual coaches to enhance their skills within the UK

scUK wants coaching in the UK to be recognised as world class, in both its practice and achievements. It is dedicated to guiding the development and implementation of a coaching system, recognised as a world leader, for all coaches in the UK.

scUK works closely with partner organisations such as the British Olympic Association, the British Paralympic Association and the home country sports councils. Vital financial support is provided by UK Sport and Sport England.

scUK has a High Performance Coaching Unit. Its role is to support elite level coaches, to improve their knowledge and skills.

scUK has a UK-wide network, including ten coaching development officers based at Sport England's Regional Training Units. It also has partnerships with the coaching units of Northern Ireland, Scotland and Wales. Vital financial support is provided by UK Sport and Sport England.

In 1998/99 the NCF had an annual turnover of around £3.4 million, consisting of:

Grant aid from UK Sport and Sport England	72.7%
Earned income	22.2%
Subscriptions	5.1%

In 1999 the NCF had 110 Premier Coaching centres in England, running coaching workshops covering a wide range of coaching themes. These workshops are designed to improve coaches' knowledge, awareness and ultimately ability to improve their performers' skills. The workshops cover a number of areas, including 'The Body in Action', 'Planning and Practise' and 'Child Protection'.

Each year 15,000 coaches and 12,000 schoolteachers participate in NCF programmes. Since its inception in 1983 the NCF has provided developmental and educational opportunities for some 130,000 coaches.

The British Olympic Association

The **British Olympic Association** (**BOA**) is an independent body that is made up of representatives of the national governing bodies of Olympic sports.

The BOA is responsible for organising the participation of British teams in the Olympic Games, setting standards for selection and raising funds (for the Sydney Olympics, British Airways, Adidas and Rover all supported the British Olympic team). Despite this support there is frequently the need for extra finance. For the Sydney

Olympics the British Olympic Appeal was launched, with the aim of raising £4 million.

Between Olympic Games the BOA makes vital contributions to the preparation of its competitors. The British Olympic Medical Centre at Northwick Park has been developed to provide a range of medical services. The governing bodies and athletes also receive specialist advice and knowledge in areas such as bio-mechanics, nutrition and psychology.

The British Paralympic Association

The **British Paralympic Association** (**BPA**) works in conjunction with the BOA and the sports councils and provides Britain's Paralympic athletes with the organisational back-up to give them the best chance of winning medals at the Paralympic Games.

The British Paralympic Association sent a 214 strong team to Sydney in 2000.

Disability sports organisations

All sports providers have a responsibility for people with disability. There are, however, specialist disability organisations whose main role is to oversee the development of disability sport. In England the English Federation of Disability Sport (EFDS) is the umbrella body that works with the seven National Disability Sports Organisations. The seven organisations are:

- British Blind Sports (BBS)
- British Wheelchair Sports Federation (BWSF)
- British Amputee and Les Autres Sports Association (BALASA)
- Cerebral Palsy Sport (CP Sport)
- British Deaf Sports Council (BDFC)
- UK English Sports Association for People With Learning Difficulties
- Disability Sports England (DSE)

ACTIVITY

Disability sport and elite performance

Choose one event from the Sydney Paralympic Games. Who was the winner?

Now choose a British medallist from the Games. State the event in which he or she was successful. Which organisation from the list above might that competitor belong to?

Now choose a swimming or athletics event that appears in both the Olympic and Paralympic Games. Identify the differences between the competitions. What was the difference in the winning times or distances between each competition? Comment on how big the gap is between the ability levels.

United Kingdom Sports Institute

The **UK Sports Institute** (**UKSI**) aims to provide the facilities and support needed to give elite sportsmen and women the best chance of winning at international level. There are ten regional institutes in England, each with a co-ordinating focal point, and institutes in Scotland, Wales and Northern Ireland.

Institutes make use of a wide variety of facilities and services in each area. Each institute is responsible for a certain area. It then has to co-ordinate and support athletes and all the other people involved such as their coaches, sport scientists and medical support.

Sport England looked at the work done by the East Midlands region at the Holme Pierrepoint centre and stated that:

'The purpose of each institute is to provide specialist training facilities, but equally importantly, nation-wide access to a range of services. In practice, the institute is a co-ordinating mechanism to harness the services in the local area.'

'In the East Midlands for example, Holme Pierrepoint will provide facilities for canoeing and rowing, and some sports medicine and some sports science, but it will also harness the services of the nearby Queens Medical Centre in Nottingham and the facilities, skills and services provided by Loughborough University.'

They also reported on the work done by the home country sports institutes:

- The **Scottish Institute of Sport** was launched in 1998 with the initial aim of supporting athletics, badminton, curling, hockey, football, rugby and swimming.

- The **Northern Ireland Sports Council** is working in partnership with Ulster University to use an £18 million budget to develop the site and training facilities.

- The **UKSI in Wales** has begun spending its £22 million capital budget, such as the £4 million national centre for cricket opened in partnership with Glamorgan County Cricket Club.

The Central Council of Recreation (CCPR)

The **CCPR** has an important role to play as an independent organisation outside of the government funded and appointed sports councils. Its role (amongst other things) is as an organisation where national governing and other representative bodies could be represented and collectively 'formulate and promote measures to improve and develop sport.'

It is divided into six divisions and each of the 285 governing or representative bodies are placed in a division that is most relevant to their activity:

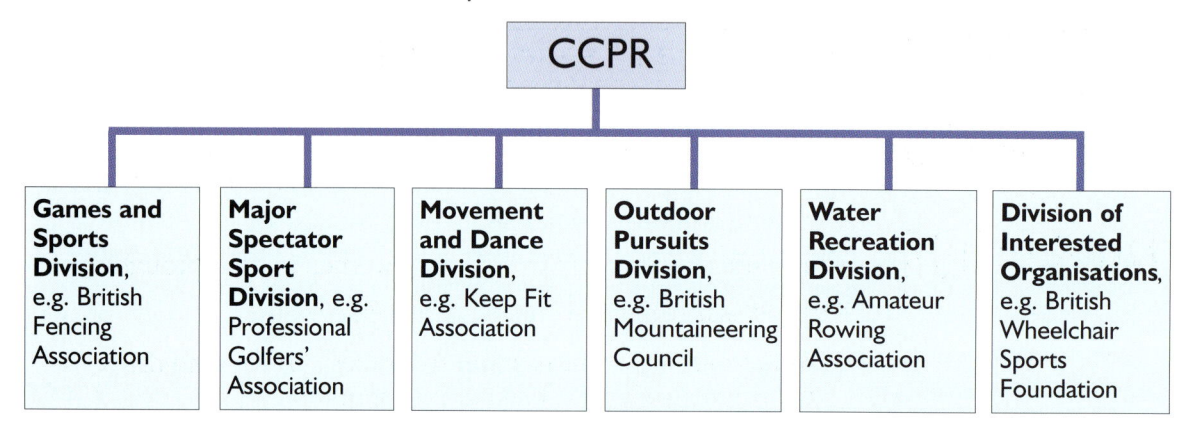

```
                              CCPR
   ┌──────┬──────┬──────┬──────┬──────┐
Games   Major   Movement Outdoor Water   Division
and     Spectator and     Pursuits Recreation of
Sports  Sport    Dance   Division Division Interested
Division Division Division                 Organisations
```

- **Games and Sports Division**, e.g. British Fencing Association
- **Major Spectator Sport Division**, e.g. Professional Golfers' Association
- **Movement and Dance Division**, e.g. Keep Fit Association
- **Outdoor Pursuits Division**, e.g. British Mountaineering Council
- **Water Recreation Division**, e.g. Amateur Rowing Association
- **Division of Interested Organisations**, e.g. British Wheelchair Sports Foundation

Each division elects a chairperson and a supporting member who supervise the divisional meetings and who sit on the executive committee of the CCPR.

In 1989 the CCPR set up a charitable arm called the British Sports Trust with the aim of providing administration and funds for its leadership awards. The most popular of these awards is the Community Sports Leaders Award (CSLA). Completion of this award allows people to work in the community assisting a coach in the delivery of sports and activity.

National Playing Fields Association

The National Playing Fields Association (NPFA) was founded in 1925 and one of the its most long lasting contributions has been the setting of the 6-acre standard, which recommends 6 acres of playing field for every 1000 of population.

The NPFA is a charitable trust, which has had a Royal Charter since 1933. The NPFA aims to stop building development on playing fields and gives advice and information to support campaigns aimed at preserving playing fields that are under threat.

Today the NPFA owns 138 playing fields and has custodial responsibility for around 1,700 others. In 1999, according to the NPFA there were over 900 sites under threat.

ACTIVITY

Playing fields – a future in doubt?

Make a list of the playing fields and green spaces in your area, and identify them on a map of your locality. Is there enough green space in your opinion? Are there residential areas that are too far away from green space for young children to reach them? Do you think anything can be done about the problem?

Look up the NPFA website (www.npfa.co.uk) to see if any playing fields near you are under threat, and to find out what you can do about it if they are.

The Women's Sports Foundation

The Women's Sports Foundation (WSF) was founded in 1984 and is the only organisation in the UK that is solely committed to improving and promoting opportunities for women and girls in sport at every level. Their vision is:

'To pursue and promote equity for women in and through sport.'

The WSF is a registered charity with five key aims:

- ◆ **To increase awareness** about the issues surrounding the involvement of women and girls in sport.
- ◆ **To support women and girls** to become involved in sport at all levels and in all capacities.
- ◆ **To encourage organisations** to improve access to sporting opportunities for women and girls.
- ◆ **To challenge instances of inequality** in sport and seek to bring about change.
- ◆ **To raise the visibility** of all British sportswomen.

The Women's Sports Foundation is committed to encouraging women to take part in sport at all levels

Organisation of sport at a national level

Organisation of sport at international level

Nelson Mandela stated that:

Sport is probably the most effective means of communication in the modern world, bypassing both verbal and written communication and reaching directly out to billions of people world-wide. There is no doubt that sport is a viable and legitimate way of building friendships between nations.

International sport is now commonplace. Football teams will travel mid-week for European Cup competition. Tennis and golf competitions are world-wide. Athletics has a European circuit. International sport and competition is the responsibility of a number of organisations.

International sports federations

International sports federations (**ISFs**) such as FIBA (International Basketball Federation) or FIH (International Hockey Association) are the governing bodies of sport at international level.

The structures of these organisations vary from sport to sport but generally their role is to administer their sport, implement policies on an international basis, make the rules and oversee the affiliated national governing bodies from each country.

The ISFs also organise international championships in their sport such as the IAAF World Athletics Championships or the FIFA football World Cup. Many sports also have international regional organisations that run competitions such as the EUFA Champions League.

ACTIVITY

Organising international competition

Identify the ISF for your sport.

Identify one international competition that the ISF is responsible for. How is the sport organised, managed and funded at International level?

The Olympic movement

The French educator Baron Pierre de Coubertin had the inspiration to revive the Olympic Games. In order to help achieve his dream he founded the International Olympic Committee (IOC) on June 23 1894, which acted as the creator of the modern Olympic movement. An Olympic Charter was developed which stipulates rules, bylaws and principles for the IOC to follow.

The Olympic movement includes the IOC, national Olympic committees, the Olympic Games organising committees, national sports associations, clubs, members and athletes. The aim of the

The site of the first modern Olympic games in 1896

movement is to provide an arena where athletes can compete fairly with mutual understanding and solidarity with fellow Olympians.

The first modern Olympics were held in Athens in 1896, with just 311 athletes competing in six sports. Since that time the Olympics have flourished into a global international movement, with an estimated 10,000 athletes competing in 296 events across 28 sports in Sydney 2000.

The summer and winter Olympic games are held every 4 years. Since 1984 the games have been staggered and summer and winter Games are now held 2 years apart from each other.

The International Olympic Committee

The IOC, based in Lausanne Switzerland, is the global organisation responsible for the administration of the Olympic movement. It is a non-profit organisation, which has no government involvement.

The IOC is responsible for selecting the host cities for both the summer and winter Olympics and running the movement's educational and commercial activities.

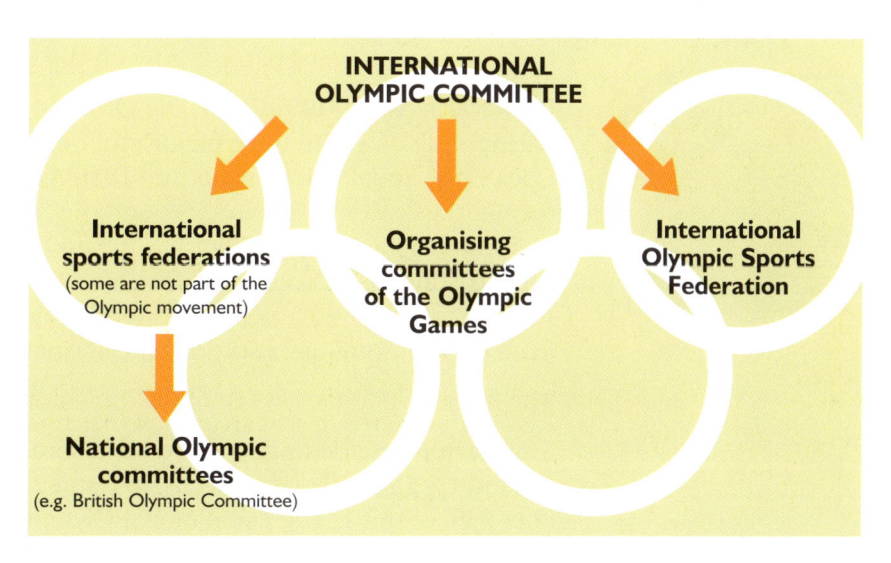

The 'Olympic family'

The figure above shows the organising structure of the Olympic movement. It is often referred to as the 'Olympic family'.

Organisation of sport at international level **265**

The IOC has 28 affiliated summer federations such as FIG (International Gymnastics Federation) and IWF (International Weightlifting Federation) and seven affiliated winter federations such as FIS (International Ski Federation).

The IOC also undertakes a preliminary selection process for cities bidding to host the games. A successful bid for the staging of the Olympics requires the foundation of an organising committee, who have the huge task of staging the Games and providing and arranging the facilities and accommodation for thousands of athletes.

In 1998 ATHOC (the organising Committee for the 2004 Athens Games) was created to allow 6 years for planning and development.

There are currently 200 national Olympic committees affiliated to the Olympic movement. Only cities that win their domestic selection through their national Olympic committee can be forwarded to the IOC for selection.

Olympic funding

In 1984 only the city of Los Angeles was prepared to host the Olympic Games. Many interested cities were put off by the enormous costs and commitment involved in being a host city. One fear was that they could be left with crippling financial problems after the Games were completed. Montreal in Canada in 1976 suffered just such problems.

Los Angeles was the first Games in recent history to make a profit and 13 cities made bids to host the 2004 Games.

The Olympic Partners

After the 1984 Games the IOC decided to restructure its system of sponsorship. As a result The Olympic Partners (TOP) was created as a sponsorship scheme involving major multi-national corporations. The Olympic partners provide revenue and services in exchange for exclusive rights in their own areas and the global coverage and image that comes with being associated with the Olympic movement.

In its fourth cycle, 1997–2001, the Olympic movement had 11 partners, all of whom were major multi-national companies such as Coca Cola, Kodak, McDonalds and IBM. All 200 national Olympic committees receive revenue through the programme. The effect of this sponsorship arrangement has meant that whereas in 1980 broadcasting rights accounted for 95% of the income, sponsorship now accounts for 36% of the IOC marketing revenue. The income from broadcasting has also dramatically increased.

The figure top left shows the breakdown of Olympic funding.

This Olympic marketing revenue was estimated to have generated around US $3.5 billion between 1997 and 2001. The IOC distributes over 93% of this to the 200 national Olympic committees and their Olympic teams, the ISFs and the organising committees for the Olympic Games.

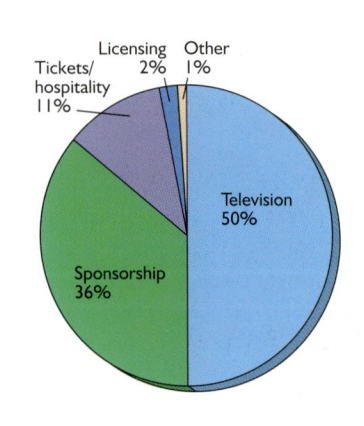

Revising organisation of sport

This section is designed to help you improve your knowledge and understanding of the organisation of sport.

In order to answer the questions you may well need to look back through the chapter to help you. Completing these questions successfully will help you prepare for your examination.

Participation in sport and recreation

1. Other than as an active participant, name three different ways in which individuals can take part in sport and recreation.
2. Give three different responsibilities of an official in sport.

Organisation of sport at a local level

1. What is meant by the term 'dual-use facility'?
2. When visiting a public sport centre you have to pay to use the facilities. However, these prices are usually subsidised. Who helps provide the funding for a local authority facility?
3. What is the role of the voluntary sport organisations?
4. Anil is a member of a football club and has been asked to undertake the position of Fixture Secretary next season. What would he have to do for the club if he is voted into this position?

Organisation of sport at a national level

1. In 1997 the GB Sports Council was abolished. Which two organisations took its place?
2. UK Sport is divided into three directorates. Can you name them?
3. What are the three main aims for the Scottish, Welsh and Northern Ireland Sport Councils?
4. Most sports are affiliated to a national governing body. What is the purpose of these governing bodies?
5. What do the initials BPA stand for?

Organisation of sport at an international level

1. Why does Britain have an international sports federation?
2. Who was responsible for the revival of the Olympic movement?
3. What organisations does the Olympic movement include?
4. Name two Olympic Partners and identify their role.

Answers to revision questions

Revising anatomy and physiology

The skeletal system

1 **A** cranium; **B** humerus; **C** radius; **D** pelvis; **E** phalanges; **F** femur; **G** metatarsals.

2

NUMBERED JOINT	TYPE OF JOINT
1	Ball and socket
2	Pivot
3	Fixed
4	Saddle
5	Hinge
6	Condyloid

3 **a** Any one of elbow, shoulder, knee, hip, fingers, wrist; **b** atlas and axis, wrist, ankle; **c** shoulder or hip; **d** hip or shoulder; **e** hip or shoulder.

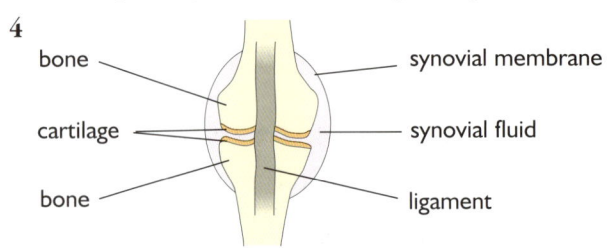

4 Diagram labelled: bone, cartilage, bone, synovial membrane, synovial fluid, ligament.

5 Ligaments.

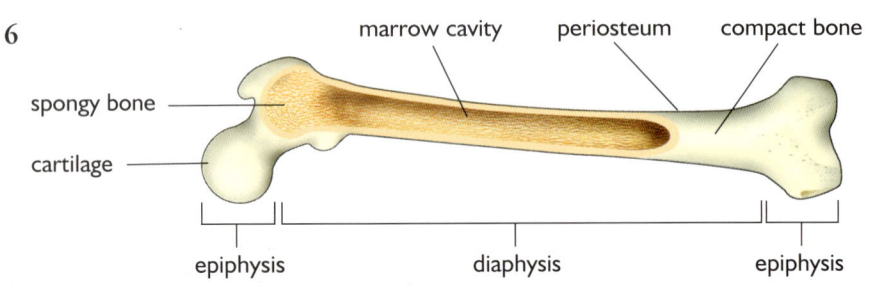

6 Diagram labelled: spongy bone, cartilage, marrow cavity, periosteum, compact bone, epiphysis, diaphysis, epiphysis.

7 **A** short bone; **B** long bone; **C** irregular bone; **D** flat bone.

8 To protect the bone from wear; to provide a smooth surface for the bones to articulate.

The muscular system

1 **a** Any skeletal muscle; **b** any part of the gut; **c** the heart.

2 Tendons.

3 Antagonistic.

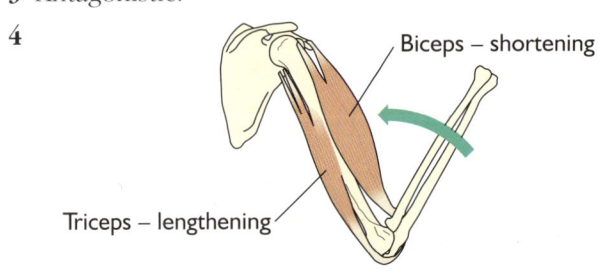

4 Diagram labelled: Biceps – shortening; Triceps – lengthening.

5 Third order.

6 Muscles are made up of **fast** twitch and **slow** twitch fibres. **Fast** twitch fibres contract quickly and can be used for **explosive** movements. **Slow** twitch fibres contract slowly and can be used for **endurance** activities.

7 **a** Isotonic contraction is when the muscle contracts and the muscle length shortens; **b** in isometric contraction the muscle is tense, but the muscle fibres do not change length; **c** in isokinetic contraction the speed of the contraction stays the same.

The respiratory system

1

FEATURE	LETTER
bronchioles	B
larynx	F
lung	D
pharynx	G
pleura	C
trachea	E
bronchus	A

2 It contracts.

3 Oxygen, carbon dioxide and nitrogen.

4 Oxygen diffuses through the walls of the alveoli and the blood capillaries into the bloodstream to be carried round the body. At the same time carbon dioxide diffuses from the blood into the alveoli to be expelled from the lungs as you breathe out.

5 The tidal volume.

6 Vital capacity is the **maximum** amount of air you can breathe **in** after breathing as deeply as you can.

7 Respiratory rate.

8 The rate of breathing and the tidal volume both increase, which increases the amount of oxygen supplied to the blood. The heart beats more quickly, pumping the blood around the body more quickly and so increasing the oxygen supply to the working muscles.

The circulatory system

1

STRUCTURE	LETTER
left atrium	D
right ventricle	G
superior vena cava	K
pulmonary vein	C
right atrium	I
pulmonary artery	B
tricuspid valve	H
pulmonary valve	J
left ventricle	F
septum	L
aorta	A
bicuspid valve	E

2 In all but one case veins carry **deoxygenated** blood **to** the heart. Arteries carry **oxygenated** blood away from the heart. The pulmonary artery carries **deoxygenated** blood from the heart and the pulmonary vein carries **oxygenated** blood back from the **lungs** to the heart.

3 White cells, platelets and plasma.

4 Red blood cells.

5 Any of: arteries thick walls, high blood pressure, no valves, more elastic; veins thin walls, lower blood pressure, have valves, less elastic.

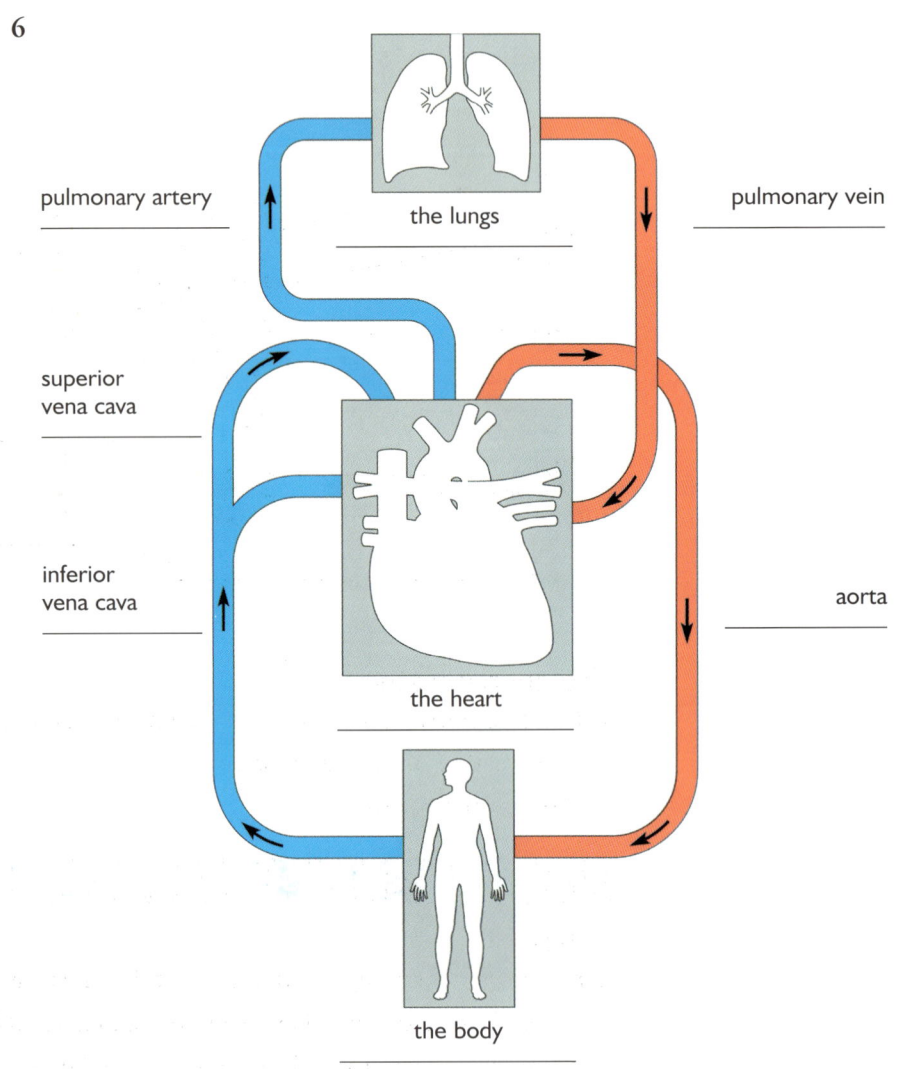

6

pulmonary artery — the lungs — pulmonary vein

superior vena cava

inferior vena cava — the heart — aorta

the body

7 Stroke volume × heart rate.

8 **a** diastolic; **b** systolic.

9 Any three from: exercise, age, stress or tension, diet, smoking habits, alcohol intake.

The nervous system

1 Brain, spinal cord, network of nerves, receptor organs.

The hormonal system

1 It is located at the base of the brain. It controls the endocrine system by producing hormones that stimulate or inhibit the other glands.

The digestive system

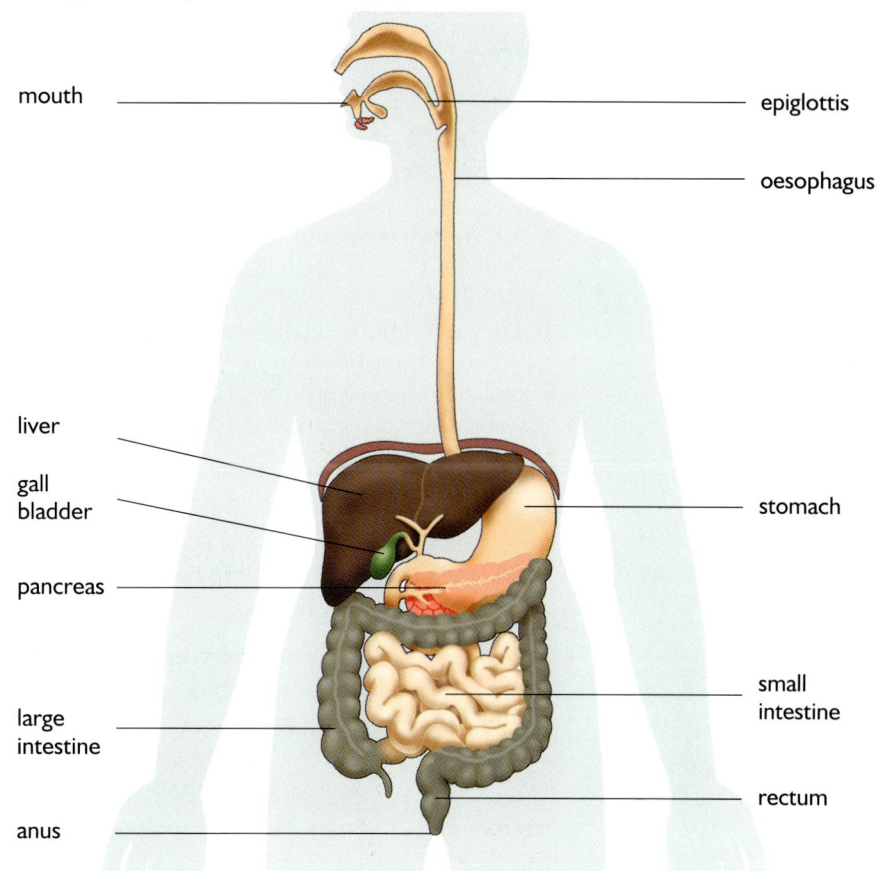

1

- mouth
- epiglottis
- oesophagus
- liver
- gall bladder
- pancreas
- stomach
- small intestine
- large intestine
- rectum
- anus

The energy systems

1. Creatine phosphate, lactic acid system and the oxygen (aerobic) system.
2. The creatine phosphate system.
3. The aerobic system.

Revising fitness, testing and training

Fitness

1. **a** Fitness = meeting the demands of the environment.
   b Health = free from disease and emotional trouble.
   c Social well being = belonging to and feeling valued in society.
2. Cardiovascular endurance, muscular endurance, muscular strength, flexibility and body composition.
3. Aerobic fitness, working the heart and lungs. Sports in which cardiovascular fitness is important include long-distance running, team games and swimming.
4. Muscular strength is the maximum force exerted by a muscle or muscle group in one single repetition, for example when doing an explosive movement like weight lifting or starting a sprint from the blocks. Muscular endurance is the capacity of the muscle or muscle group to exert a force repeatedly, or hold a fixed contraction for a period of time – such as in long-distance running or holding a pose on the rings.

5 Agility, balance, co-ordination, power, reaction time and speed of movement.

SPORT	SKILL-RELATED FITNESS COMPONENT
Sprint hurdling	Agility
Weight lifting	Power
Receiving a tennis serve	Speed of movement

6 **a** Speed of movement and speed of reaction. Examples of both occur in saving a penalty goal, beginning to sprint after hearing the starting gun fire.
  b They need both cardiovascular stamina and local muscular stamina, because their heart must be able to pump blood from the working muscles for a long time. The muscles involved in the activity also need to be able to continue working for long periods.

7 **a** dynamic strength; **b** explosive strength; **c** static strength.

8 Suppleness is the range of movement that someone can perform at a joint. Some sorts need more suppleness than others, for example throwing a javelin or doing the splits in gymnastics.

Body types

1 **a** Body size; **b** Body composition; **c** Body type.

2

BODY TYPE	SPORT
Ectomorph	High jump, basketball, middle and long-distance running
Mesomorph	Rowing, contact sports
Endomorph	Sumo wrestling, shott putt, hammer throw

Testing physical fitness

1 $$\text{BMI} = \frac{\text{weight}}{(\text{height in m})^2}$$
$$= \frac{63}{1.7^2}$$
$$= 21.8$$

2 MHR = 220 minus age
   = 220 − 27
   = 193 beats per minute.

3

COMPONENT OF FITNESS	TEST
Cardiovascular endurance	Havard step test, Cooper 12-minute run, multi-stage fitness test
Dynamic strength	Press up test or abdominal curl
Suppleness	Sit and reach test

Effects of exercise and training

1

BODY SYSTEM	LONG-TERM EFFECTS
Circulatory	Heart becomes larger, heart rate falls, increase in the number of blood vessels to the muscles, more red blood cells produced
Respiration	Lungs become bigger, breathe deeper with a stronger rhythm, increase in gaseous exchange
Muscular	Bigger blood network, body adapts to using more oxygen, increased muscle tone

Methods of training and programme design

1.

PRINCIPLE	EXPLANATION
1 Specificity	The effects of training need to be specific for the exercise or the muscle group that is being trained
2 Progression	Gradually put more stress on the body system being trained as you increase the amount of exercise, to build up the system
3 Overload	As you increase the amount of stress put on your body (overload it), it will adapt to deal with the extra demands and performance will improve
4 Reversibility	If you reduce or stop training your body will adapt to the reduced workload and fitness will decrease
5 Tedium	Use a variety of methods of training or activity types to prevent getting bored with your training

2. Your answer should include exercises similar in intensity and frequency to the ones shown below.

DAY	ACTIVITY	INTENSITY (WEIGHT/DISTANCE)	FREQUENCY (REPS/SPEED)
1	Fartlek	2 miles jog, 50 m sprint	Four times
2	Weight training	Light weights, 10–15 kg	1 set of 20–25 reps
3	Interval training	Medium pace	Run 200 m, rest 2 minutes
Repeat 6 times			
4	Rest		

3. Warm up and cool down.

4. To become more successful in a specific sport; to reduce weight; to improve muscle tone; to develop muscle bulk; to increase general fitness; to help recovery from injury; social reasons such as companionship.

5. 60–80%, 10–15 reps.

6. Increase his work rate, an increase the load or weight he is using for training and do the same amount of work/distance in a shorter amount of time. These use the principle of overload and will all increase the stress on his body, which will adapt to the extra work

7. It will reduce significantly – it takes only 2 or 3 weeks to become out of condition.

8. Naseem's MHR is 220 − 22 = 198 beats per minute
80% of that is 198 × 80/100 = 158
So Naseem must exercise at a rate that will keep his heart rate at 158 beats per minute.

9. Caz should stretch each muscle group twice, holding each stretch for 15–30 seconds.

Revising factors affecting performance

Diet and nutrition

1. Insufficient high-energy food, such as carbohydrates, in the diet, not taking in enough water, too much fat in the diet, not taking in the right amount of vitamins.

2. Energy, growth and repair, general good health.

3 Carbohydrates, fats, proteins.

4 The liver and muscles.

5 Saturated fats, found in animal products (e.g. meat, milk, butter, cheese), and polyunsaturated fats, found in fish oils, nuts and seeds.

6 Potassium. Milk, oranges and bananas.

7 Drink plenty of water.

8 Age, gender and lifestyle.

9 Increase.

10 You may experience cramps, a 'stitch' – or may even vomit.

Physiological factors

1 At puberty the increase in testosterone causes boys' muscles to develop and so boys become stronger and more powerful.

2 Arteries begin to lose their elasticity, blood pressure tends to increase, blood flow to working muscles reduces, maximum stroke volume decreases, vital capacity of lungs decreases, amount of body fat increases.

Drug use and abuse

1 Relieve pain, remove anxiety, induce sleep, fend off sleep, control weight.

2 Co-ordination becomes poorer, balance may be affected, hearing and speech will be affected, the user can become dehydrated, muscles do not work properly. Long-term effects include kidney and liver damage.

3 Nicotine. Nicotine increases heart rate and blood pressure, which puts a strain on the heart. Carbon monoxide in the cigarette smoke prevents oxygen getting to the tissues. Tar in the smoke blocks the tubes that carry air and so breathing becomes less effective.

4 Stimulants, beta-blockers, diuretics, anabolic steroids.

5 Anabolic steroids include nandrolone, stanozol, artificial testosterone, clenbuterol. They enhance performance by building up muscle mass and aid in recovery after injury. Side-effects include high blood pressure, heart disease, bone, tendon and ligament weakness, infertility, cancer, facial hair growth and deepening of voice in women, liver damage and aggressive behaviour.

6 In competition they need their muscles to work most efficiently. To do this the muscles need as much oxygen as possible. By increasing the amount of blood in the body, the amount of oxygen carried to the tissues is increased.

Safe practice in sport

1 Shin pads, gloves, goalkeeper also needs a helmet, leg guards, kickers, chest protector.

2 To prevent injuring herself or others involved in the sport by catching on the jewellery.

3 Stretch to the point before it feels uncomfortable; hold the stretch for 8–10 seconds; relax muscle as it is stretched; keep a good balance; release stretch slowly; repeat stretch to make a slightly greater improvement; do not bounce.

Sports injuries

1 Chronic or overuse injury. May be caused by over-training, insufficient recovery time, poor technique, badly designed footwear or equipment.

2 Pain, swelling and bruising.

3 **R**est, **I**ce, **C**ompression, **E**levation.

4 Repeated friction against the skin, opening up layers between the skin where fluid (serum) fills the gap. Treatment: cover with an adhesive dressing; if blister is large drain with a sterile needle and cover with a sterile dressing.

5 Simple or closed fracture. Other symptoms include pain, tenderness, loss of full movement, swelling and bruising.

6 **D**anger, **R**esponse, **A**irways, **B**reathing, **C**irculation.

7 **Hypothermia** is when a person's body temperature falls below normal – perhaps as low as 35°C. They start to shiver, look pale (almost blue), have shallow breathing and a weak pulse.

Hyperthermia is when a person's temperature rises above normal – perhaps as high as 39°C. They sweat, become dehydrated and could have heat exhaustion.

Revising acquisition of skill in sport

Skill in sport

1 True. You are taught a skill by using your innate ability.

2 He or she must be able to run, dribble, pass, receive, tackle, shoot and have good timing.

3

SPORTSPERSON	COMPONENT OF SKILL
Ice hockey goalkeeper	Agility
Gymnast	Balance
Archer	Co-ordination
Shot putter	Power
Sprinter	Reaction time
Cricket batsman	Speed of movement

4 **a** the environment in which it is performed.

Classifying skill

1 A closed skill takes place in a stable, predictable environment where the performer knows in advance what to do and when. An example is a high dive.

2 **a** Any example that shows the athlete takes full control, e.g. golf swing;
  b any example which demonstrates that the environment plays a part in the athlete's decision process, e.g. passing a ball in football.

3

TYPE OF SKILL	DEFINITION
Serial	They string discrete moves together
Continuous	Skills have no fixed start or end point
Discrete	Skills have a definite start and end point

Stages of learning
1 **a** cognitive; **b** associative; **c** autonomous.
2 Explanation of the aim of the technique, a physical demonstration, breakdown of the skill into parts (but avoid giving performer too much information), rest and recovery periods, praise for correct action.
3 Feedback obtained through the body's sense organs. It allows the performer to feel if he or she has executed the movement correctly.

Learning and skills practice
1 Guidance, practice and feedback.
2 Practice.
3 **b** break it down into sub-routines.
4 Mental rehearsal.
5

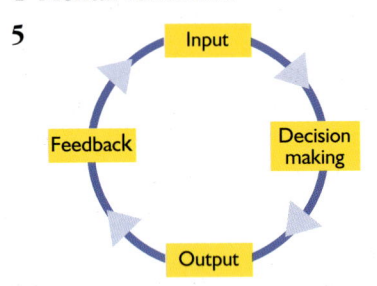

Input → Decision making → Output → Feedback → (cycle back to Input)

Revising psychology and sports performance

Personality
1 Someone who performs intricate skills well and has a low pain threshold, has a low level of excitement and performs better at low levels of arousal. Introverts would take part in individual non-contact sports such as tennis or marathon running
2 Extrovert.

Arousal and performance
1 Heart and breathing rates increase, palms become sweaty, mouth is dry. The person may have 'butterflies' in their stomach and may even feel sick.
2 The performer could start to worry or become anxious and their performance will be adversely affected.
3 They need to keep quiet during the putt, as Tiger needs low levels of arousal in order to complete the task. He needs to be able to perform with great attention to detail.
4 Call a time-out and 'psych up' the team, give a positive game plan, encourage them and give praise where possible.
5 High level of arousal.

Aggression
1 No, because he was not being harmful towards others.
2 Direct aggression is when an athlete takes the opportunity to actively harm an opponent. An example would be using a tackle in a game of football to knock the opposing player down.

Motivation
1 Intrinsic motivation.

2 Where the performer is able to focus completely on the task in hand and achieves success with perfection.

3 Motivation that comes from something or someone else. An example would be receiving a cash prize for a winning performance.

4 Outcome goals are the result of competition. Performance goals are standard of performance. Individuals have more control over performance goals.

Revising current issues in sport

Participation in sport

1 Training for a particular sport; general health; mental well being; social reasons; recreation; excitement; because they want to participate.

2 The environment provides the location for the activities. The closer you live to a particular environment the more likely you are to have easy access to the facilities that environment provides. This therefore influences your choice of sports. For example, if you live within easy reach of a large lake you are more likely to take part in water activities such as sailing, windsurfing or angling.

3 Any two of: confidence, comfort, choice and convenience.

4 Any three of: make sure facilities are accessible by providing ramps, wide doors etc.; provide audio tapes, Braille, large print signs and documentation; make provision for sign language interpretation; special staff training.

5 Plan the delivery of their PE lessons, introduce different sports, relax the policies on PE kit and showers, single-sex and single-ability groups and more female role models.

Sport in society – current issues

1 Violation of rules of a game or organisation. An example would be purposely irritating your opponent during competition.

2 Racism, interaction of fascist groups, organised gangs. Precautions include high fences, segregation of fans, high police profile, all-seater stadiums, ticket touting to become an offence, CCTV and the hoolivan.

3 Use of drugs and match fixing. As an example use any published event you have thought of.

4 Examples include: etiquette, fair play and shaking hands with opponent.

5 Examples include: aggressive tactics, stalling to put opponent off.

Women in sport

1 It was thought that women were not physically capable of competing in sport.

2 It reduces the risks of developing osteoporosis or heart disease.

3 1980

4 Positive discrimination.

5 Women's Sport Foundation.

6 Any three from: both men and women compete at this event; Wimbledon has a high media profile; players' fashion; players' looks; players as role models.

Revising finance and funding in sport

Money in professional sport
1 Where clubs obtain the money they need to pay for their activities.
2 Any four from: merchandise; advertising; product endorsement; conferences; corporate entertainment; TV rights; sponsorship.
3 Players wear or use a product in matches, which helps encourage others to buy the same goods.
4 Expenditure.

Amateur and professional sport
1 An amateur plays for love of the sport and does not get paid for playing. He or she has a job to support him or herself. A professional receives payment for taking part, and relies on the sport to make a living.

Government spending in sport
1 The Leisure and Recreation Department.
2 Any four from: sports facilities help keep people healthier, keep children off the street, help social development, invest in talent at grass-roots level, provide a better quality of life and provide green spaces in urban areas.
3 To obtain money to help top athletes perform at the highest level.

Sports clubs and the sports governing bodies
1 From membership fees, joining fees and subscriptions.
2 To manage the finances of the club.

Sport and the media
1 Any three from: more people can watch the event, it encourages participation, helps stars become household names, helps promote product endorsement.
2 Any three from: radio, magazines, newspapers, the Internet and fanzines.

Sponsorship
1 The company receives mass exposure, reaches a wide audience, company gains positive image of being associated with the healthy image of sport.
2 Advertise products, promote image of the company and sell products through the club.

The National Lottery
1 3.8p
2 £1,449.5 million
3 To support top athletes, to supply sport in the community.
4 Any two from: to encourage more people to take part in sport, to make people in the country feel good, to generate money that can be put back into sport to fund improvements in facilities and performance standards.

Revising organisation of sport

Participation in sport and recreation

1 Any three from: manager, coach, official at matches, club administrator, spectator, trainer.
2 He or she must understand the rules that govern the game, ensure there is fair competition, be neutral, apprehend players who commit fouls and ensure the game is played in a safe environment.

Organisation of sport at a local level

1 A facility that provides sport and recreation for both an educational institute and the local community.
2 National and local government through taxes, rates and the council tax.
3 To provide a service that may not otherwise be catered for by the public or private sectors.
4 Organise the club's home and away fixtures for the playing season.

Organisation of sport at a national level

1 UK Sport and Sport England.
2 Performance services, ethics and anti doping control, international relations and events.
3 Scottish: to widen participation, develop potential and achieve excellence. Welsh: to increase participation, raise standards, improve facilities and provide information and advice. Irish: Starting well, staying involved and striving for excellence.
4 To administer their sport in their home country and represent their sport abroad by affiliating to the ISF.
5 British Paralympic Association.

Organisation of sport at an international level

1 To administer particular sports in the country, implement policies on an international level, make rules, oversee affiliated national governing bodies, organise international championships in their sport.
2 Baron Pierre de Coubertin.
3 The IOC, national Olympic committees, national sports associations, clubs.
4 Coca-Cola, Kodak, McDonalds, IBM. Their role is to provide revenue and services in exchange for exclusive rights in their own area and global exposure of their image that is associated with the Olympics.

Useful websites

Home Country Sports Councils

England	www.english.sports.gov.uk
Northern Ireland	www.sportscouncil-ni.org.uk
Scotland	www.sportscotland.org.uk
Wales	www.sports-council-wales.co.uk
United Kingdom	www.uksport.gov.uk

Other Partners

Assocn. of Chief Executives of National Voluntary Organisations	www.acenvo.org.uk
British Association of Sport and Exercise Sciences	www.bases.co.uk
British Olympic Association	www.olympics.org.uk
Child Safe	www.childsafe.co.uk
SPRITO	www.sprito.org.uk
National Council for School Sport	www.schoolsport.freeserve.co.uk
National Sports Medicine Institute	www.nsmi.org.uk
Womens Sports Foundation	www.wsf.org.uk
National Coaching Foundation	www.ncf.org.uk

National Governing Bodies

All England Netball Association	www.england-netball.co.uk
Amateur Rowing Association	www.ara-rowing.org
Badminton Association of England	www.baofe.co.uk
British Association of Ski Instructors	www.basi.org.uk
British Canoe Union	www.bcu.org.uk
British Cycling Federation	www.bcf.uk.com
British Gymnastics	www.baga.co.uk
British Mountaineering Council	www.thebmc.co.uk
British Orienteering Federation	www.cix.co.uk/~bof/
British Tenpin Bowling Association	www.gotenpin.co.uk
British Tenpin Bowling Instructors Federation	www.users.dircon.co.uk
British Water Ski Federation	www.britishwaterski.co.uk
Clay Pigeon Shooting Association	www.cpsa.co.uk
England and Wales Cricket Board	www.lords.org
English Karate Governing Body	www.ekgb.org.uk
FA Coaches Association	www.coach-soccer.livjm.ac.uk
Lawn Tennis Association	www.lta.org.uk
OTC National Mountain Bike Award Scheme	www.otc.org.uk
Royal Yachting Association	www.rya.org.uk
Scottish Football Association	www.scottishfa.co.uk
Scottish Rugby Union	www.sru.org.uk
Squash Rackets Association	www.squash.uk.com
UK Athletics	www.ukathletics.org

Other Useful Sites

Gatorade Sport Science Institute	www.gssiweb.com/site.html
News Now -sports news updates	www.newsnow.co.uk
Online Sports Directory	www.onlinesports.com/pages/top, sprt.html
Sports On Line	www.sportsonline.co.uk

International Sites

Australian Sports Commission	www.ausport.gov.au
European Commission Sport and the European Union	www.europa.eu.int/comm/dg10/sport/index.html
European Sports Information Network	www.asn.or.at/esc/esin.htm
Commonwealth Games Federation	www.commonwealthgames-fed.org
Federation Internationale de Football	www.fifa.com
Federation Internationale de Hockey	www.fihockey.org
Federation Internationale de Natation Amateur(Swimming)	www.fina.org
International Amateur Athletic Association	www.iaaf.org
International Badminton Federation	www.intbadfed.org
International Basketball Federation	www.fiba.com
International Council of Sport Science and Physical Education	www.icsspe.org
International Cycling Union	www.uci.ch
International Federation of Rowing Associations	www.fisa.org
International Federation of Netball Associations	www.netball.org
International Gymnastics Federation	www.worldsport.com/sports/gymnastics /homex.html
International Ice Hockey Federation	www.iihf.com
International Modern Pentathlon and Biathlon Union	www.pentathlon.com
International Olympic Committee	www.olympic.org
International Orienteering	www.n3sport.no
International Paralympic Committee	www.paralympic.org
International Powerlifting Federation	www.ipf.com
International Sailing Federation	www.sailing.org
International Skating Union	www.isu.org
International Table Tennis Federation	www.ittf.com
International Triathlon Union	www.triathlon.worldsport.com
International University Sports Federation	www.ulb.ac.be/assoc/fisu
International Volleyball Federation	www.fivb.ch
International Water Ski Federation	www.iwsf.com
International Weightlifting Federation	www.iwf.net
International Working Group on Women and Sport	www.iwg-gti.org
US Olympic Committee	www.olympic-usa.org
Union of European Football Federations	www.uefa.com
World Squash Federation	www.squash.org/wsf

Index

acute injuries 131, 132
adaptation to exercise 71, 82, 85
adenosine triphosphate *see ATP*
adrenaline 39, 44, 46, 120
advertising 220
aerobic energy system 49, 51, 52
aerobic fitness *see stamina*
aerobic training zone 88
aerobics classes 89–90
age 39, 112–14, 199–200
aggression 176–8
agility 62, 146
alcohol 117
alveoli 27, 29–30
amateur sport 224–5
amphetamines 119
anabolic steroids 121
anaerobic energy systems 49, 50, 52
anaerobic threshold 88
anaerobic training zone 88
anaerobic working 49, 51, 52, 88
analgesics 119–20
analysing performance 186–94
antagonistic pairs 22, 23
anxiety 172, 173, 174
appendicular skeleton 11
arms 11
arousal and performance 171–5
arteries 33, 34, 35
    around the heart 32, 36
    around the lungs 29
    and blood pressure 38, 39
    during exercise 40
arterioles 34, 35, 40
associative stage 151, 153
asthma attacks 136
ATP (adenosine triphosphate) 49, 50, 51
autonomic nervous system 41, 44
autonomous stage 151, 154
axial skeleton 9–10

backbone 9
balance 62, 146
balanced diet 104–6
basal metabolic rate (BMR) 108, 109
beta blockers 120
blood 7, 35–6
    circulation of 33–4, 38
blood cells 7, 35, 122
blood doping 122
blood pressure 38–9, 113
blood vessels 33, 34–5, 40
    around the heart 32, 36
    around the lungs 27, 29, 31
BMI *see body mass index*
BMR *see basal metabolic rate*
BOA *see British Olympic Association*
body composition 62, 67, 69, 71, 72–3
body fat 62, 69, 72–3
    and ageing 113
    and gender 115
body mass index (BMI) 72
body movement *see movement*

body systems 4–5
    circulatory system 31–40
    digestive system 47–8
    energy systems 49–52
    hormonal system 46
    muscular system 16–26
    nervous system 41–5
    respiratory system 27–31
    skeletal system 6–15
body temperature 138–9
body types 67–9
bones 6–14
    injuries to 134–6
BPA *see British Paralympic Association*
brain 41, 42
breathing 5, 27–9
breathing rate 30
    and adrenaline 44, 120
    and exercise 31, 40, 51
British Olympic Association (BOA) 259–60, 280
British Paralympic Association (BPA) 260

cable television 232–4
capillaries, blood 33, 34, 35
    in the lungs 27, 29, 31
carbohydrates 48, 49, 50
    in diet 102, 104, 110
carbon dioxide 51
    transport 33, 34–5, 36, 40
        breathing 27, 29
        in the lungs 29–30, 31
cardiac muscle 16, 32, 36
cardiac output 37–8, 40
cardiovascular endurance *see stamina*
cardiovascular system 31–40, 82
cartilage 7, 8, 10, 12
cartilaginous joints 12
CCPR *see Central Council of Physical Recreation*
Central Council of Physical Recreation (CCPR) 262
central nervous system 41, 42
cheating 206–7
chronic injuries 131, 132
circuit training 92–3
circulatory system 5, 31–40, 82
clenbuterol 121
closed skills 147–8
closed-circuit television (CCTV) 205
clothing 127
clubs 229–30, 252, 253–4
    football, money in 218–23
co-ordination 62, 146
coaches 155–7, 175, 247
    and learning 152, 153
    in performance analysis 186–94
    and practice 158, 159
    sports coach UK 182, 259
cognitive stage 151, 152
cold and hypothermia 138
commercial organisations 251–2
community sport, Lottery funding for 241
components of fitness 62–6, 70–81

composition, body 62, 67, 69, 71, 72–3
conditioned reflexes 44, 45
conferences, income from 221
continuous skills 149
continuous training 89–90
contractions, muscle 7, 16, 17, 21–4
control systems 41, 46
cooling-down 94, 129, 130
Cooper 12-minute run 75–6
creatine phosphate 50, 51
creatine phosphate system 49, 50, 52
cricket, professional status in 224–5
current issues 195–216

decision making 45, 162, 163–4
dehydration 106, 111, 138
deoxygenated blood 29–30, 32–5, 36
Department of Culture, Media and Sport 228, 233, 255
development, physical 112, 114–15
deviant behaviour 203
diastolic pressure 38–9
diet 39, 102–11 *see also food*
digestive system 5, 47–8
direct aggression 177, 178
disability 201–2, 260–1
Disability Discrimination Act (1994) 201
discrete skills 149
dislocations 135–6
distributed practice 158–9
diuretics 120
DR ABC routine 136, 137
drinks, sport 111
drugs 117–25, 206–7
dynamic strength 65, 71, 78–9, 91

ectomorphs 68
endocrine system 5, 46
endomorphs 68
endurance
    aerobic *see stamina*
    aerobic system for 51, 52
    muscular *see dynamic strength*
energy from food 47, 107–9
energy systems 5, 49–52
environment 126–7, 147, 162, 199
equipment 127
evaluation 191
excretory system 5, 48
exercise
    and diet 47, 108–11
    effects of 37, 38, 39–40, 51
        long-term 81–2
        and lung capacity 30–1
    and fitness 116
    and programme design 83–96
exercise environment 126–7
exhaling 5, 28
explosive activity, energy for 50
explosive strength 65, 71, 79–80, 91
extroverts 168–70

facilities 126, 199, 241
    local authority 226–8, 250–1
    playing fields 262–3
fanzines 235

fartlek training 90
fast twitch fibres 20
fat, body 62, 69, 72–3
    and ageing 113
    and gender 115
fats 48, 49, 103, 104, 110
    burning in training 89
feedback 153, 160–1, 162, 164
    in performance analysis 192–3
fibre in diet 106
fibrous joints 12
finance and funding 217–44
    and drug use 206
    of governing bodies 230–1
    by local authorities 226–8, 251
    by the National Lottery 239–41
    and the Olympic Games 259–60, 266
    and participation 199
    and the private sector 252
    in professional sport 218–23
    and the voluntary sector 229, 230, 254
fitness 31, 59–66
    aerobic *see stamina*
    testing 70–81
fitness instructors 248
fixed joints 12
flexibility 62, 66, 71, 80–1, 94
food, digestion of 47, 48
    see also diet
football 218–23, 238
    hooliganism in 204, 205
    women in 212, 213
fractures, bone 134–5
freely movable joints 12
funding *see finance and funding*

gamesmanship 203, 208–9
gaseous exchange 29–30, 31, 33
gender issues *see women in sport*
global television rights 235
glucose 50, 51, 102
glycogen 50, 102, 110
glycolysis 50, 51
goals 83, 84, 181–3
golf, gamesmanship in 208–9
governing bodies 230–1, 240, 258
    international 264
    websites 280
government 226–8, 250–1
growth 112, 118
guidance 155–7

haemoglobin 35
Harvard step test 74–5
health 61
    and diet 107–11
health-related fitness 60, 62, 71, 72–3
heart 32, 36–7
heart rate 37–8, 73
    drugs affect 119, 120
    and exercise 40, 51
    and training 88
heat 51, 138–9
HGH *see human growth hormone*
hooliganism 204, 205

hormonal system 5, 46
hospitality, corporate 221
hostile aggression 177, 178
human growth hormone (HGH) 118
hypertension 39
hyperthermia 138–9
hypothermia 138

immovable joints 12
impulses, nerve 5, 43, 44
indirect aggression 177, 178
information processing 62–4
inhaling 5, 28
injuries 128–39
input 162–3
International Olympic Committee (IOC) 118, 235, 264, 265–6
international sport 264–6, 281
international sports federations (ISFs) 264
Internet 235, 236
interval training 91
introverts 168–70
involuntary muscle 5, 16, 47
involuntary nervous system 41, 44
IOC *see International Olympic Committee*
ISFs *see international sports federations*
isotonic drinks 111

joints 7, 11–15, 21, 25–6
    injuries to 134–6
    and suppleness 66

knees 12

lactic acid system 49, 50–1, 52
lean body mass 69
learning 151–4
    and performance 162–4
    and skills practice 155–61
legs 11
leisure time 197
levers 25–6
ligaments 7, 12, 21
local authority spending 226–8, 250–1
local muscular stamina 64, 65
local sport 250–4
lung capacity 30–1
lungs 27, 28, 29–30, 36

magazines 235, 236
Manchester United, sponsorship of 238
manual guidance 157
massed practice 158–9
match fixing 207
maximum heart rate (MHR) 73
    and training 87, 88–9, 91
maximum strength *see static strength*
mechanical guidance 157
media 213–14, 232–6
    see also television
medulla oblongata 42, 44
membership fees 229
memory 163–4

mental rehearsal 159–60
merchandising 219–20
mesomorphs 68
MHR *see maximum heart rate*
minerals in diet 105
minute volume 30
mobility exercises 129, 130
money *see finance and funding*
motivation 116, 179–80
movement 11–15, 21–2, 25–6
    and proprioceptors 43
    skeleton in 7, 8, 9, 10
    speed of 64, 146
muscle 7, 16–24
    and body composition 69, 72
    drugs build up 121
    injury to 132–3
    location and names 18–19
    working muscles 22, 40, 50
muscular endurance 62, 91
    see also dynamic strength
muscular power *see explosive strength*
muscular stamina, local 64, 65
muscular system 5, 16–26, 82
musculoskeletal system 21

nandrolone 121
narcotic analgesics 119–20
National Curriculum 246, 247
national level sport 240, 255–63
National Lottery 239–41
National Playing Fields Association (NPFA) 262–3
NCF multi-stage fitness test 76
nerve impulses 5, 43, 44
nerves 41, 42–3
nervous system 5, 41–5, 119, 162
neurones 42–3
newspapers 213–14, 235, 236
non-governmental public organisations 228
NPFA *see National Playing Fields Association*
nutrition 102–1

observing performers 188
officials in sport 248
Olympic Games 118, 235, 264–6
    British association 259–60, 280
    women in 211, 212
open skills 147, 148
organisation of sport 245–67
    at international level 264–6
    at local level 250–4
        voluntary sports clubs 229–30
        national governing bodies 258, 280
    at national level 255–63
output 162, 164
overload in training 85–6
overuse injuries 131, 132
oxygen
    in energy systems 49, 51, 52
    transport 31, 39–40, 113, 115
        breathing 27, 29–30
        and exercise 31, 40, 51
oxygen system 49, 51, 52
oxygen transport system 39–40
oxygenated blood 29–30, 32–5, 36

Index **283**

pacing 150
painkillers 119–20
pancreas 46, 48
Paralympic Games 202, 260
parasympathetic nervous system 44
parental influences 197–8
part practice 157–8
participation 196–202, 246–9
   and women 211–12
performance
   analysing 186–94
   and arousal 171–5
   factors affecting 101–41
   and feedback 160–1
   and learning 162–4
   and psychology 167–84
performance-enhancing drugs 118–22
peripheral nervous system 41, 42–3
personality 168–70
physical demonstration 155
physiological factors 112–16
physique 67–8
planning 94–5, 191–2
plasma, blood 35
platelets 36
playing fields 262–3
power 62, 146
   muscular *see explosive strength*
practice 157–60
prevention of injury 128–30
prime movers 22, 23
private sector 251–2
product endorsement 221
professional sport 218–23, 224–5
progression in training 85
proprioceptors 43, 45, 153, 162
proteins 48, 49, 103, 104
psychology and performance 167–84
public sector 228
pulmonary circulation 36
pulse 37, 73, 128, 130

racism 204
radio 235, 236
reaction time/speed 62–3, 64, 146
receptors 41, 43, 153
   proprioceptors 43, 45, 153, 162
recovery 74–5, 88
red blood cells 7, 35, 122
reflexes 44, 45
residual volume 30
respiration 27, 40
respiratory rate *see breathing rate*
respiratory system 5, 27–31, 39, 82
rest 116
reversibility and training 86
ribs 9, 10, 12, 27
RICE treatment 133, 134, 135
rotation, joint 15

safe practice in sport 126–7
satellite television 232–4
schools 198, 246, 247, 250
scUK *see sports coach UK*
selective attention 163–4

semi-professionals 225
serial skills 149
shape, body 16, 68
shock 136–7
size, body 67, 68
skeletal frames 9–10
skeletal muscle *see voluntary muscle*
skeletal system 5, 6–15, 21
skeleton 6, 9
skill 41, 143–66
   definition 144
   and practice 155–61
   and reflexes 44, 45
skill-related fitness 62–3
skin injuries 133–4
skin-fold measurements 72–3
skull 7, 9, 12, 25, 42
slightly movable joints 12
slow twitch fibres 20
SMARTER goals 182–3
smoking 39, 117
smooth muscle *see involuntary muscle*
somatotyping 68–9
specificity in training 84–5
spectators 249
speed 62–3, 64, 146
speed training zone 88
spinal cord 41, 42
spine 9
sponsorship 221–2, 237–8, 266
sport
   current issues 195–216
   and diet 108–11
   energy systems in 51–2
   government spending on 226–8
   organisation of 245–67
   participation in 196–202
   professional 218–23, 224–5
   safe practice in 126–7
   women in 210–14
sport drinks 111
Sport England 228, 255–6, 280
Sport Scotland 257, 280
sports coach UK (scUK) 182, 259, 280
sports councils 122, 228, 255–7, 280
sportsmanship 207
stamina (aerobic fitness) 62–5
   testing 71, 74–6
   training for 86, 88, 89–91
stanozol 121
starch 48, 102
static strength 65, 91
   testing 71, 77–8
stereotypes, gender 211–12
steroids, anabolic 121
stimulants 119
strength 62, 65, 71, 77–80
   training for 89, 91–3
stress 39, 115–16
stress fractures 135
stretching 94, 129–30
stroke volume 37–8, 40, 113
student participation 246

sub-routines 152, 157, 158, 189
subscription television 232–4
subscriptions, members' 229
subsidies 226, 227, 251
suppleness 62, 66, 71, 80–1, 94
sweating 40, 138
sympathetic nervous system 44
synovial joints 12
systemic circulation 36
systolic pressure 38–9

tax 226, 228
Taylor Report 205
teachers and participation 247
technique 144–5
tedium in training 86
television 232–5, 236, 249
   broadcasting rights 221, 234–5, 266
   and women 213
temperature, body 138–9
tendons 12, 16, 21
terrestrial television channels 232–4
testing for drugs 122–4
testing physical fitness 70–81
testosterone 46, 121
tidal volume 30, 31
total lung capacity 30
training 81–96
   principles of 83–6
   and programme design 83–96
tranquillisers 120
turnover 215, 222

UK Sport 122, 228, 256
UKSI (United Kingdom Sports Institutes) 240, 261
unconsciousness, treating 136

veins 33, 34, 35
   around the heart 32, 36
   around the lungs 29
venules 34, 35
verbal guidance 156
vertebral column 7, 9–10, 12
video recordings 194, 248
visual guidance 155
vital capacity 30, 113
vitamins 104–5
$\dot{V}O_2$ max 31, 76, 113
Vodaphone sponsorship 238
voluntary muscle 5, 16–19, 22
voluntary sector 229–30, 253–4, 280

warming-up 94, 128–30
water in diet 106
websites 280–1
weight training 91–2
white blood cells 35
whole practice 157–8
women in sport 210–14
   and participation 196, 198, 200
   physical development 114–15
Womens Sports Foundation (WSF) 213, 263, 280
working muscles 22, 40, 50
WSF *see Womens Sports Foundation*